Democracies

Also by Yves Mény

ADJUSTING TO EUROPE (*co-edited with P. Muller and J.-L. Quermonne*)

GOVERNMENT AND POLITICS IN WESTERN EUROPE (*3rd edition, with Andrew Knapp*)

LA CORRUPTION DE LA RÉPUBLIQUE

PAR LE PEUPLE, POUR LE PEUPLE: Le Populisme et les Démocraties (*with Yves Surel*)

THE FUTURE OF EUROPEAN WELFARE: A New Social Contract? (*co-edited with M. Rhodes*)

Also by Yves Surel

L'ANALYSE DES POLITIQUES PUBLIQUES (*with Pierre Muller*)

L'ÉTAT ET LE LIVRE

Democracies and the Populist Challenge

Edited by

Yves Mény
Former Director of the Robert Schuman Centre for Advanced Studies
and
President of the European University Institute
Florence
Italy

and

Yves Surel
Professor of Political Science at the IEP
Grenoble
and
Research Associate at the Centre d'étude de la vie politique française
Sciences Po
Paris

With the editorial assistance of
Clare Tame and Luis de Sousa

palgrave

in association with
Palgrave Macmillan

Softcover reprint of the hardcover 1st edition 2002 978-0-333-97004-1

Published by
PALGRAVE MACMILLAN
Houndmills, Basingstoke, Hampshire RG21 6XS and
175 Fifth Avenue, New York, N.Y. 10010
Companies and representatives throughout the world

PALGRAVE MACMILLAN is the global academic imprint of the Palgrave Macmillan division of St. Martin's Press, LLC and of Palgrave Macmillan Ltd. Macmillan® is a registered trademark in the United States, United Kingdom and other countries. Palgrave is a registered trademark in the European Union and other countries.

ISBN 978-1-349-42911-0 ISBN 978-1-4039-2007-2 (eBook)
DOI 10.1057/9781403920072

A catalogue record for this book is available from the British Library.

Library of Congress Catalog Card Number: 200106875

Contents

List of Tables and Figure

Tables

Figure

Foreword

This book is the result of a project on the study of populism which started in the mid-1990s. A first publication (in French) appeared in May 2000, focusing on its constitutive – and elusive – elements. More specifically, this volume addresses, through a comparative study, the problem of the definition and manifestations of populism in democratic regimes. This collective work has been made possible thanks to the dedication of its contributors, to the senior commissioning editor for politics at Palgrave, Alison Howson, and to their external editorial consultant, Nick Brock, but also to some 'invisible hands' who helped us to rescue time from pressing administrative tasks of a day-to-day nature. Our gratitude goes to the staff of the Robert Schuman Centre who combine efficiency, dedication and enthusiasm in the best possible way. A special thanks to Alex Howarth, who brought her British sense of humour when the French team was overwhelmed, to Luís de Sousa, who took care of the many details involved in a collective enterprise, and last but not least to Clare Tame, so efficient in preventing the English language from being destroyed by its non-native users.

YVES MÉNY and YVES SUREL
Florence

Notes on the Contributors

Hans-Georg Betz is Associate Professor of Political Science at the Canadian Centre for German and European Studies, York University, Toronto. The main focus of his recent work has been on social change and the rise of exclusionary forms of populism in Western Europe. His publications include *The New Politics of the Right* (co-edited with Stefan Immerfall) (1998) and a number of comparative articles on the populist right in Austria, Switzerland, and Northern Italy.

Margaret Canovan is Professor of Political Thought in the School of Politics, International Relations and the Environment at the University of Keele, England. Her books include *Populism* (1981), *Hannah Arendt: a Reinterpretation of her Political Thought* (1992) and *Nationhood and Political Theory* (1996). Recent publications on populism include 'Trust the People! Populism and the Two Faces of Democracy', *Political Studies*, 47 (1999).

Luìs de Sousa is a research assistant at the European University Institute where he is completing a doctorate on corruption control in Britain, France and Portugal.

Herbert Kitschelt is Professor of Political Science at Duke University. He has published on parties and party competition in contemporary West European democracies, in, for instance, *The Transformation of European Social Democracy* (1994) and *The Radical Right in Western Europe* (1995). More recently he has completed a study of new East European democracies: *Post-Communist Party Systems* (co-authored with Zdenka Mansfeldova, Radoslav Markowski, and Gabor Toka) (1999) and has written on the political economy of welfare state retrenchment in Western democracies. He is also co-editor of *Continuity and Change in Contemporary Capitalism* (1999).

Peter Mair is Professor of Comparative Politics at Leiden University in the Netherlands, and is co-editor of *West European Politics*. His main publications have been in the field of parties and party systems, and he is the author, most recently, of *Party System Change* (1997) and

Representative Government in Modern Europe (with Michael Gallagher and Michael Laver) (third edition, 2000).

Yves Mény is Professor of Political Science, former Director of the Robert Schuman Centre and President elect of the European University Institute in Florence, Italy. His most recent publications include *Par le Peuple, Pour le Peuple. Le Populisme et les Démocraties* (2000, co-authored with Y. Surel), *The Future of European Welfare: a New Social Contract?* (1998, co-edited with M. Rhodes), *Government and Politics in Western Europe* (third edition, 1998 with A. Knapp) and *La corruption de la République* (1992).

Cas Mudde is lecturer in the Department of Politics at the University of Edinburgh. He has written extensively on the field of extremism and democracy. His publications include *The Ideology of the Extreme Right* (2000) and *Extreem-rechts in Nederland* (1998, co-edited with Joop van Holsteyn). He is currently finishing co-edited works on democracy in the Netherlands (2001) and uncivil society in post-communist Europe (2002). His new project is on xenophobic nationalist parties in Eastern and Western Europe.

Wolfgang C. Müller is Professor in Political Science at the University of Vienna. He has published widely on Austrian and comparative politics. His recent publications include *Policy, Office, or Votes? How Political Parties in Western Europe Make Hard Decisions* (1999) and *Government Coalitions in Western Europe* (2000), both co-edited with Kaare Strøm, and *Die österreichischen Abgeordneten* (2001).

Yannis Papadopoulos is Professor of Swiss Politics and Public Policy and Director of the Institut d'Etudes Politiques et Internationales at the University of Lausanne. His current research interests are on the question of democratic legitimacy in policy-making. He has written extensively on issues of governance and participation, and his publications on these topics include *Complexité sociale et politiques publiques* (1995), and *Démocratie directe* (1998). He recently co-edited the *Handbuch der schweizerischen Politik* (second edition 2000).

Yves Surel is Professor of Political Science, IEP, Grenoble and research associate at the Centre d'étude de la vie politique française in Paris. His most recent publications in the field of political science are: *Par le* *peuple, pour le peuple. Le populisme et les démocraties* (2000, with Yves Mény); *L'analyse des politiques publiques* (1998, with Pierre Muller) and *L'État et le livre* (1997).

Paul Taggart is Lecturer in Politics and Jean Monnet Lecturer in Contemporary European Studies at the Sussex European Institute, University of Sussex and is a Visiting Scholar at the BMW Center for German and European Studies at Georgetown University, as well as being co-editor of the journal *Politics.* He has written on political parties, populism and Euroscepticism and is the author of *The New Populism and the New Politics* (1996) and *Populism* (2000).

Clare Tame is a freelance social science editor based in Florence and a former research assistant at the European University Institute.

Marco Tarchi is Associate Professor of Political Science and Political Communication at the University of Florence. His publications include *Partito unico e dinamica autoritaria* (1981), *La 'rivoluzione legale'. Identità collettive e crisi della democrazia in Italia e Germania* (1993), *Cinquant'anni di nostalgia. La destra in Italia dopo il fascismo* (1995), *Esuli in patria. I fascisti nell'Italia repubblicana* (1995), *Dal Msi ad An. Organizzazione e strategie* (1997).

Alan Ware is a Professor of Politics at the University of Oxford and a Fellow of Worcester College. His books include *Political Parties and Party Systems* (1996), and *Funding Democratization* (1998, edited with Peter Burnell). He is currently completing a book on the origins of direct primary elections in the United States (*Why the Direct Primary?)* and is conducting research on change in the American party system between the 1880s and the 1990s.

1
The Constitutive Ambiguity of Populism

Yves Mény and Yves Surel

Has the Weberian disenchantment with the world finally freed people from the illusion that democracy is a panacea? For the past decade, once the glory and triumph of the western model over the socialist regimes had evaporated, we have been able to observe the numerous manifestations of popular misgivings about political participation and democratic institutions. Democratic malaise (Dahl 1998), the politics of resentment (Betz 1994, 1998a, b), political anomie, and protest movements are among the most frequent manifestations of this disillusion in many western democracies. Both electoral turnout and opinion polls testify to the endurance and extension of the problem. Nor have the new democracies which emerged from the collapse of the socialist systems escaped this general phenomenon of disillusion as shown by the return to power – in sheep's clothing – of former communist party officials. These challenges to democratic governance vary according to the specificity of each national polity, but share some common features such as the decline of electoral support for political incumbents, a marked increase in electoral abstentionism, the volatility of the electorate, the growing fragmentation of the party system, the emergence of ad hoc social movements unrepresented by traditional political organisations, and the emergence of single-issue and/or radical parties.

Over the past ten years these phenomena have been extensively studied and documented on a case-by-case basis or in a more comparative and systematic way (see, for example, Dalton and Küchler 1990; Klingemann and Fuchs 1995; Held 1993). However, there has been some difficulty in making sense of these new manifestations of democratic malaise. Do they really constitute a challenge to democratic institutions or is it merely a transitory and recurrent problem of adaptation or adjustment? How should we classify these new social movements, actors and organisations? And should we analyse the transformations taking place within the party systems as simple conjunctural adjustment or as major political, ideological and institutional realignments?

These questions have been made more complex by the emergence, or rather the re-emergence, of the concept of populism as an empirical reality and an academic issue. For a long time, the word had a rather circumscribed application and was mostly applied to North American political movements advocating the power of the people against the corporate 'fat cats' and corrupt political parties. In the 1950s and 1960s, it was loosely extended to a completely different phenomenon, that of political mobilisation as the mixture of relatively formal electoral politics and charismatic leadership found in less developed countries, the archetype of which was Perónism in Argentina. The concept was again stretched by applying it to dictatorial regimes in the Third World where elections effectively 'rubber-stamped' dictators with the semblance of popular legitimacy. With this extension, both the concept and the word lost most of their heuristic utility and were generally used as a convenient label to designate unfamiliar or unusual forms of political mobilisation. This qualification was often applied retrospectively, for instance to political movements such as General Boulanger's campaign in late nineteenth-century France, or to the *Mouvement Poujade* at the end of the Fourth Republic. This eclectic collection of situations, phenomena and data have led many observers and analysts to believe that there is no such thing as 'populism', but, rather, a mix of extremely heterogeneous situations which can be analysed according to type, but which cannot be reduced to any form of comprehensive unity. Ionescu and Gellner (1969) and Canovan (1981) reached more or less the same conclusion – the extreme difficulty, not to say, impossibility of coming up with a definition or an approach capable of subsuming the differences. Since these early and stimulating studies, however, the landscape has changed. First of all, populism has returned both as an empirical reality and as an academic concern. In addition, the concept is no longer used to describe, almost exclusively, Third World countries governed by charismatic leaders, but has increasingly been applied to situations in Western Europe. Although populism is still the favourite concept used to designate the Chavez regime in Venezuela for instance, it is increasingly associated with European leaders, movements or parties, which has meant that the new approach is much closer to the North American tradition than was previously the case.

However, this transformation in the use of the concept does not resolve the problems of identification and meaning. On the contrary, and using the image ironically proposed by Isaiah Berlin 30 years ago, the Cinderella complex is not yet resolved: there is a shoe – in the shape of populism – but no foot to fit it! Over the past ten years, populism has more often than not been an easy way to deal with unusual political manifestations as if the term alone were enough to explain the new forms of political mobilisation. Populism has become a catchword, particularly in the media, to designate the newborn political or social movements which challenge the entrenched values, rules and institutions of democratic orthodoxy. In this way, within the space of a few years, populism has become equated with the pathology of democracy.

Populism: the pathology of democracy?

One of the first interpretations of populism as a pathology of democracy can be found in the contributions of Peter Wiles to the classic work on populism edited by Ghita Ionescu and Ernest Gellner in 1967. Since the publication of this seminal work, it has been customary to consider the variegated forms of populism as the multifaceted expressions of political pathology. As underlined recently by Taguieff,

> In the ordinary language of today, populism makes the ideas of demophily and demagogy coexist. This means that 'populism', in its constitutive ambiguity, can be considered an ideological corruption of democracy if we consider that democracy, founded upon transmissible principles, implies, in Proudhon's words, the willingness to teach and educate the people rather than to seduce it. (Taguieff 1997)

However, this definition of populism implies being able to measure its degeneration by reference to an accepted standard. A pathology is meaningful only by comparison with a situation defined as normal, a definition which in this case is, to say the least, problematic. Indeed, democracy is not only a system of fundamental values, but also a set of institutional or procedural mechanisms, understood as 'the rules of the game'. This complex varies by time and place. De Tocqueville's America was a democracy by the standards of the time, but would probably not be strictly classified as such today. Similarly, the French in the 1930s had no doubt about the democratic character of the Third Republic, although women did not have the right to vote. Today, many American citizens and politicians consider the death penalty as an unavoidable instrument in the fight against crime, whereas in Europe, most political elites would reject such a view as being populist and unacceptable.

The same applies to participatory politics: can we assume that only peaceful and politically correct forms of participation, such as the vote, are democratic? Or should we be more inclusive and accept that other forms of involvement can contribute to the democratic process? Once again, there is a need for a relativist approach to this question: the French tend to consider 'lobbying' as a dirty trick, closer to corruption than to politics, while many British or American observers view the style of French social movements as a form of violence and political primitivism. Any reference to pathology will inevitably include a definition of democracy, and this definition is likely to differ markedly from one political setting to another.

The definition of ideal regimes and of their degeneration has a long tradition dating back to Aristotle and Montesquieu. When it comes to populism, understood as a perversion of democracy, we can distinguish three distinct components.

The first, and most recent, relates to the almost exclusive identification of populism with the extreme Right. While some nineteenth-century forms of populism – such as in America – were perceived as modern and reformist, there is now a propensity to equate populism with political movements on the Right. Le Pen in France and Haider in Austria have been labelled neo-Nazi or neo-fascist as well as populist. In France, some observers and political scientists have coined the term 'national-populist' to characterise these political movements. But what is the value of a classification which is nearer to an ad hoc, and at times misleading, conceptualisation than to a carefully formulated definition? Many parties on the extreme Right are not populist and many populist movements are too specific, heterogeneous or eclectic to be identified with the extreme Right (see, for instance, Di Pietro's movement in Italy or the mobilisation of the French electorate behind the 'hunters' party', *Mouvement Chasse, Pêche, Nature et Tradition*). Traditionally, the parties of the extreme Right have a declared aversion to democracy and claim to combat its existence, but at the same time populist parties insist that they are the only democrats, because they want to restore power to the people. Thus, democracy is not challenged in principle, but in its organisational form.

Another reason for defining populism as a pathology regards the contribution of the so-called realist (or elitist) school. Those who have contributed to the disenchantment of democracy – Ostrogorski, Michels, Schumpeter, Mosca, Pareto – have exposed democracy's fundamental elitism, stressing that the people's contribution to democracy is little more than the participation in the selection of their rulers. If this is democracy, then any additional involvement of the people can indeed be seen as disturbing, pathological and overloading the system – precisely what Crozier, Huntington and Watanuki had in mind when they presented the Trilateral Report on 'The Crisis of Democracy' in 1975. A well-functioning democracy is an elitist democracy or, to give Sartori's blunt definition, 'Democracy is the pompous word for something which does not exist.' Seen from this perspective, populism can indeed be viewed as a disturbing pathology of democracy.

Even if the identification of populism as a democratic pathology is problematic, the contribution of elitist theory is important insofar as it allows us to analyse in sociological and political terms (the constitution of ruling elites) what constitutes the vital principle that animates modern democratic regimes, that is, the representative principle (Pitkin 1967). Probably no one has defined the iron rules of representation with more brutal clarity than Edmund Burke when addressing his fellow citizens in Bristol and declaring that once elected he would follow nothing but his own informed judgement! If indeed democracy is representative democracy, in the political rather than the sociological sense, then it is more appropriate to follow the indications of Paul Taggart (2000) and to analyse populism as the 'pathology of representative politics'. Thus defined, the problem is no longer the inherent contradiction between populism and democracy, but rather that between populism and the most usual form of democracy – representative democracy. However, as this specific form of democratic rule has become the dominant and almost universal variant, it is also tempting to consider alternative forms as pathological, utopian or simply unrealistic. The confusion stems, as Margaret Canovan (1999) points out, from the fact that the reference to the people is the common feature which unites all those who are, or claim to be, democratic. Although 'the people' is the common denominator, the role and place of the people in any political system is highly contentious. Today, even authoritarian or dictatorial regimes pretend to govern in the name of the people. Governments that make no attempt to invoke popular legitimacy are rare, and those that attempt to offer an alternative foundation of their political regime are the exception.

As such, populism cannot be described as anti-democratic per se. Indeed, many populist claims are well-founded, even if the way in which they are articulated is highly problematic: the sociological distance between the people and the elites is probably unavoidable, but it does not mean that this tension should not be debated and, where possible, reduced. The closed nature of the policy process and of the policy agenda has been stressed out by many observers and not just by populists, and the search for the more direct involvement of citizens is a central question for any democracy. Many solutions (such as referenda or popular initiatives) advocated by populist parties have been introduced into political systems, helping to balance the principle of representation with direct modes of popular expression.

One may wonder why populism is perceived so negatively given this proximity to, and affinity with, the democratic principle. The reason is quite simple. Populism, as with many other concepts, is, by itself, an empty shell which can be filled and made meaningful by whatever is poured into it. This helps account for the difficulty of defining populism and finding common features across time and space when considering its manifold manifestations. Paul Taggart emphasises that 'Populism has an essential chameleonic quality that means it always takes on the hue of the environment in which it occurs' (2000, 4).

The problem, then, is not only the 'loose' character of populism highlighted by Peter Wiles in Gellner and Ionescu's 1967 study, but also the fundamental ambiguity of the main and ultimate reference, 'the people'. In English and French (but also in many other languages), people or *peuple* simultaneously designates both the whole and the part (Finley 1983).[1] A third meaning, sometimes added, is that of the people in relation to a heartland, usually the nation, but sometimes a fraction of a nation-state which wishes to establish itself as a cultural and/or political community, best illustrated by the term *das Volk*. A recent debate in France highlighted this ambivalence when the Constitutional Court struck out the first article of a bill dealing with Corsica which referred to the 'peuple Corse', arguing that there was only a 'peuple français' and that the French nation was not made of peoples but of a single people.

This blurring of the main ideological reference explains why the same word may refer to such different specific realities. The classic democratic orthodoxy uses 'the people' as an abstract construction (Anderson 1991, 4), while the populist ideology or rhetoric may add other dimensions and also perceive 'the people' as a community of blood, culture, race, and so forth. The first conception is republican, the second more traditionalist, organic and nationalistic. However, these are ideal-types rather than empirical realities. The republican model has had to make some exceptions to its highly abstract construction in order to accommodate sectoral or territorial claims. The 'ethnicist' variant of 'the people' is present in some democracies (for instance, Germany), but its potential capacities for exclusion are kept under control by the *Rechtsstaat*. The same confusion occurs when the concept is transposed from one level to another – for instance, from the nation-state to the European system. The very same advocates of the republican concept at the national level argue that a European democracy is a contradiction in terms given the absence of *a* European people.

When they define the people as an *ethnos*, rather than the more abstract *demos*, populist movements are placing themselves on a slippery slope. Once again, however, this is not fatal. Take the case of the Federal Republic of Germany where immigrants were long considered simply as 'guest workers', whilst German nationality was guaranteed to the descendants of Germans who had emigrated generations earlier! The tension in the German situation has been attenuated by a strong democratic regime and a generous asylum policy, but in most cases, an ethnicity-based conception of the people leads to exclusion, racism and xenophobia. Looking at their ideologies, in recent years, many populist movements appear to have fallen into this mould where populism is equated with the extreme Right. By the same token, immigration has become a central issue in their discourses. Foreigners are perceived to be a threat not only to the welfare state or the employment of domestic nationals, but also to the constitutive nature of the nation itself, its homogeneity and identity.

Representative politics and populism

Representation has helped to make democracy workable. Constitutionalism has guaranteed its survival. As stressed by Jean Leca (1996), democratic systems are characterised by an intrinsic tension between the power of the people on the one hand (the popular/populist will), and, on the other, the constitutionalist provisions which protect the citizen from the government, and the arbitrary exercise of power, even when this power derives from the political majority responsible for government.

Democracy was made possible in practical terms through the unexpected combination of popular sovereignty and the representative principle. The establishment and functioning of democracy certainly did not conform to the ideals of the philosophers or the idealised model of the Greek city-state. The absolute power of the people had to compromise with the need to devolve authority to an elite selected through competition within the boundaries of a polity. This ambiguous mix has become part of the genetic code of democratic regimes and many elements which are not, strictly speaking, 'democratic' (such as the rule of law or the welfare system) have become essential parts of modern democratic systems.

Unfortunately we have to live with this contradiction because neither social scientists nor politicians have been able to provide a more appealing or workable alternative. The present model can be adjusted and improved but it remains deeply marked by its original flaw – the constitutive tension between its ideology (the power of the people) and its functioning (the power of the elites chosen by the people). This contradiction is a permanent feature of democratic systems, and whilst it will not disappear, it may evolve and change in both form and intensity. This tension is underlined in a radical fashion by those who deny any merit to this historical and incomplete construction and suggest radical alternatives to the ambiguity of the democratic order. The communist parties and the anarchic movements on the Left, and the fascist/corporatist or authoritarian ideologies on the Right, are cases in point. Both have challenged the existing democratic regimes by proposing a new set of potential options, ideas, values and institutions, normally embodied within a political party, considered to be outside the system by the other government parties. But there are also other forms of challenge, of a different nature, offered by political movements or organisations which do not reject the democratic system as such but its organisation, and in particular, its foundations and constitutive arrangements. Democracy for them can be identified in Lincoln's motto of 'government of the people, by the people, for the people', with the emphasis on '*by* the people'. They reject, in more or less sophisticated ways, the modalities or even the principle of representation so congenial to contemporary democratic systems. Democracy (as it works) is challenged in the name of democracy (as it is imagined). As underlined by Margaret Canovan in this volume, it is 'the people' that constitutes the 'ideology' of those movements which sporadically emerge and disappear on the political scene of most democratic regimes. In other words, democracy means the power of the *demos*. Before 1787–89, most political thinkers would have argued that it was *only* the power of the *demos*, and this illusion lasted throughout the nineteenth and twentieth centuries. At the same time, during the past two centuries, democracy has become a composite regime which combines the rule of the people in many different ways (through representation and the majority principle) with the rule of law as a counterweight to the discretionary or arbitrary power of the people's representatives. Amongst the analysts and observers of the political systems there is broad agreement as to this mixed character of democracy and for once the empirical evidence converges with normative approaches. There is a certain amount of discussion and disagreement over the correct balance between these two components but, on the whole, there is a broad consensus that all democracies are founded on these two 'pillars'.

This realist analysis may help us understand why populist movements contest the functioning of the democratic systems as they now stand. All populist movements speak and behave as if democracy meant the power of the people and *only* the power of the people. Indeed, this feature is probably the sole element shared by populist movements and parties. They have defied all attempts to find comprehensive definitions or adequate typologies both from a longitudinal and/or spatial perspective. As noted by Paul Taggart '[A]ttempts to capture the essence of populism have sprung up at different times and in different places, but it is very difficult to see a consistent pattern' (Taggart 2000, 10).

This reductionist definition of democracy by populist leaders and voters is paradoxically facilitated by the representatives themselves who, more often than not, talk or act as if democracy were the pure expression of popular will. In doing so, they not only pave the way for more radical discourses, such as populism, but also prepare the rod to beat their own backs. Unable to deliver on the promises they have given, the structural, functioning conditions of democratic systems and their representatives become the target of demagogic discourse, being accused of betrayal, corruption, unaccountability, and incompetence.

From the outset, populist movements opposed the institutions or procedures which impeded the direct and full expression of the people's voice. For instance, in America at the end of the nineteenth century, the favourite scapegoats of the populist movements were not only the representatives themselves, but also the Federal Bank or the nascent regulatory agencies, who were accused of being insensitive to the needs of the people and too intimate with 'big business'. When populists did manage to gain influence, mainly at the state and local levels, they introduced mechanisms of direct election in order to strengthen the popular input within the institutions. In fact, the history of American democracy can be analysed in terms of the in built tension between the popular element and the sophisticated tools introduced to check and balance the power of the masses (Kazin 1995; Hertzke 1993; Manin 1997).

The European development was quite different. Not only did democracy develop later and more slowly, but the two versions experienced in France and Britain, while being different in content, style and speed, shared a common view: power lay in the hands of the people, but only through its representatives or delegates. France used universal suffrage to strengthen its authoritarian powers, while Britain affirmed the principle of parliamentary supremacy. In both cases, instruments of control (the courts), or the balance-of-power (the central banks), were weak or limited because they were perceived as incompatible with the power of the people. The French and British influences were often antagonistic, but converged in their emphasis on rule by the people (that is, parliamentary majority). Most of the new democracies emerging from the collapse of authoritarian empires after the First World War were built following this dominant paradigm. The main exception, under the influence of the prominent lawyer, Hans Kelsen, was Austria, which set up a Constitutional Court. In any case, the inter-war period was disastrous for most continental democracies which at best functioned badly, and at worst, simply collapsed. It soon became clear that non-democratic regimes, even fascist or Nazi governments, could achieve power through democratic elections.

The lesson was learnt and after the Second World War, with the notable exception of France and Britain, the new constitutional developments took a different course. The influence of the American model combined with the collapse of the fragile European democracies helped shift attention to the 'checks-and-balances' dimension of the constitutional arrangements. Democracy was still the power of the *demos*, but the *demos* was now only one component of democracy. Constitutionalism – that is, the development of counterweights to the unbalanced supremacy of the people – developed rapidly: enforceable human rights, constitutional courts, the territorial and functional division of powers, and the autonomy of the central banks all became key features of the new regimes. However, not all systems adjusted smoothly to this new order and to this revised view of democracy, particularly where radical or extremist parties challenged the new political arrangements.

Looking back over the past 50 years, the most remarkable phenomenon is the sheer continuity and consistency of the trend. The first changes were driven by the legacy of the past. The successive waves were linked to the transformation of the market and the progressive unleashing of economic forces still under the control of political and bureaucratic actors. The building of the Common Market, followed by the processes of privatisation and liberalisation, produced new exigencies, rules, and institutions. Once the shared domain of politicians and businessmen, the market now became a force in its own right, regulated by 'independent authorities' instead of representative government, and unaccountable to the people through the political process.

This second, constitutionalist, dimension of democracy is becoming so developed that some believe it jeopardises the very existence of democracy itself – that is people's democracy. Have we now gone too far? There is no clear answer to this question because each democratic system constitutes a 'mix' whose content varies over time and space. Some argue that the present dissatisfaction with democratic institutions or representatives is the result of inappropriate expectations on the part of the citizens (see, for example, Majone 1996), and that politics needs to be stripped of the illusion that it has a supreme ability to resolve human and social problems. Others, such as Fritz Scharpf (1999a), stress that democracy can work in two ways: via inputs (such as popular vote), or through an evaluation of the outputs produced by the political system. However, this dichotomy has a limited value as retrospective (output-oriented) assessment constitutes – thanks to the electoral process – an input for the incoming government. When this assessment is applied to non-democratic institutions (such as the courts or the central banks), the legitimacy of these bodies mainly depends on the quality of their choices and policies (as, for example, in the case of the *Bundesbank*).

These arguments are certainly pertinent and often based on empirical evidence, but they will prove to be useless if the public perception of the democratic deficit weakens the legitimacy of the political system. Feelings of powerlessness, of not being able to voice dissatisfaction effectively, or of not being able to make oneself heard, are all fertile ground for populist parties. Populist movements or parties are a by-product of the democratic malaise which they, in turn, exacerbate when the political elites and their democratic institutions are unable to address the challenge with vigour or efficiency.

Voice or exit? The populist mobilisation

In spite of their heterogeneity, populist movements all tend to develop their arguments in three distinct steps. In the first place, they emphasise the role of the people and its fundamental position, not only within society, but also in the structure and functioning of the political system as a whole. The people stand at the centre of their vision of the world and of the political institutions which organise the community. Community is indeed a fundamental concept as the definition of the people tends to integrate only those who are considered to be the 'true' people. This exclusion is more or less symbolic, depending on the type of populism (the wealthy or corrupt elites, for instance, are the favourite targets of most populist movements), or may approach the exclusion and racism found in Haider's or Le Pen's discourse. Populist movements tend to deny horizontal cleavages (such as the Left/Right divide) and to promote the fundamental unity of the people, while introducing a new vertical dimension, which may exclude, for instance, elites at the top and foreigners at the bottom.

Edward Shils (1956) was among the first to highlight this division and to emphasise the relationship between masses and elites as a key dimension. By extension, the populist resentment spreads to the institutions which embody and execute the principle of representation. In practice, when political elites are thus constituted, it means the rejection not only of the representatives but also of the mechanisms and institutions which organise this 'division of labour'. Drawing a line between the top and the bottom, the rich and the poor, the rulers and the ruled produces an effect similar to the classic division along social or economic cleavages – that is, a sharp contrast between the privileged and the underdogs. However, populism usually goes beyond the traditional opposition between competing political parties and/or parliamentary groups and, like the extreme parties, the political discourse is often based on the twin pillars of resentment and exclusion.

This rhetoric, based on the celebration of the good, wise, and simple people and the rejection of the corrupt, incompetent and interlocking elites, permeates the populist discourse. The condemnation of plutocrats and their political servants often has an anti-system flavour, more reminiscent of the extreme parties or movements than of traditional patterns of party politics. But, in the same way as the radical parties of the Left and Right, the populists draw a different type of division between the 'vast majority of the population', as the Communist parties used to say, on the one hand, and the tiny minority of rulers and exploiters, on the other. In this 'black and white' picture there is no room for more nuanced approaches or analysis.

Secondly, populist movements usually claim that the people have been betrayed by those in charge. Although the frequency of such changes may vary across time and country, this accusation is directed at some time or another against all political elites. Elites are accused of abusing their position of power instead of acting in conformity with the interests of the people as a whole.

Thirdly, the primacy of the people has to be restored. In the words of the *Mouvement Poujade* in France in the late 1950s (*'Sortez les sortants!'*), the elites in power have to be ousted and replaced by leaders capable of acting for the good of the community. This also means drastic changes in the institutions by means of a greater use of the tools of direct democracy, and by placing independent bodies such as central banks or independent (regulatory) agencies under strict political control. This challenge to established democratic regimes has two main targets: representation on the one hand, and non-elected independent bodies on the other. The ideal populist political system comes close, at least on paper, to a 'pure' democratic regime where the people are given the first and final word. However, this democratic stance is generally counteracted by the central position taken (or assumed) by the leader who is, supposedly, the best qualified to take on board, defend and protect the popular will.

These three basic components of populist claims are flexible enough to leave room for a great variety of populist movements, leaders or programmes. For instance, they may be partially taken on board by parties integrated into the system and to which the label 'populism' has rarely been applied, as in the case of the French Communist Party. As rightly pointed out by Georges Lavau (1969), this party played a key role in integrating those working-class voters who might otherwise have rejected the political system. He defines this role as the *'fonction tribunicienne du parti communiste français'* – that is, the party's capacity to control and steer anti-system feelings among the working classes. In other cases, political leaders or parties borrow the political rhetoric of populism for electoral opportunism. It is indeed ironic to listen to Jacques Chirac criticising the French elites of whom he is the epitome.

Populism should not be studied solely for its programmes and ideological standpoints, but also as a specific form of political mobilisation which differs both from classical modes of interest articulation and from political action through the channel of political parties. In this sense, populism may be interpreted as one possible reaction to the malfunctioning of the political system. Dissatisfaction with the way democracy works does not always mean mobilisation. Political action is costly and many people choose to exit by simply not voting. Absenteeism has increased everywhere, even in countries long characterised by a very high electoral turnout or mandatory voting. Populism is often the opposite and more demanding option: it is a political mobilisation designed to 'send a message' to those who govern. The sources of dissatisfaction may stem from different levels of the political system:

- from the political parties accused of being unable to propose programmes which match the aspirations of sectors of the population, or from the defence of specific interests;
- from the gap between electoral commitments and actual policy output;
- from the inability of the political class to put problems on the agenda and to debate solutions;
- from the lack of proper procedural or institutional instruments capable of channelling non-conventional views or ideas which disturb the internal equilibrium of political parties or institutions;
- from political or economic outputs, particularly in relation to economic and social policies;
- from the loss of trust in politicians or institutions.

Dissatisfaction is a relatively common phenomenon in any society and democracy is designed to allow, or should allow, the expression of this dissatisfaction and its translation via the change in governing elites and adopted policies. However, this universal character of democracy is modified by the institutional arrangements of particular systems and their specific capacity to manage the expression of the popular will, by the preferences citizens give to the various options for political involvement (vote, pressure, participation, protest, and so on.), and by the capacity of the system to make people's rights meaningful.

Voicing this dissatisfaction in various ways, including through 'populist' claims and strategies, may be interpreted as a crisis of democracy (see Crozier et al. 1975). It may also be seen as a challenge, associated with the functioning and transformation of representative democracy. All democracies are faced constantly with the need to justify the institutional and political channels of representation to new societal demands and needs. Rather than the manifestation of crisis, it is the expression of an in-built feature: if representation is an ad hoc and second-best solution to 'pure' democracy, it is condemned to constant adjustment. As underlined by Klingemann and Fuchs (1995), rather than a crisis of democracy (which by itself is not at stake), what we are facing is a challenge to the functioning of political systems.

Populist manifestations can also be seen as a 'reminder' to the elites. As pointed out by Dalton (1996, 84–5), 'Democracies must adapt to survive ... Democracy is threatened when we fail to take the democratic creed literally and reject these challenges'. In this sense, populism can be read as a fever warning which signals that problems are not being dealt with effectively, or points to the malfunctioning of the linkages between citizens and governing elites. Klingemann and Fuchs, for instance, do not see any contradiction between non-institutionalised participation and the emergence of new political actors on the one hand, and the institutional framework for democratic participation on the other. They conclude, rather optimistically, that 'the capacity of the representative democracy of Western societies to absorb and process problems arising from the transition to post-industrial society has apparently been adequate' (1995, 438).

This generally positive assessment may, however, overestimate the integrative capacity of western political systems. Most of them have been able to deal successfully with the various challenges faced in recent years, ranging from terrorism to forms of social protest. However, this capacity has not been uniform in the nature or swiftness of its response. In particular, explicit or hidden consensus among the political elites, or between the elites at large, has helped fuel the feeling that change was difficult or impossible when channelled via established political parties and 'normal' politics. Moreover, the European integration process has had a deep impact on national politics and policies, shaking up the traditional cleavages, threatening ideological and political alignments, and calling for a restructuring of interests, parties and institutions.

This uneasiness with 'politics as usual' can be observed in many countries, including those with a more balanced relationship between the power of the people and the constitutional system of checks and balances. Neither the United States nor Switzerland, which both make extensive use of the tools of direct democracy, have escaped the pitfalls of popular claims and protests. In both countries referenda and popular initiatives are so prolific that many politicians and observers have suggested reducing their scope and objectives. Populist movements and discourse are accentuated rather than reduced by the existence of opportunity structures favouring forms of popular expression. This is not particularly surprising given that the purpose of instruments giving voice to the people without the mediation of political parties is not to suffocate this direct expression, but, rather, to offer a complementary access to the political process. But far from challenging the power of the elites, these popular/populist tools may help strengthen the political system by preventing elites from becoming exclusively gatekeepers or rent-seekers. By placing problems and topics which do not appeal to the interests or ideologies of the governing elites on the political agenda, the popular input can reinforce the legitimacy of the system and contribute to a more lively and open public debate. This is often the case in the United States, where many issues arrive on the national agenda thanks to intense political debate during local or state referenda. The issue is not the more or less progressive or conservative character of popular involvement (which is a matter of taste), but rather the positive or negative impact that these forms of direct democracy may have on the working of representative democracy.

A similar observation can be made in the Swiss case where the use of referenda has been criticised as conservative and, more recently, as over-frequent and counterproductive: the *vox populi* all too often run counter to government by the elites making the country increasingly difficult to manage in the right direction (membership of the European Union being a case in point). In a recent publication, Trechsel and Sciarini (1998) challenge this common interpretation and lend empirical support to the hypothesis according to which the risks of negative feedback through popular referenda push the political elites into striking deals, implying a broader consensus than would be strictly necessary for a parliamentary adoption through majority rule. Paradoxically, the consensus among the elites is strengthened and becomes in its turn a problem, as the results for the Swiss populists in the recent general election in Switzerland would seem to indicate. The referendum has a veto function and allows voters to reject the legislation prepared by the political elites when they dislike it. It means that parliament and government work in the shadow of the people, which can threaten any reforms adopted.

> This has led to the development of the initial phase of the legislative process – the so-called pre-parliamentary phase – and strengthened the preferences of the elites for co-operative behaviour. Hence, the pre-parliamentary phase has, according to Neidhart, transformed the Swiss 'plebiscitarian democracy' into a 'bargaining democracy'. (Trechsel and Sciarini 1998, 302)

Democracy and populism are intimately interlinked. Both, in their own way, deal with the place and the role of people in democratic institutions. While democratic systems are constantly struggling with the uneasy association between the, at times clashing, principles of democracy and representation, populism tends to reject the principle of representation outright or at least to limit its use as much as possible. From this point of view, populism constitutes the most acute tension between the power of elites and the role of the masses. The ambiguous status of populism derives from the fact that it often places itself in a 'middle-of-the-road' position. It does not fully accept the usual instruments of representative democracy, but neither does it adopt strictly unconventional forms of political participation. Its repertory of action belongs more to the traditional tools of electoral politics than to the instruments of social mobilisation. Populism rejects parties but usually organises itself as a political movement; it is highly critical of political elites, but runs for elections; it advocates the power of the people, yet relies on seduction by a charismatic leader. In other words, populism is a warning signal about the defects, limits and weaknesses of representative systems. In spite of its often unpleasant tones, it may constitute an effective reminder that democracy is not a given, but is instead a constant enterprise of adjustment to the changing needs and values of society.

In the past, populism had been studied as a phenomenon in the form of protest movements, radical parties, and anti-system organisations. All too often observers have been puzzled by its loose, volatile and unstable definition and, at the same time, not enough attention has been paid to its relationship with democracy and democratic institutions. In this volume, we have attempted to tackle the complexity of populism by taking a slightly different approach. Our concern has not been so much the specific content of the populist party programmes as their position *vis-à-vis* the organisation and creeds of the democratic systems. While there is little doubt that the programmes of these parties are important, especially in view of the overt or covert ideologies they help propagate, focusing exclusively or mainly on this component may impede rather than promote a full understanding of the phenomenon. As observation shows, populist parties are generally very opportunistic. The same party can be pro-European or anti-EU within a very limited period of time according to its interests. It can be pro- or anti-globalisation according to the changing mood of its leader. Populist parties can be vociferous and extreme in opposition and more moderate and compromise-oriented when in power. In addition, as already underlined, it is precisely by identifying populism with specific programmes or ideologies that we miss out on its crucial specificity.

All of the chapters of this volume address the issue by examining precisely how populism amplifies the inherent tension between the democratic and 'non-democratic' components of democratic systems. Populist parties are by nature neither durable nor sustainable parties of government. Their fate is to be integrated into the mainstream, to disappear, or to remain permanently in opposition (as is the case in the United States for instance). Their weakness lies in the dream of an alternative form of democratic regime that they have been unable to articulate clearly, let alone establish. Their strength – and probably their permanence – derives from the drawbacks, failures and inconsistencies of the democratic regimes themselves insofar as democracy is both an ideal and a pragmatic, yet incomplete, reality. As long as the discrepancy between the ideal – and idealised – vision of democracy and the less than perfect political reality remains, there will be room for populism, in one form or another.

Populism puzzles observers and makes it difficult or even impossible to place it in a clear-cut category. In Part I of the volume, the contributions by Margaret Canovan, Yannis Papadopoulos, Paul Taggart and Peter Mair deal with the intricacies of the relationship between populism and representative democracy. As Margaret Canovan indicates in chapter 2, its only core ideology is 'the people' which allows for versatility and chameleonic positions according to time, place, needs and strategies. The weak and vague content of this ideological framework makes it more opportunistic and flexible than the more value-laden dominant ideologies. This intrinsic vagueness is exacerbated by the widespread and overextended use of the populist label, particularly in the media. As soon as a new political grouping tries to challenge the political establishment and does not match the familiar categories, it is tempting to denominate it as populist, a classification generally perceived as negative or even dangerous.

Populism cannot be labelled as a social movement given its preference for political action via the channels provided by the political system such as elections, referenda, and so forth. At the same time, however, populist organisations often derive from the protest of specific social groups (shopkeepers, owners of small businesses, employees faced with the threat of change and adaptation), and use instruments of mobilisation borrowed from the repertoire of protest movements. As neither pure social movements nor political parties in the classic definition of the term, populist organisations prefer alternative labels (Movement, League, Front). The use of the word 'party' is more the exception than the rule and often relates to the transformation of an old-style party (such as the FPÖ in Austria), or to the reliance upon the traditional and oldest denomination, 'the people's party' (this is particularly true in Scandinavia or in the Anglo-Saxon world). Whatever the word used to identify or, alternatively, to stigmatise, populism does indeed constitute a challenge to the party system. Not only can it try to destroy the party system by openly condemning its cartelisation (for example, in many instances Le Pen opted for '*la politique du pire*', preferring to defeat candidates on the Right by helping the candidates on the Left), but it can also try to 'join the club' and to 'take over' its weakest members (as Berlusconi has done since 1994). Not only can a populist party be an antidote to the cartel party system, but it can also contaminate the other parties by influencing the style of leadership, the type of political discourse, and the relationship between leader and followers. As Peter Mair states in his contribution,

> There is a fragmentation of once powerful collective electoral identities, there is a blurring of the ideological and organisational distinctions that once defined electoral choice and, to paraphrase Kornhauser, we see the emergence of a genuinely mass electorate whose relations with the institutions of government are no longer mediated to any significant extent.

Part II of the volume goes into more detail by considering the variegated forms of populism in four distinct national settings. Alan Ware emphasises the distinct character of populism and underlines that it 'appears less to be the politics of outsiders who are seeking a voice for themselves, and, instead, it forms one aspect of the political mainstream'. It has become a strategy. In his contribution on Italian system, Marco Tarchi analyses the roots of populism since the foundation of the Republic and the prolific mushrooming of populist parties and movements during the last ten years. The crisis of the First Republic in the wake of the corruption scandals of the 1990s has contributed to the birth of very different populist styles embodied in leaders as different and distinctive as Bossi, Di Pietro or Berlusconi. The elusive and transitory character of some of these parties and the progressive institutionalisation of others (*Forza Italia*) is a clear demonstration that populism is not a stable phenomenon, and that adaptation and adjustment to the rules of the game, whilst simultaneously contributing to changing those very same rules, is the price that must be paid to avoid political elimination. The same type of challenge can be observed in Austria, where Haider's party faces the risk of being transformed from a protest party into a party of government. As Wolfgang

Müller indicates in this volume, 'Such a transformation would require the FPÖ to abandon precisely the strategy responsible for its electoral breakthrough'.

In his contribution on France, Yves Surel shows that, whilst populist movements are not an unknown phenomenon in the Republican tradition, until the 1980s, the Fifth Republic managed to avoid being faced with the problem thanks to the populist components introduced under the Gaullist regime, in political discourse as well as in the formal institutions. Only when the Left came to power in France and the Right was unable to integrate all its internal components into mainstream politics, did populism re-emerge as the transformation of social cleavages and the shortage of available political space for newcomers initiated a process of realignment within the party system. It was briefly interrupted by the election of Chirac in 1995, curiously enough thanks to his use of the populist rhetoric for short-term and electoral campaign purposes.

Part III of the volume addresses the problem through a number of comparative case studies. Hans-Georg Betz analyses the sort of popular dissatisfaction which can breed populism and concludes that among the factors accounting for the rise of populist movements, perhaps the most important is the ability to appeal to and mobilise popular *ressentiments* generated by specific events or experiences. However, he points out the persistent differences between the various populist movements and concludes that 'We need to gain a better understanding of the specifics of each individual case'. This view is shared by Kitschelt who calls for a careful approach to the question and concludes that there is not much point in 'vague and generalised theorising about "rightist" and "populist" currents in developed post-industrialising democracies'. Finally, Cas Mudde extends the comparative investigation by examining the forms of populism emerging in the new democracies of Central and Eastern Europe.

The contributions in this volume depict a rather variegated and, at times, confusing situation which seems to discourage any attempt to find a common denominator. At the same time, however, the idea that so widespread a phenomenon cannot be anchored to some core commonalties or unifying principles is theoretically unacceptable. Part of the problem undoubtedly stems from the loose way in which the term is used. In this book we have reserved both the word and the concept for those ideas, parties or movements which place themselves within the democratic framework, rather than applying it to those regimes whose reference to the people is a poor fig-leaf concealing their dictatorial nature. However, the confusion may sometimes also derive from an overly restrictive and partial definition, particularly in the recent past, where populism has been equated with extremism or radical right-wing movements. Such movements are indeed part of the landscape, but they are only one part.

The fate of populism, as defined here, is associated with democratic regimes. Populism is the exacerbated expression of the people's place within democratic institutions, particularly at times when the political systems do not function properly, when tensions become too acute, when the channels for expressing discontent work badly, or when the political elites are perceived as breaking faith with those they represent. Representative democracy is challenged in the name of (people's) democracy. This explains why, in spite of this core constitutive element, populism presents itself in so many different guises: the nature of protest, and the channels and instruments used by the populists are very much conditioned by the structure of the political system, the nature of the problems at stake, the role and place of political parties, the adversarial or consensual style of politics, and so forth. But in spite of these variations in time and place, and in spite of its constitutive ambiguity, populism cannot be seen and analysed merely as a kind of democratic sickness. Rather, it is the indication of a democratic malaise that political actors and citizens would do well to take seriously. It is a valid and timely reminder that democracy is not a given, but is instead a permanently renewed construct.

Note

1. Moses Finley traces this dual meaning in Greek democracy and republican Rome. The English term is more likely to indicate a collection of individuals, whilst *'le peuple'* refers to the whole community constituted by the association of citizens and, at times pejoratively, to the lower strata of society.

Part I

Making Sense of Populism

2

Taking Politics to the People: Populism as the Ideology of Democracy

Margaret Canovan

Introduction

> Our government has lost touch with the people. (Ross Perot in Westlind 1996, 175)
>
> The parties and governments in most countries in Europe are isolated from their people. (Jörg Haider 1995, 88)
>
> What are democratic processes but the people? (George Wallace in Lipset and Raab 1971, 355)

Although populist[1] movements are usually sparked off by specific social and economic problems, their common feature is a political appeal to the people, and a claim to legitimacy that rests on the democratic ideology of popular sovereignty and majority rule. Analyses of populism often point to the tension within western democracy between this populist tradition and liberal constitutionalism. Certainly, there are difficulties in reconciling the project of giving power to the people with the drive to restrain power within constitutional limits, but concentration on this particular problem leaves unexplained the enduring strength of populist-democratic ideology and the ways in which it sustains populist movements. In this chapter I will argue that in order to understand populism we need to be aware of a complex and elusive paradox that lies at the heart of modern democracy. Crudely stated, the paradox is that democratic politics does not and cannot make sense to most of the people it aims to empower. The most inclusive and accessible form of politics ever achieved is also the most opaque. Precisely because it *is* the most inclusive form of politics, democracy needs the transparency that ideology can supply, and yet the ideology that should communicate politics to the people cannot avoid being systematically misleading.

This democratic paradox may be summed up as a contradiction between *bringing the people into politics,* that is, providing avenues and mechanisms to allow their concerns to be fed into the political process, and *taking politics to the people,* by allowing them to form an intelligible and persuasive mental picture of it. To simplify the issue, we contrast democracy with personal dictatorship. Under autocratic rule the mass of the people are completely excluded from power. Nevertheless they can form a mental picture of where power lies, so that the system that leaves them powerless is at least intelligible. Democracy, by contrast, is about widening the political arena to include the entire population. But the more successful the project of inclusion, the more crowded and dynamic the political arena, and the more interests and opinions exert some small influence on policies, the harder it is for any particular voter to form a picture of the location of power or to trace a clear path through the maze.

Ideology, which reduces the complexity of politics to dogmatic simplicity, is ill-fitted to deal with these intricacies, and yet it is indispensable in mass politics. As democracy becomes more inclusive, the need for a simple and vivid ideological map of the political maze becomes even more pressing. But the ideology of democracy, continually reaffirmed by politicians and the mass media, is full of populist themes that belie the current trend of democratic politics, stressing sovereignty and the exercise of the general will against compromise and accommodation, popular unity against multiplicity, majority against minorities, and directness and transparency against complex and intricate procedures. The paradox, in other words, is that while democracy, with its claims of inclusiveness, needs to be comprehensible to the masses, the ideology that seeks to bridge the gap between people and politics misrepresents (and cannot avoid misrepresenting) the way that democratic politics necessarily works. This contradiction between ideology and practice is a standing invitation to populists to raise the cry of democracy betrayed, and to mobilise the discontented behind the banner of restoring politics to the people.

In this chapter I will explore the democratic paradox through an analysis of the workings of populist democratic ideology. The first section elaborates the fundamental problem of how to *take politics to the people,* in the sense of presenting an intelligible mental picture, whilst simultaneously *bringing the people into politics,* and thereby generating an unavoidably opaque political system. The core of the analysis, an examination of the populist ideology in terms of which democracy continues to be popularly visualised, draws on Michael Freeden's theory of ideology as a specific form of political thinking. The final section argues that the democratic paradox appears to be insoluble. Ideology is indispensable as a bridge between people and politics, but the yawning gulf between democratic ideology and political practice is growing wider, partly as a result of more inclusive (and therefore more democratic) political practices. The ambiguities involved have been articulated by some of the most subtle of contemporary democratic theorists, including Jürgen Habermas and Claude Lefort, but not in terms that are communicable to voters. These deep tensions within the democratic project are a standing invitation to populist mobilisation.

People vs politics

The central populist message, repeated by diverse leaders and movements in many established democracies, is that politics has escaped popular control. The message is, 'this is *our* polity, in which we, the democratic sovereign, have a right to practise government by the people; but we have been shut out of power by corrupt politicians and an unrepresentative elite who betray our interests, ignore our opinions, and treat us with contempt'. Unlike officials, politicians and opinion-formers, populist leaders articulate a view from the grassroots. Their characteristic strategy is to highlight those issues where strongly held popular views have been neglected by decision-makers. Immigration, crime and employment are typical concerns, although the issues vary from one country to another. Whilst it is the negative aspects of populist movements that attract most attention, they are able to claim legitimacy by appealing to the people and calling for the restoration of democracy.

In the face of sporadic populist upsurges in many established democracies, some commentators have focused on the ability of manipulative leaders to attract those alienated from the political system by the strain imposed by economic and social change (Taggart 1996; Betz 1994; Immerfall 1998). Others have examined the political context, conceding that populism may in some instances be a rational response to systems that have been monopolised by a cartel of parties (Katz and Mair 1995; Mair 1995; Helms 1997). These approaches are fruitful, as is the familiar point that liberal-democratic traditions and institutions incorporate tensions between liberal and democratic priorities

(Beetham 1992). But the focus of this analysis is the way in which populist movements gain legitimacy as a result of a neglected paradox at the heart of democracy. The paradox is this: democracy is the most inclusive and 'popular' form of politics, taking politics to ordinary people, giving them political rights and access to multiple channels of influence. But it is for that very reason by far the most complex form of politics, so bafflingly tangled and opaque that the vast majority of its supposed participants can form no clear picture to help them make sense of it. *The fundamental paradox of democracy is, in other words, that empowerment undermines transparency.* Attempts to give a political voice to the population at large tend to produce institutions that separate people and power in the very process of mediating between them. Examples are easy to find. Consider the most fundamental of democratic practices, free elections. These require elaborate and obscure technical arrangements, and attempts to bring politics closer to the people by making elections more representative of ordinary citizens tend to generate greater obscurity. There is a trade-off between representativeness and transparency in the working of national electoral systems. In Britain, for example, the 'first-past-the-post' system produces relationships between votes and seats that are arbitrary and discriminatory, but its advantage lies in transparency: not just in being simple, but in offering a vivid mental picture of politics to the voters. 'first-past-the-post' portrays elections at the national and constituency level as sporting contests where the winner takes all. Though offensive to notions of representative fairness, this makes sense to voters, for whom an electoral victory after a recount has some of the drama of a winning goal scored in extra time. Its critics can choose from a variety of systems with lists, quotas, multiple votes, the Borda Count, the d'Hondt Formula and so on (Reeve and Ware 1992), but cannot escape the paradox that arrangements designed to give maximum effect to voters' choices throw up a smokescreen of technicalities that obscure their transparency to the citizen, and present voters with 'behind the scenes' coalition-building instead of the chance to 'throw the rascals out'.

It is not simply the fault of lazy voters or corrupt politicians, then, if democracy eludes the grasp of those it seeks to empower. There is an inescapable trade-off between transparency to ordinary citizens and properly functioning institutions that allow them access to politics. Everyone can understand the personal power of a visible boss, even as they cower under his rule, but the kind of politics that may empower and include them cannot help becoming opaque in proportion to its democratic effectiveness. Contemplating this dilemma, we can hardly be surprised if voters are periodically attracted by the populist dream of combining transparency and empowerment by entrusting their interests to a personal leader who is directly chosen by the people and who continues to defer to, and consult, them (Westlind 1996, 106, 177). Neither is it surprising that professional politicians enmeshed in highly institutionalised party machines should seek on occasion to present themselves to the electorate in a quasi-populist guise.[2] Our main concern here, however, is with the way in which these populist and quasi-populist attempts to bridge the gulf between politics and people are aided by the populist ideology of democracy.

Ideology and democracy

In general, ideology as a type of political thought is a response to the problem of linking political leaders with their followers. Unlike traditional rulers, no modern government, democratic or otherwise, can afford simply to ignore its population. Political activities that were once the personal affair of a more or less tiny elite have been transformed into *mass* politics, drawing in more and more of the population and requiring the latter's support or acquiescence. The gap between power and people has been spanned by ideologies – that is, by conceptual structures that provide a simplified map of the political world and motivate their followers by bestowing an almost religious significance on political doctrines and symbols.

But the end of the millennium saw a sharp reaction against ideology, found guilty of having damaged theory and practice alike. Ideological commitments had imprisoned too many theorists in dogmatic blinkers, blinding them to reality, and the practical effects had been even more serious, leaving the world littered with the ruins of the ideological projects of both Left and Right. Reacting against these experiences, many political actors have retreated into pragmatism, while political thinkers have replaced ideological faith with postmodern scepticism. Despite its obvious dangers and costs, however, political ideology is hard to do without. As political parties have found, dropping ideological commitments can make it hard to motivate activists and may encourage cynicism and corruption among the elite, and indifference or distrust among voters. And if the loss of ideological faith is a problem for political parties, it represents a more serious difficulty for democratic systems themselves. Democratic ideology, which is, as we shall see, thoroughly populist, is still needed to legitimise the system to voters and to mobilise them for participation. It is reaffirmed with every election campaign, as politicians in search of votes pay lip-service to this picture of democracy. But since the ideology contradicts the way democratic politics necessarily works, populists – who do take it seriously – are encouraged in their belief that they, rather than the politicians, are the true democrats. A closer look at this populist ideology of democracy should help us to understand why modern democratic politics persistently generates populist movements.

Populist ideology: some objections answered

First a caveat: 'ideology' is not used here in the Marxist sense, nor in any other sense that identifies ideology with delusion and manipulation. I am using the term in a more neutral sense, drawing on the approach developed by Michael Freeden. Freeden understands ideologies as conceptual maps of the political world, and regards them as important forms of political thinking that merit examination in their own right, not just as poor relations of political philosophy (Freeden 1996). Fully developed ideologies such as liberalism and socialism are indeed very elaborate conceptual structures, but the particular interest of ideologies, in Freeden's view, is that they do not shut themselves away in ivory towers but are closely linked to political action and mobilisation and '... straddle the worlds of political thought and political action, for one of their central functions is to link the two' (Freeden 1996, 76). They do so by cutting through complexities to provide clear guidance, reducing the kaleidoscopic permutations of ideas to something manageable, and at the level of practice 'converting the inevitable variety of options into the monolithic certainty which is the unavoidable feature of a political *decision*, and which is the basis of the forging of a political identity' (Freeden 1996, 76 – 7).[3]

The relative crudity and dogmatism of ideological thinking is, in other words, the price of political effectiveness, generating a creed able to mobilise and guide a movement. Ideology bridges the gap between politics and people by converting opaque complexities into a picture that voters can grasp. Where philosophical analysis calls everything into question, continually opening up for debate the concepts with which it deals, in Freeden's view the most salient feature of ideologies is that they are configurations of 'decontested' concepts, built around a core of concepts whose significance and range of meanings are beyond question. Whilst ideological traditions are themselves battlegrounds where different factions try to capture the sacred standards and to lead the fight into a different territory, the bitterness of such struggles owes much to the shared assumption that within the framework of a particular ideology, the most important things are settled, and certain questions are 'not in order'.

In applying Freeden's theory to populism and democracy I shall supplement it by focusing more on the motivational aspects of ideology, that is, its ability to inspire faith and bestow legitimacy. Because he wants to rescue ideologies from philosophical contempt, Freeden concentrates on the most intellectually elaborate versions, taking care to stress their intellectual content by insisting that they must be treated as configurations of concepts rather than as expressions of emotion. This approach tends to underplay the emotional charge implicit in ideological concepts and their capacity to inspire faith and commitment, features that matter a good deal in the present context.[4] For an ideology motivates its followers by offering a redemptive vision, promising salvation through politics by pointing the way to a better world. Indeed, ideologies demand not only faith but dedication from those who have seen the vision of that transfigured world. The quasi-religious qualities of ideologies such as socialism, liberalism, nationalism or green politics have often been recognised. What is less often noted, however, is that democracy, too, has its ideological aspect, promising a better world through the return of power to the people. Without this inspiration it is hard to see how democratic reforms could ever have been achieved. From the Levellers to the Chartists, from 'People Power' in the Philippines to the students of Tiananmen Square, those who struggled for democracy have always believed that what was at stake was a new beginning.

Before examining this ideology in detail it may be wise to forestall some objections to connecting democratic ideology with the sporadic populist movements characteristic of contemporary democracies. Can anything resembling ideology really be attributed to the latter? In the first place, students of these movements may object that populists have no settled views on most political issues, and that their utterances have too little intellectual content to amount to an ideology. As Hans-Georg Betz says, 'Populist parties are generally held to lack grand visions or comprehensive ideological projects' (Betz 1994, 107). A second objection is that insofar as populists do take up firm positions, these are merely reactive and do not constitute a positive vision. Thirdly, it may be argued that instead of searching in vain for the conceptual structure that an ideology requires, we should instead analyse populist utterances as a characteristic *discourse*, the strength of which lies precisely in its lack of content, and hence its readiness for use in a range of different contexts for a variety of different purposes. While these are all significant objections, they do not constitute insuperable barriers to my present undertaking. Whilst Freeden himself does not discuss populism (or democracy) as an ideology, aspects of his analysis of other ideologies are significant.

On the first point, that of lack of intellectual substance, Freeden makes a pertinent distinction between 'full' ideologies (such as liberalism or socialism) which provide a comprehensive map of virtually the entire political world, and 'thin-centred' ideologies 'with a restricted core attached to a narrower range of political concepts' (Freeden 1998, 750). Nationalism, feminism and ecologism may all be candidates for analysis, despite falling more or less short of ideological comprehensiveness (Freeden 1996, 485–7, 550). Since our main concern here is with populism as the ideology of democracy, lack of substance outside such a core is of no interest to us.[5]

The second objection, that populism has no ideological content because it is merely reactive, is more interesting. Students of populist movements agree that a very large part of the populist message is negative and critical. Populists always attack the power elite of politicians and bureaucrats for their privileges, their corruption, and their lack of accountability to the people. They also attack those they identify as clients of the elite and beneficiaries of taxes paid by ordinary, hard-working people: typically, asylum-seekers, immigrants, minorities who have been granted special treatment, welfare recipients and so on. They protest against the internationalist cultural elite who despise the majority's traditional habits and opinions and foist politically correct and 'progressive' policies upon them.[6] They identify external forces (from international capitalists to Brussels bureaucrats) as threats to the way of life and economic security of 'ordinary people'. All of this is clearly defensive (Taggart 1996; Immerfall 1998), but there is also a positive element which lies in the promise to look after 'our people', the faith in 'the common sense of the common people', the call for the voice of the people to be heard and power restored to them (Haider 1995; Manning 1992). It is indeed this core set of concerns with 'the people', combined with an antagonistic critique of the powers that be, which generate positions that are recognisably populist.

The third possible objection to examining populism as ideology is that it is better treated as *discourse,* that is, as a kind of language and rhetoric, a particular style of simplicity and directness, or the communication of a specific political mood. There is no doubt that analysis of this kind has much to recommend it (Canovan 1999; Kazin 1995; Westlind 1996), but discourse is not the end of the matter (Freeden 1996). Populism also has a characteristic core of *concepts* that it asserts, prioritises and decontests – democracy, popular sovereignty, the people understood as a collectivity with a common will, and majority rule. These cannot be dismissed as empty rhetorical flourishes. Not only are they sacred banners under which generations of radicals have fought for democratic institutions, but they trail behind them the weight of the western tradition of democratic ideals articulated by (among others) Paine, Jefferson, Lincoln and (in his more populist mood) Rousseau. It is precisely this confident appeal to democratic tradition that makes populism such a worrying phenomenon to many non-populist democrats. Following Freeden's insight that ideology operates in the middle ground between philosophy and political action, we need to pay serious attention to populists' use of central democratic concepts while conceding their philosophical limitations.

Populist ideology: an analysis

Freeden's claim is that any genuine ideology contains a core structure of tightly interrelated concepts. No ideology has a monopoly of its preferred concepts, and within the wider discourse of politics those same concepts may be understood in many different ways, but within the framework of a particular ideology great efforts are made to 'decontest' them – that is, to put them beyond question by giving them a particular meaning and significance. Since the key concepts are bound together in a structured core, the prescribed meaning of each one shapes the ways in which the others are understood, while the ideological core itself affects the interpretation of a range of less central concepts. None of this implies that ideological thinking excludes all ambiguity (Freeden 1996, 77), but the key point is that within the bewildering maze of available political ideas, an ideology gives priority to certain topics rather than others, and interprets concepts within strict limits.

The key concept that lies at the heart of populist ideology is undoubtedly 'the people', followed by 'democracy', 'sovereignty' and 'majority rule', each defined through its links with the others. Thus, democracy is understood as government by the sovereign people, *not* as government by politicians, bureaucrats or judges. Furthermore, the linked concept of sovereignty implies that much more is involved than mere popular elections or consultation: democracy demands that political decisions be under popular control. Within this conceptual context there can be no doubt that so-called 'direct democracy' (the use of popular initiatives and referenda) has a much better claim than representative institutions to be the real thing. The point of voting is to declare the will of the people, identified by means of the associated principle of majority rule. The meaning of majority rule is in turn influenced by the concepts that surround it. No mere device for settling disputes by counting individual votes, it is raised to the dignity of the oracle who declares the will of the sovereign people. The emphasis on sovereignty reinforces the implication that democracy is a politics of will and decision rather than accommodation and compromise; furthermore it is a matter of public decision open to the people, not an opaque practice whereby the leaders of factions work out compromises behind closed doors. Attributing sovereignty to the people emphasises and sharpens the distinction between the sovereign people and those ruling in their name.

Above all, what this conceptual configuration does is to give a vivid outline to the central concept of 'the people'. Instead of referring to a mere agglomeration of individuals with no manifest links or boundaries, 'the people' acquires unity and definition. As sovereign and rightful rulers, 'the people' must be understood as an entity, a corporate body with a continuous existence over time, capable of having common interests and a common will. Furthermore that body must be capable of action, able to express its will and to take decisions. While a numerical majority of votes may be the way that the will is expressed, a prime characteristic of 'the people' is unity. So are boundaries: the contrast between 'us' and 'them', between those who are and are not included in the notion of 'the people', is a crucial aspect of the ideological picture (Westlind 1996). Popular sovereignty implies boundaries of two kinds. As legitimate sovereign, 'the people' is distinguished from, and counterposed to, the power elite, from whom power is to be retrieved. But its sovereign independence of external powers also gives it territorial definition, linking its borders to the boundaries of the polity, while its essential unity narrows down its identity, making it equivalent to the nation.

The attraction of an ideological picture of this kind is that it promises to make politics transparent, offering a short-cut that bypasses philosophical disputes and institutional niceties. Philosophically, the point about ideological thinking is that key concepts are, to use Freeden's term, 'decontested'. That is to say, they are interpreted in such a way that some key questions are simply not asked. It is worth enumerating a few of the troublesome philosophical problems that this ideological picture of democracy enables its adherents to avoid thinking about. For example, the decontested notion of 'the people' as the nation sweeps under the ideological carpet awkward questions about the criteria to be used in determining where democratic boundaries fall, and who should or should not be entitled to vote in referenda on crucial issues such as secession or immigration. The ideology also dodges the problems related to identifying majority decisions with the authoritative voice of the people. Apart from the concerns this raises about minority rights in the face of a sovereign majority, there are well-known theoretical difficulties involved in trying to combine individual votes in a collective decision able to present itself as 'the will of the people'. In a classic critique, William Riker took aim directly at 'populist democracy', setting out to demolish the notion of 'the people's will'.

> The populist interpretation of voting (i.e., that what the people, as a corporate entity, want ought to be public policy) cannot stand because it is inconsistent with social choice theory. If the outcomes of voting are, or may be, inaccurate or meaningless amalgamations, what the people want cannot be known. Hence the populist goal is unattainable. (Riker 1982, xviii)

But if Riker (see also Weale 1999, ch. 7) expected his dissection of 'populist democracy' to kill it off, he might just as well have saved himself the trouble. The ideology of 'government by the people' and 'majority rule' survives unimpaired by philosophical refutations and retains the power to bestow or withhold political legitimacy. For an ideology's core concepts are not just decontested and defended against philosophical debate, but are also charged with sanctifying force. Ideology infuses humdrum political arrangements with faith in redemption through politics, putting beyond question not only the meaning of popular sovereignty, but also its virtue and saving power.

The practical impact of this ideology can be illustrated by examining referenda, devices favoured by populists and, for that reason, feared by many democrats. Although these institutions are often referred to as 'direct democracy', a label that would appear to endorse the populist picture, they need not in themselves be infused with populist ideology. Precisely for this reason they can help us see just how confusingly entwined ideology is with the workings of democracy. It must be emphasised first of all that referenda (like elections) *can* be looked at (and sometimes used) in a thoroughly non-ideological way. They can be treated simply as one set of technical devices among others in the repertoire of modern politics, to be assessed in a dispassionate and pragmatic manner. Viewed in this way, direct consultation of the voters is rich in complexities and technicalities, for there are many different kinds of referendum, carrying different political implications (Smith 1976; Butler and Ranney 1994; Gallagher and Uleri 1996; Kobach 1993). Beyond the framework of ideology, few useful generalisations can be made about referenda, and arguments for or against them are necessarily complex and technical. One can discuss their complexity and argue for their increasing use without departing from that dispassionate, non-ideological tone, as some political scientists have recently done (for example, Budge 1996). But in order to grasp the potential political significance of referenda we need to take account of the way they may appear when seen through the spectacles of the democratic ideology analysed above. Some instances of this political device are particularly likely to attract an ideological halo because they offer the opportunity of translating all the core concepts examined here into practice. Take, for example, the promised British referendum on whether or not to adopt the Euro in place of sterling. From a dispassionate, non-ideological point of view, this could be regarded simply as a convenient decisional mechanism for dealing with an issue that causes divisions within political parties. It is, however, highly unlikely to function in that pragmatic manner; indeed, the use of a referendum to resolve such a major political issue seems certain to endorse and emphasise the populist ideology of democracy.

Let us consider how well the case fits the ideological picture. A polity-wide referendum on such a major issue would seem to imply an understanding of democracy as popular sovereignty. Sovereignty will be stressed in many ways, not just because the anti-Euro campaign will warn of a possible loss of British independence, but because those living in this distinct territorial polity will themselves be taking the decision, emphasising the boundary between 'us' and 'them'. Furthermore, the vote cannot avoid appearing as an exercise of sovereign will, for a single-issue referendum implies a clear decision rather than an intricate compromise. What is at issue is, of course, *popular* sovereignty, since the decisive act of will is shifted from politicians and the elite to the mass of the electorate. This also means that those campaigning on both sides have to translate the issues at stake from the complexities of elite negotiation into terms that the electorate can understand, thereby confirming the ideological expectation that politics ought to be simple enough for everyone to grasp. Meanwhile, campaigning itself is bound to emphasise the importance of the decision made. The rarity of referenda in British politics can only accentuate the solemnity of this appeal to the ultimate authority, emphasising the contrast between politicians and people.[7] The sovereign people who take this momentous decision on behalf of the polity, binding themselves and their successors, cannot be seen merely as a conglomeration of individuals but as a *corporate* people, identified with the historic nation not only by the issue at stake but by the referendum process itself. Furthermore, the process confers an extra dignity on the counting and assembling of individual votes; *majority rule* means that the entire sovereign people speak through the balance of votes. The legitimacy conferred by such a procedure must far outweigh the legitimacy of any mere parliamentary decision, thereby vindicating the populist ideology of democracy.

It is for reasons of this kind that many democrats (including some committed to increasing popular participation in politics) have grave misgivings about the wisdom of holding referenda (see Magleby 1984). But the crucial point to note is that the ideological simplification and intensity considered here should not be seen simply as dangers that are hard to avoid in conditions of mass politics: they can also have an invaluable function as sources of political legitimacy. Referenda, such as those on the Maastricht Treaty, or the votes North and South of the Irish border on the 1998 Belfast Good Friday Agreement, can carry great political weight when they are seen through ideological lenses and taken as the voice of the people.[8] But these are only especially dramatic instances of a process of legitimation that is to some degree needed at every election. However hard it may be to square ideology with philosophical critiques and institutional technicalities, it is not something that democratic politics can safely do without.

It may be objected that even if the importance of ideology is conceded, the *populist* ideology of democracy may still be challenged. Many democrats would call into question its understanding of democracy as a politics of will and decision rather than of accommodation and compromise, and its monolithic concept of the people, identified with the majority. Such critics often accuse populists of misunderstanding or misrepresenting what democracy is really about. Disputes of this kind follow the characteristic form of ideological argument, where the object is to capture a central concept (in this case 'democracy'), and to decontest it in a different way, anchoring it with appropriate concepts to hold it in place and control its implications.

Although populist democratic ideology is more or less deeply entrenched in the political culture of most established democracies,[9] there are alternatives that are also charged with redemptive energy. The most influential draws on the rich resources of liberal ideological traditions to maintain that what democracy is really about is securing universal human rights through the rule of law, so that concepts such as 'people', 'sovereignty' and 'majority rule' must be modified and reinterpreted in the light of that central concern. It is highly probable that tensions between the liberal and the populist ideological will be heightened by the increased use in many democracies of referenda on the one hand and of judicial review of political decisions on the other, the latter often influenced by liberal beliefs about human rights (Knopff 1998). From the populist point of view, lawyers (especially *foreign* lawyers) form as attractive a target as political parties and big business.

The insoluble paradox of democracy

Since there is indeed an ideological contest between populist and liberal understandings of democracy, attention tends to be concentrated on that particular battle. My thesis is, however, that the tensions that spark off populism within democratic polities have even deeper roots. The problem, then, is how to reconcile ideology of any kind, populist or liberal, with the way democracy does or could function. The problem would appear to be insoluble: ideology is indispensable as a bridge between people and politics, and of all forms of politics, democracy most needs to make that link, yet democracy as we know it is peculiarly hard to capture in ideological terms.

Consider some of the practical developments that tend to make the practice of democratic politics more opaque, particularly in Europe. One aspect is the legalism already mentioned – that is, the increasing involvement of courts of various kinds in political decisions. Instances in which decisions by the elected governments of EU states are overruled by EU law or by the European Court of Human Rights also illustrate the increasing institutional complexity of a world in which international linkages of many kinds are eroding state sovereignty and blurring the territorial boundaries of polities. At the national and international level it is becoming harder to say exactly where power lies. Even the jealously guarded sovereignty of the British Parliament is being eroded by European institutions on the one hand and devolution on the other. Elsewhere in Europe decision-making power is diffused in the practice of coalition politics and consociationalism, together with the ever-increasing network of lobbyists and pressure groups. Moreover, this process of diffusion should not be thought of simply as increasing domination by elites. More politicisation of the grassroots and a greater willingness on the part of citizens to campaign against GM foods or Third World debt only wind further strands into the tangle of democratic politics. In contrast to the ideological stress on concentrated will and decision, practical democracy is a politics of diffuse *talking*, some of it public debate, some of it legal deliberation, and much of it the formulation of elaborate deals and compromises by political professionals. Politics of this kind is democratic in the sense that the laws and policies that come out at the end of the process have been influenced by inputs from many sources, including channels to which every citizen has some access. Compared with the various forms of dictatorship, its relative inclusiveness is indeed impressive. From the point of view of most citizens, however, the route from inputs to outcomes is far from transparent, and it is hard to see how this could be otherwise.

In recent decades, some of the more influential contemporary democratic theorists have tried to articulate this democratic practice, repudiating the preoccupations of democratic ideology in the process. The terminology of rule, sovereignty, will, and decision-making is increasingly being displaced by a focus on talk, discourse, and deliberation. While some theorists hanker after an ideal of deliberation that would give rise to a transparent rational consensus (for instance, Dryzek 1990), there is among the most sophisticated an increased and significant readiness to identify democracy with the actual process of political deliberation, recognising that its conduct is labyrinthine and its outcomes contingent and not necessarily rational. The tendency is to define democracy in terms of the rules and procedures that prevent any group from monopolising power, to encourage the representation of plural views and interests, to protect the citizen's right to participate, and to set the stage for policy to emerge from a complex process of discussion and negotiation not confined to formal bodies nor sharply limited by territorial boundaries.

This procedural understanding of democracy has been most cogently articulated in the writings of the German philosopher, Jürgen Habermas (Habermas 1996). Habermas' position is particularly interesting in the populist context because he retains notions of 'popular sovereignty' and 'will-formation', but reinterprets them in a thoroughly non-populist way. Within his 'discourse theory' of 'deliberative politics', popular sovereignty is 'proceduralised'[10] and the collective sovereign of populist ideology vanishes into the diffuse channels of public opinion and influence. Rejecting the picture of a unified body of citizens that can take collective action (or, indeed, a Riker-style dissolution of the people into distinct individuals), he thinks in terms of a 'decentred society' in which public opinion emerges from a dense network of communication and discussion that includes official and unofficial channels. This complex process of public discussion forms the link between people and power. 'Informal public opinion-formation generates "influence"; influence is transformed into "communicative power" through the channels of political elections; and communicative power is transformed into "administrative power" through legislation' (Habermas 1994, 8). In this process no one is sovereign. Many different views and perspectives affect the outcome, and the need to offer public justification for policies rationalises and refines interests and opinions, but the procedure offers no scope for populist notions of the direct exercise of the people's will. Interestingly, however, Habermas denies that the intricate democratic process he describes simply excludes popular sovereignty.

> This is not to denounce the intuition connected with the idea of popular sovereignty but to interpret it in intersubjective terms. Popular sovereignty, even if it becomes anonymous, retreats into democratic procedures and the legal implementation of their demanding communicative presuppositions only in order to make itself felt as communicatively generated power. Strictly speaking, this communicative power springs from the interactions between legally institutionalised will-formation and culturally mobilised publics. (Habermas 1994, 10)[11]

While Habermas does not discuss populist ideology, his account does recognise the democratic contradiction explored above, between the complexity of democratic politics and the indispensability of 'the intuition connected with the idea of popular sovereignty'. But he does not address the problem of *how* people recognise their sovereignty in the procedures he describes, particularly if (as populists claim) such procedures systematically exclude many of the issues that most concern 'ordinary people'. His own account is as forbiddingly complex and opaque as the democratic procedures he is analysing, and is certainly not calculated to make them transparent to baffled voters.

Turning from Habermas to the very different writings of the influential French political thinker Claude Lefort we find some interesting parallels. Once again we encounter a theory that attempts to articulate the peculiar complexity and open-endedness of democratic politics, that treats 'the people' with ambiguous subtlety, and is expressed in an equally opaque style. Lefort's best-known insight is his observation that whereas monarchy means power exercised by a king, democracy does *not* mean power wielded by the people, but rather that 'the locus of power becomes an empty place' (Lefort 1988, 17). The point about democracy is that power is dispersed, continually contested, and not possessed by any single person or collective body. The idea of popular sovereignty was originally modelled on kingship, and was an attempt to cast a collective 'people' in the role previously occupied by the sacred person and body of the king. But the achievement of democracy was actually to dissolve that corporate unity into a dynamic and multifaceted form of politics. Lefort sees the seeds of totalitarianism in attempts to put this fragmented and unpredictable society back together again, and to organise politics as if 'the people' really *were* a single body, arguing that the social unity and transparency that totalitarianism seeks to recreate by force are quite alien to democracy.

Although Lefort does not discuss populism, in his terms its craving for transparency in the exercise of popular sovereignty must harbour totalitarian possibilities. His sensitivity to the dangers of imagining 'the people' as one and sovereign therefore makes it all the more striking that he should nevertheless (like Habermas) acknowledge democracy's need for legitimation through the image of popular sovereignty. As he sees it, democracy is balanced on a knife-edge between totalitarianism and mere corruption. If we are to be able to stop politicians behaving as if the polity were their private possession, we need to believe that 'the people' are the source of power, but at the same time we cannot operationalise popular sovereignty without heading toward totalitarianism.

> The legitimacy of power is based on the people; but the image of popular sovereignty is linked to the image of an empty place, impossible to occupy, such that those who exercise public authority can never claim to appropriate it. Democracy combines these two apparently contradictory principles: on the one hand, power emanates from the people; on the other, it is the power of nobody.[12] And democracy thrives on this contradiction. Whenever the latter

> risks being resolved or is resolved, democracy is either close to destruction or already destroyed. (Lefort 1986, 279)

Despite his claim that 'democracy thrives on this contradiction', Lefort (like Habermas) does not deal with the problem of how this subtle intuition might be conveyed to those who think that they *are* 'the people'. Politicians seeking votes do not even try, but instead continue to reinforce the ideological picture with every election fought.

Theories such as those of Lefort and Habermas are interesting because they articulate in theoretical terms the way modern democratic politics works, *including its contradictions*. On the one hand, they highlight the fact that democracy as practised is quite unlike the picture of it painted by populist ideology. Power is diffuse rather than concentrated; policies emerge from adjustments between multiple initiatives rather than by clear acts of will; and countless political actors and interests, many of them spanning territorial frontiers, replace the populist image of a unified and sharply defined sovereign people. On the other hand, that same decentred, proceduralised, internationalised democratic politics cannot do without 'the image of popular sovereignty' as a kind of patron saint inspiring and presiding over it.

What we seem to be left with, in other words, is the impasse from which we began. The most sophisticated theorists of democracy, observing the increasingly complex way in which democratic politics actually works, confirm that, of all forms of politics, democracy is the hardest to render transparent. It is agreed that the picture of democracy sustained by populist ideology is misleading, but it is also conceded that the intricate procedures and processes which constitute democratic politics require legitimation by means of symbolic references to the authority of the people, even though such symbols are dangerous if construed literally. It would appear that voters need to swallow a democratic equivalent of Plato's 'noble lie', whilst not believing in it to the point that they attempt to act on it.

Conclusion

I have argued that in order to find the sources of populist protest, it is not sufficient to look at socioeconomic difficulties, the defects of party systems, or even the tensions between the liberal and the democratic strands in modern 'liberal democracy'. Instead, we need to be aware of a fundamental contradiction which lies at the heart of the democratic project. This can be summed up as a contradiction between *bringing the people into politics,* and *taking politics to the people.* Democracy is about widening the political arena to include the entire population instead of a few powerful interests. But the more successful that project of inclusion, the more crowded and congested the political arena, and the harder it is for any particular voter to have a clear picture of democracy. Ideology, which reduces the complexities of politics to dogmatic simplicity, is ill-fitted to deal adequately with these intricacies, and yet is at the same time indispensable in mass politics. Indeed, as democracy becomes more inclusive, that mass public becomes ever larger and the demand for a simple and persuasive ideological map more pressing. I have tried to show that the traditional and dominant ideology of democracy is full of populist themes that cut across the current trend of democratic politics, stressing sovereignty against accommodation, majority against minorities, transparency against intricate procedures. In contrast to the present tendency for democratic politics to flow across territorial frontiers, populist ideology also stresses the boundedness of the people and their territory, a particularly explosive theme in an age of economic globalisation and international migration. No wonder, then, if populist leaders and their followers interpret the contradiction between ideology and politics as a clash between shining ideal and corrupt practice. We may indeed concede that, since the institutional complexities that aid inclusiveness also help to conceal corruption, they may in many instances have a case.[13]

Notes

1. This analysis is concerned with political populism in established democracies, meaning movements that appeal to 'the people' against both the existing structure of power and the dominant ideas and values of the society. For a justification of this structural account see Canovan 1999, 3–5. On broader uses of the term 'populism', see Canovan 1981, Ionescu and Gellner 1969.
2. Consider some of the soundbites in Tony Blair's speech to the Labour Party Conference following his landslide victory in the British general election of 1997: 'Ours was not a victory of politicians but of people', 'As one woman put it to me, "We've got our government back"'; 'On May 1, the people entrusted me with the task of leading their country into a new century' (excerpts from the speeches at the 1997 Labour Party Conference, 8–9).
3. Emphasis in original.
4. For a brief discussion of emotion in ideology see Freeden 1996, 29–30. On the place of emotion in nationalist ideology, see Freeden 1998, 754.

5. Fuller populist ideologies of different kinds can be found in the American People's Party of the 1890s and in the Russian *narodnichestvo* of the 1870s. For summaries see Canovan 1981. For contemporary versions of full-scale populist ideology (formulated, of course, by intellectuals) see Lasch 1991 and Piccone 1994, 173–208.
6. In the words of George Wallace, whose slogan was, 'Nobody is for Wallace but the People', 'the average American is sick and tired of all those over-educated ivory tower folks with pointed heads looking down their noses at us' (Lipset and Raab 1971, 350).
7. By contrast, the constant use of popular decision in Switzerland may help to dilute the ideological charge attached to any particular referendum, making for a politics that is popular but less populist (Helms 1997, 47).
8. On the significance for voters of the sense that the Agreement represented a 'new beginning', see Hayes and McAllister 1999.
9. See Article 3 of the French Fifth Republic's Constitution: 'National sovereignty belongs to the people, which shall exercise it through its representatives and by means of referendums' (Butler and Ranney 1994, 49).
10. Compare Norberto Bobbio's assertion that democracy is above all 'a set of procedural rules' (Bobbio 1987, 63).
11. See also Appendix I, 'Popular Sovereignty as Procedure' in Habermas 1996.
12. Compare Giovanni Sartori's claim that in democracy, the principle 'all power to the people' has to be modified into *'all power to nobody'* (Sartori 1987, 72) (emphasis in original).
13. I am grateful to John Barry, April Carter and John Horton for helpful comments on a previous version, and to the SPIRE Theory Group at Keele and participants in the workshop from which this volume originates.

3
Populism, the Democratic Question, and Contemporary Governance

Yannis Papadopoulos

Introduction

There is now a substantial body of research on populism which focuses, in particular, on what motivates people to support successful *national*-populist parties, such as '*Verdrossenheit*' (frustration) with established parties (Schedler 1996), reactions against the success of 'left-libertarian' movements (Kitschelt and McGann 1995), or the concern of the losers in the modernisation process triggered by internationalisation (Kriesi 1999), and the fears of those negatively affected by post-industrial forms of social organisation (Ignazi 1999). In contrast to these important empirical findings, this chapter is guided by more theoretical and conjectural considerations. As it is reductionist to consider populism as either a pathology of, or a threat to, democracy, I shall focus on the ambivalent link between populism and democracy, which in turn requires a certain familiarity with major debates taking place in democratic theory. In this analysis I will attempt to formulate new hypotheses as to the origins of populist successes, and possible links with the transformations taking place in democratic decision-making, which in turn requires an understanding of the lessons of policy analysis.

Populism and democracy: an uneasy partnership

Hermet refers to the day-to-day routines of democracies, somewhat ironically, as a '*savoir-vivre démocratiquement sans trop faire référence au peuple*' (Hermet 1992, 15), and Canovan (1999, 15) notes that 'many of the themes of populism are easily familiar to ... the theories of participatory democracy that emerged out of the radical movements of the 1960s and have dominated philosophical discussion of the subject ever since'. Populism does not lack sound academic credentials,[1] and its creed of the damage to popular sovereignty caused by representation resembles the conclusions reached by 'principal-agent' approaches in economics, or the theory of 'goal displacement' in organisational sociology.

Thus, we need not return to the Athenian democracy or even to Rousseau in order to understand the foundations of populism. One must, however, remember that the notion of representative government, so much distrusted by populists, is feudal in origin, and initially had nothing to do with either democracy or elections. Originally, democracy was conceived exclusively in its direct form, or in conjunction with the selection of leaders by lot, allowing everyone the same chance to rule. Representative government, which is, alongside other institutional techniques, an arbitrary social construct, has regularly been challenged in theory and practice (see Papadopoulos 1998). Far from belonging to political folklore, many populist-inspired instruments, designed to avoid principal–agent problems between the citizenry and representatives, are part of the arsenal of 'immediate democracy' (Max Weber), and regularly feature on the agenda of institutional reform.[2]

Populism at the heart of democratic tensions

At the same time, distrust with populist forms of democracy is not new either, especially since the advent of universal suffrage which lent credibility to the belief that representative government would gradually evolve into democracy (Manin 1995, 171). In ancient Greek political thought, moderate and mixed forms of government were designed to prevent perversions of democracy such as demagoguery or oligarchy. James Madison and l'abbé Sieyès, the two major drafters of the American and French revolutionary constitutions respectively, were careful to deny any link between their programmes for modern representative democracies and conceptions of 'pure' democracy (Fontana 1994). Among modern political theorists, Max Weber and Joseph Schumpeter are known for their defence of leadership and their reluctance to equate democracy with extensive self-government. However, the elitist approach may itself be criticised for its lack of coherence, since elites can hardly question the wisdom of the very people they claim to represent (Hermet 1991, 50). The contemporary philosopher Jürgen Habermas (1989, 29) asserts that if we dismiss the extensive participation of the mass public on the grounds of its incompetence this may logically induce us to dispute the rationality of those delegatory mechanisms which are also based on popular acquiescence. These controversies deserve closer examination.

In much the same way as the Communists attacked the 'dictatorship of the bourgeoisie' hiding behind the veil of democratic regimes, populists define democracies as façades which conceal autocracies dominated by the oligarchic interests of corrupt elites (Hermet 1997, 34, 47; Schedler 1996, 297). Canovan (1999, 2–3) maintains that 'we cannot afford to brush these claims aside', and suggests that the sources of populism be sought in the tensions inherent in democracy, more precisely between its 'redemptive' and its 'pragmatic' aspects, so that populism is, in her words, 'a shadow cast by democracy itself'. This view is not dissimilar to that expressed by William Riker (1982), who identified a contradiction in democracies between populism and liberalism, or more recently by Jean Leca (1996), who noted the difficult coexistence of a 'populist' and a 'constitutional' dimension in democracies, which allows populist challengers to discredit with ease any prevalence of formal liberal institutions over the norm of popular sovereignty. In criticising the literature on democratic transition and consolidation for its poor conceptualisation of the quality of democracy, Wolfgang Merkel (1999, 369) made a further distinction between constitutionalism, the rule of law, and democracy by classifying democracies legitimated exclusively by vertical accountability mechanisms of the populist type as '*defekte Demokratien*'.[3]

The likelihood that populism is driven by the institutional architecture of democracies has seldom been systematically explored (see Mény and Surel 2000), let alone empirically tested. Populism may well be fed by the 'broken promises' of democracy (Bobbio 1987), such as the survival of oligarchies and the ensuing persistence of group power as opposed to the 'one man, one vote' principle, the prevalence of particularisms as opposed to the general interest, a lack of decisional transparency, the poor results of democracies in the domain of citizens' civic education, or the confinement of democracy to the narrow political sphere and its lack of spillover into other social arenas such as the economy.

Populism as the outcome of the structural ambiguity of electoral democracy

This analysis does not simply argue that populists are, in a sense, right – when they, for example, blame the elite conspiracy for an alleged authoritarian drift of democracies – but maintains, rather, that the problem rests with the *inherently* oligarchic dimension of representative democracy. Both Montesquieu and Rousseau associated elections with an aristocratic principle (Rosanvallon 1993, 13), since they enable people to select the best rather than taking the risk of being ruled by incompetent, dangerous or corrupt leaders because of the caprices of random choice. This nation of the aristocratic principle of election is still valid, insofar as potential office-holders receive consideration only as long as they are considered *'des citoyens distingués'* (Manin 1995, 95).[4] Hence we select office-holders who we believe will do the job better than ourselves – for example, because they have greater skills or more free time (Sartori 1987, 280), considering that ignorance is rational given the high costs of information-seeking. This conception of electoral democracy is sustained by the belief that politics is not merely a vocation, but a genuine profession (*'Politik als Beruf'*). As a result we deliberately select those who command our respect, precisely because they *differ* from us. In this conception of election, representatives are legitimate not because they are close to the citizenry, but because they are somewhat remote, like genuine professionals whose credentials set them apart from amateurs or *dilettanti*. Clearly, societal complexity and differentiation justify this view, first because the political job can be a highly technical and time-consuming one, but also because specialised activities in other functionally defined social sub-systems (the economy, health, research, the arts, education or the legal system, and so on) require a high investment on behalf of individuals, so that they may consider devoting themselves to politics a rather unrewarding activity.[5]

In democracies this principle is also challenged by an alternative principle of populist inspiration. This unavoidable cohabitation of the populist with the aristocratic principle makes populist notions of democracy both legitimate and contestable. Democracy also entails the *unbiased* representation of citizens' viewpoints and its legitimacy includes a sort of 'specular' conception of decision-making. Similar to the rationale of selection by lot practised in ancient times (and today in citizens' juries), but as a result of deliberate choice, we expect rulers to be replicas of the man in the street, and to come from the same background, express the same preferences, or share the same values as ourselves (Strøm 1997). Given the absence of any guarantee that once in office those elected will *continue* to maintain this profile, populist techniques of 'immediate democracy' (referendum, recall, limited mandates, etc.) are sometimes used to constrain them.

Ideally, we would like to be represented by those we consider our replicas and, all other things being equal, whom we regard as more able than ourselves to do the job in hand. We may also want to elect pure replicas, irrespective of their competence or availability, or professionals, even though they do not do things the way we would like (since they know better). But, in all likelihood, we usually seek a trade-off, by balancing the risk of being disappointed or deceived in either respect. In general, voters also experience the, irreconcilable, tension between the specular and the aristocratic principle of electoral democracy. Quite apart from other contradictions between democratic principles, we must keep this particular ambivalence, linked to the *electoral* nature of representation in democracies, constantly in mind. Thus, the populist criticism – quite apart from any other sources of concern due to the excessive role played by corporation, organised interests, partitocracies, technocracies, and so forth – is sustained by the structural ambiguity of electoral mechanisms that entail at the same time representation and selection. In a *demo*cracy the aristocratic dimension must remain under control, but precisely how this control should be exerted is a matter of some controversy.

The quest for an *'effet de justice'* (Manin 1995, 97) by replacing elites is indeed an integral, and multifunctional, part of democratic ideology. In the first place, the likelihood of elite replacement is a sword of Damocles hanging over incumbents' heads, minimising their room for manoeuvre and maximising their responsiveness (for a discussion of this 'deterrence', see Elster 1999). It is also instrumental in avoiding the formation of a homogeneous political class, cartel or caste, with its own esprit de corps, able to exploit long periods in office to argue the need for (its) indispensable skills for ruling. Elections as a mechanism of elite replacement are expected to generate more *empathy* among office-holders vis-à-vis their constituencies. In his seminal work, Bernard Manin demonstrates that the obstacle of *re-election* makes representatives more responsive in that they are induced to *'anticiper le jugement rétrospectif des électeurs sur la politique qu'ils mènent'* (Manin 1995, 228). Although the threat of electoral sanction is a major defensive weapon in the hands of the subjects, it may not, populists argue, suffice to ensure elite responsiveness. Manin is certainly aware of some, but not all, of its weaknesses, and resorts to the prevailing argument that coalition government renders the accountability of individual partners more problematic. Empirically speaking, the difference between majority and coalition systems does not appear to have had the anticipated impact on the responsiveness of incumbents,[6] or to account for the uneven success of anti-establishment parties.

On the other hand, Manin does not extensively state the limits of retrospective voting, although he does admit that voters do not always vote on retrospective considerations. If voters are oriented towards the future rather than the past, then the margin of politicians will in all probability increase: if they are able to make attractive pledges, their previous sins will be forgiven (although for pledges to be credible, they must already have acquired a good reputation in the past). Furthermore, adjustment to voters' preferences will only occur if politicians possess adequate information about their voting intentions and are able to anticipate their reactions – daring assumptions indeed (Bartolini 1999, 464). Furthermore, we cannot take for granted that parties in office either desire, or are able, to set clearly identifiable goals and to select between alternative means in order to achieve them ('bounded rationality'). Moreover, several other factors tend to weaken elite responsiveness *vis-à-vis* voters: pressure from purists in the party organisation which impairs adjustments to the alleged preferences of the average voter; a captive electorate sufficiently loyal not to threaten with exit if disappointed by the party's performance; the capacity to bind voters through the clientelistic allocation of club goods, and so forth. On the part of the voters, retrospective behaviour requires the capacity or the will to act rationally and instrumentally rather than ideologically. This presupposes an encompassing view of politics that may be hard to achieve: voters must be considered capable of regularly making causal links between policy outputs and the outcomes that affect them. In sum, retrospective voting as an incentive to responsiveness places an unrealistic burden of rationality on politicians and voters alike (see, in particular, Papadopoulos 2001). The degree of responsiveness generated by elections is clearly an empirical issue, depending on ad hoc constellations, and populists have a point when they argue that betting on elite responsiveness through elections is simply too optimistic.

The conflict between populism and deliberation

Bearing in mind the limitations in ensuring responsiveness via elections, populists propose that pressure be exerted to make elites' behaviour more dependent on the risk of sanctions. Taking an example from American constitutional history, in the debate over the length of mandates in the bicameral Congress, the Founding Fathers expected that frequent rotation would prevent the formation of a cohesive group of opinion-makers instead of opinion-followers. The debate a century later on the recall of officials, went one step further than short mandates, by placing agents under a *permanent* threat of sanctions by principals.[7] Other devices are preventive, and designed to secure *in advance* the contiguity of principals and agents typical of the reflective notion of representation. The imperative mandate is the best case of a prospective, as opposed to retrospective, control of politicians' actions (Elster 1998, 3), and is a perfect substitute when the direct democracy of the town meeting becomes impracticable for reasons of size.

Nevertheless, the problem with populist techniques is that they are hostile to deliberation. Populists suspect elite interactions of collusion at the expense of third parties. However, modern notions of representation do not only favour deliberation on elitist grounds and may, for example, rule out the imperative mandate. Edmund Burke feared the dominance of local particularisms over the 'general good' and believed the 'judgement' of representatives to be necessary. A few years later James Madison concluded that representation was necessary to 'refine' the world views of political actors. Madison was not so naïve as to think that such an improvement would be produced by aristocratic rule, but he was convinced that deliberation was a precondition of refinement, and the fragmentation of power was in turn a precondition for deliberation. He understood perfectly how positive and negative incentives in political action are much the domain of institutions. Checks and balances would constrain circumstantial majorities to formulate their arguments so as to successfully overcome multiple tests and to withstand criticism from their adversaries.

Together with the aristocratic dimension of elections, deliberation is part of the principle of 'distinction', and distinction cannot simply be written off as irrelevant in democratic polities (Manin 1995). Whilst those adhering to the aristocratic notion of elections anticipate refinement through selection, deliberation also heightens the level of political debate. Deliberation must, however, respect some sociological conditions, and these conditions are absent in populist democracy. In order to learn from deliberation, representatives need to enjoy the sort of autonomy that is not even compatible with de facto imperative mandates (Fishkin 1991). Furthermore, deliberating actors must engage in durable face-to-face interactions to ensure they respect their mutual commitments.[8] Under the normalising effect of the '*Gesetz des Wiedersehens*' (Offe 1992), actors are unlikely to push exclusively selfish arguments for self-preservation, and will have to submit their claims to debate without being able in the long run to ignore those of their partners, since the costs of opportunistic behaviour may be prohibitive.

Deliberation seems to go hand in hand with what Elster (1998, 3) describes as the 'civilising force of hypocrisy',[9] which is a powerful incentive for co-operation.

What we face is a major trade-off between deliberation, which is a functional requirement in modern fragmented societies, and its prerequisites, which are problematic for democratic legitimacy. Populists offer good reasons to be suspicious it, especially as the deliberative component of democracy remains a pure abstraction for most citizens (Hermet 2001, 16). On the other hand, the populist 'direct-majoritarian' (Fishkin 1991) creed is likely to undermine the foundations of coexistence in societies where 'factionalism' prevails. Institutions built on populist principles tend to impede the development of mutual empathy and of other-regardingness in social environments where feelings of 'sameness' and collective identification are weak (Offe 1987; Scharpf 1993). Therefore populist direct-majoritarianism may not be the most appropriate route to collective welfare when the latter requires the *conciliation* of competing interests instead of the abrupt domination over minorities.

In addition, good government cannot merely be responsive government, for the latter may be tempted to give priority to the shifting preoccupations of majorities and thereby eschew long-term problems.[10] Good government must also be 'responsible' government (Sartori 1994, 73), and probably the best illustration of the contested nature of democratic government comes once again from the constitutional debates in the United States. Preference for a system of horizontal accountability resting on checks and balances (a bicameral legislature, the presidential veto, judicial review) was preceded by heated debate as to the adequate degree of elite autonomy. The anti-federalists, for example, advocated a specular conception of democracy, and supported the idea of an Assembly composed of a larger number of parliamentarians, arguing that this would be more representative of the population at large (Manin 1995, 143–6). They wanted elections to be held more frequently, and the Senate was their major target, as federalists had imposed indirect election of this body and a six-year mandate (Manin 1994), in order to secure representation for the wealthy, and to isolate senators from pressure. Good government must mirror public opinion and enlighten it *at the same time*: a difficult conciliation, seeing that populist devices are all oriented toward the first goal, and elitist devices toward the second.

Populism and the transformations in policy styles

Although we may expect majoritarian democracies, closer to the populist model of direct electoral accountability of office-holders, to be more immune to populist protest than consensual democracies subject to the fragmentation of power, this does not appear to be the case. Countries with the most successful populist movements include consensus model democracies such as Austria, Switzerland, Belgium, and the Scandinavian countries, and also countries with bipolar party systems, such as Italy and France. Given the diffusion of populism across systems with different institutional configurations, it may help to make a supplementary interpretation of its roots so as to accentuate once more the impact of 'systemic' factors. I will examine an, apparently new, problem at the origin of contemporary populist protest, unlike the dilemma between populist or Madisonian democracy, or the issue of the broken promises of democracy,[11] and argue that the dominant contemporary policy 'style' tends to impede accountability *regardless* of whether or not incumbents behave responsively, and that this is likely to nurture populist protest. Responsiveness and accountability do not necessarily co-vary: office-holders may not just be more remote from the citizenry, they may simply be harder to identify and to induce to account for their choices. Bartolini (1999, 448–9) is right to assert that these concepts are not synonymous: responsiveness refers to the substantial content of policy choices (that must conform to voters' wishes), whilst accountability is related to the availability of adequate instruments which oblige incumbents to report on their deeds, and enable voters to respond with electoral sanctions. Institutional complexity may prejudice accountability insofar as it tends to reduce the visibility of decision-makers. The increasing complexity of decisional processes is a matter of (increased) *social* complexity.

Governance and policy networks as responses to complexity

Following the theory of differentiation, the more complex a society, the more likely it is to be fragmented by a plurality of interests that manifest heterogeneous and frequently conflicting claims. Under the pressure of particularisms of professional sectors, interest groups, lifestyle communities, territorial subdivisions, or even of individuals, complex societies run the risk of disintegration. This aspect of social complexity is currently supplemented by technical complexity: problems have complex origins, and their parameters tend to evolve in unpredictable ways. Hence complexity is closely associated with contingency: there is no unanimously accepted hierarchy of values (for example, in contrast to theocratic societies), and most choices are considered with some degree of scepticism or anxiety, given the difficulty of anticipating their consequences. Political decision-making has clearly become a difficult exercise; how, for example, can one ensure the correctness of policy choices under conditions of high uncertainty, and how is sufficient support on decisions to be achieved under conditions of fragmentation?

In order to cope with contingency in most developed democracies the style of conduct in policy-making has undergone some substantial changes during the last few decades. A new model emerged, more strongly orientated toward collaboration of the state with social segments, clearly as a response to societal complexity (the 'law of requisite variety' see Ashby 1956). What has often been portrayed as a shift from 'government' to 'governance' entails the co-production and co-implementation of public policies by different bodies forming networks. These networks are intergovernmental as in 'multi-level governance' ranging from European Union institutions to the local level, or mixed, as in policy domains where public bodies jointly act with interest associations or private firms. In most democracies there are a number of informal procedures where public authorities draft legislation in close co-ordination with major interest groups.[12] Sometimes official bodies merely ratify proposals made by public bureaucracies after concertation with the representatives of organised interests. It is no exaggeration to say that these procedures are frequently opaque and selective. Likewise, if public officials wish to avoid failure in reaching their targets when attempting to implement policies, they must often bargain and make compromises with blatantly 'nimbyist' local actors. This carries the risk that short-term and concentrated interests will prevail over the less visible public interest, especially because collective mobilisation is much easier to achieve on particularistic grounds.

Today it is no longer sufficient to interpret the rise of populism simply in terms of the contradiction between liberal constitutionalism and populism. Pure legal-rational domination is also perceived as increasingly problematic with respect to state efficiency, so that a *déformalisation* process occurs (in the sense of decisional processes being largely uncoupled from official democratic circuits), which in turn fosters populism. We can therefore argue that this current antinomy is not so much between populism and the advent of informal modes of governance, as between populism and the (decreasing) formalism of the *'Rechtsstaat'*. This is not a certainty, however, and will consequently be presented as a hypothesis to be tested in future empirical research.

The democratic question: governance and populism

The representativeness of the collective voice heard in procedures typical of 'governance' is indeed disputable. Moreover, an informed view of complex problems requires a degree of professionalisation that excludes ordinary citizens, not to speak of the declining role of standard democratic procedures. Although supporters of governance may well be right to argue that these are more horizontal and less statist processes, their inclusiveness is nevertheless *selective*. It depends on the blackmailing power of some subsystems and organisations, so that negotiated agreements based on participatory procedures cannot be equated with more democracy (Duran 1999, 85). While it is true that the degree of closure in policy networks typical of governance differs from case to case (for example, specialists distinguish between loose issue networks and cohesive policy communities), these networks are usually confined to the circle of public bureaucrats, experts, representatives of interest groups or private firms, and prominent local politicians. As a result, they are likely to generate significant negative effects (Benz 1998, 206): resistance to change, goal-displacement, rent-seeking, the externalisation of costs, and so forth (Bobbio's 'broken promises').

The legitimacy of policy networks is mostly internal, self-referential, and based on mutual trust and acknowledgement between participants. As a result, there is a real risk of democratic legitimacy being substituted by more fragmentary forms of legitimacy, frequently with a strong bureaucratic or, in the case of non-state actors, corporate-professional flavour. Even though this form of consent is by no means unproductive, mutual adjustment between actors with high blackmailing potential provided by knowledge, finance, organisation, mobilising skills or whatever, cannot be considered a sufficient source of legitimacy. Curiously enough, these forms of less hierarchical state–society relations are not easily compatible with democratic standards, because of the ensuing de-differentiation of state action.

The vertical bottom-up delegation of power *to* the state in democracy is traditionally associated with its counterpart – that is, a vertical top-down regulation *from* the state. The transformation of policy styles weakens this linkage and may also be at the root of populist protest, but has not yet been clearly identified as such. The articulation of 'politics' with 'policy' has not been dealt with in depth in the study of populism, while there may be straightforward links between some policy styles and negative perceptions of elite behaviour. The uncoupling of administrative steering from the parliamentary complex and the removal of key issues from the public agenda are likely to cause the periodic re-emergence of the 'democratic question' (Habermas 1992, 389).[13] Policy networks tend to gain considerable autonomy from circuits of democratic control, to be disconnected from citizens or even from parliamentary bodies,[14] and to rely heavily on feedback from 'customers' or 'users', whose influence is proportional to their exit power: we are evidently still miles away from the democratic-egalitarian principle of 'one man, one vote'.

Given the 'polycentric' component of governance arrangements and the co-production and co-implementation of collectively binding decisions by a mixture of public and private bodies, traditional accountability mechanisms may well be obsolete. Does it make sense to hold formally elected officials, who are the most visible but not necessarily the most powerful part of the decisional chain, accountable if effective authority is largely out of their hands? Pluralist democracy is poorly equipped to deal with the increasing complexity of the links between the political system (assuming that this system is horizontally and vertically unified among decisional bodies), and other social subsystems (Zolo 1992, 109–14). The problem is that no alternative, credible and uncontroversial accountability mechanisms have been found, leaving populists free to occupy a market 'niche'.

In addition, governance arrangements frequently lack social visibility and tend to be weakly codified. The legal system is also faced with social complexity insofar as it must resort to softer means, such as information and persuasion, instead of ordinary law and the threat of sanctions, and must incorporate more feedback from environments (through process such as sunset legislation and monitoring; see Morand 1999) if it is to be more respectful of the autonomy of recipients of public policies. Instability and ad hoc choices are likely to supplant the rule of law in its general and abstract form. Incorporating complexity by awarding more room to flexibility may damage the functionality of law in ensuring predictability and in stabilising social relations. When normative uncertainty is tied to decision-making through policy networks, accountability deficits may well proliferate: not only does overcrowding in multiple policy arenas inhibit the identification of power-holders, but legal fluidity impedes the identification of their acts. Representative democracy presupposes the ability to identify actors who can be sanctioned positively or negatively depending on their performance. Citizens have taken up this assumption, and still use cognitive models of command in assessing public policies that leave little legitimatory room for bargaining and negotiation. Decisions are viewed as the object of implementation at the bottom from a legitimate top, while governance tends to dissolve political roles and political performance, rendering this command model to a large extent illusory. Yet, this model remains a centrepiece of democratic legitimacy, and governments are still considered responsible for policy failure, despite the heavily circumscribed nature of their role. Due to changes in forms of governance 'the sense of top-down authority exercised through state actors has been diminished or lost' (Pierre and Peters 2000, 45), and this opens up avenues to populist movements.

Conclusion: the populist potential in modern democracies

In this chapter I have attempted to identify two major dimensions of the essentially ambivalent relation between populism and democracy. On the one hand, the populist claim for more inclusiveness is largely driven by democratic ideology and sustained by the failure of democratic practice to keep some of the central promises of this ideology, and by the ambivalent structural properties of electoral representation. This claim has remained controversial throughout democratic history so that well-worn alternative notions of government still compete over the correct balance within democratic polities of constitutionalism, rule of law, populism, majority principle, or checks and balances. The limitations of the populist conception of democracy are clearly visible when it comes to dealing with social fragmentation, which requires the sort of deliberative mechanisms that are not compatible with direct majoritarianism.

On the other hand, institutional techniques available to deal with 'complexity management' are likely to nurture populism. This populism is generally the reaction to an excess of constitutionalism that is increasingly combined with deficits in decisional visibility, due to the proliferation of informal governance arrangements that jeopardise accountability. Populist claims for order may thus be considered as alternatives to the prevailing bargaining models of decision-making, whatever the formal (majoritarian or consensual, unitary or federalist) features of institutional architectures.

Populism is paradoxically sustained by the very requirements of democratic legitimacy, which in the last instance rests on popular sovereignty even in representative democracies, notwithstanding any mediations or filters that may be deliberately introduced between governors and governed. The prevalence of this source of legitimacy helps us understand why opinion poll democracy grows, or why it may be hard to portray what is populist as a vice when 'being popular' is not disputed as a virtue. We can indeed protect our reputation as democrats by claiming that we only disapprove of the excesses of the populist principle when it prevails in an unbalanced combination with the constitutional or Madisonian principle. Yet one cannot deny that the populist principle is consubstantial with democracy, and that thresholds between principles are contingent.[15]

Today we can observe a broader consensus on democracy as the most appropriate form of government: between the onset of the so-called 'third wave' of democratisation in 1974 and 1996 no less than 89 states (about the half of UN members) shifted from authoritarian to democratic regimes (Merkel 1999, 361). This was accompanied, however, by controversies over the appropriate form of democracy: parliamentary or presidentialist, majoritarian or consensual, unitary or federalist, and so forth. Institutional designers must resolve puzzles regarding the adequate mix of the elitist and the populist principle, the limits to successive stages of power delegation, and the degree of extension of citizenship rights; in short, the degree of inclusiveness, and correlatively, the acceptable (and inescapable) exclusivist component, of democratic systems. Democratic theory has explored some of these dilemmas by distinguishing between input-oriented and output-oriented legitimacy (Scharpf 1970), and – in its economic version – by sketching the trade-off between transaction or external costs that decision-makers try to minimise alternately (Buchanan and Tullock 1962).

We now know that this epistemological uncertainty as to the appropriate character of democracy (Ossipow 1994, 13) leaves room for populists and feeds their arguments. It should be added, however, that, much like democracy, populism is not immune to strains and uncertainty (Taguieff 1997, 11–12). The dilemmas of populism are similar to those faced by democracies with respect to the 'inclusion – exclusion' question (Taylor 1998). While democracy requires more participation than authoritarian regimes, participation requires mutual recognition and trust – in other words a feeling of collective belonging that inevitably generates exclusion. Likewise, populists push and campaign for more direct involvement of, and control by, the citizenry, which is only possible in a homogeneous community fostering exclusion.[16] This dilemma is particularly visible in the populist project to strengthen the direct-majoritarian component of democratic institutions.

It is difficult to object to this project without being accused of elitism or authoritarianism. Yet in complex societies, where a feeling of sameness is lacking,[17] fragmentation facilitates 'legitimate indifference' (Schimank 1996, 158), the externalisation of costs, rent-seeking, particularism and 'free-riding' or, in Madison's words, facilitates factionalism (whatever its sources: business or professional interests, territorially based groups, lifestyle communities, and so on), direct-majoritarianism is indeed problematic. The populist-inspired institutional design assumes – somewhat imprudently – that ordinary people are depositories of wisdom and, as such, possess the necessary civic virtues to act in the common good (or, more accurately, for the good of common people). Individuals may in reality lack these virtues, while direct-majoritarian institutions have no mechanisms to foster those 'moral resources' (Offe and Preuss, 1991) vital for the proper functioning of democratic decision-making, especially as the individual voter is the sole link in the decisional chain not accountable for their choice (Papadopoulos 1998, 131–2).[18] In order to guarantee inclusion, differentiated societies need political systems that mirror fragmentation, which in turn carries the risk of undermining accountability. On the other hand, the similarity of the inclusiveness – exclusiveness dilemma faced by democracy and populism alike is an integral part of their ambivalent relation as populist claims and pledges simultaneously represent both an extension and a negation of what most of us would wish to preserve in democracies.

Notes

1. See, for example, Barber's (1990, 145) negative views on representation.
2. See, for example, the proposals to set up referenda as remedies for the 'democratic deficit' within the European Union in Zürn (1996), Abromeit (1998), or Schmitter (2000).
3. But mechanisms designed to safeguard horizontal accountability ought not to be idealised either. Maravall (2000) offers several examples of how politicians can, for example, instrumentalise the judicial system in order to eliminate competitors.

4. Newton writes that 'politicians are less likely to be trusted because they are "one of us" (Catholic, black, Southerner, farmer, gentleman), but because of their policy record and personal performance and appearance' (Newton 1997, 147); in other words because of their 'capacity' rather than their 'fidelity' (Pharr and Putnam 2000a, xx).
5. This process is best studied by the sociology of differentiation (Schimank 1996).
6. Using two measures to compare the distance between governmental choices and voters' preferences in both systems, Lijphart (1999, 287–8) is able to show that it is shorter in coalition systems. See also Maravall (1999, 164) who also cites older studies.
7. In Athens all magistrates, elected or more often chosen by lot, could be ousted at any moment by a vote of the Assembly. The recall was also conceived as a protection against incompetence, a major risk of selection by lot and the Achilles heal of the specular conception of representation (Manin 1995, 25).
8. Benz (1998, 212) states it bluntly: effective co-operation is only possible in oligarchic, elitist, non-transparent and selective political structures.
9. Or, rather, the civilising force of the constraint to provide reasons for one's preferences, that must be acceptable to the audience; whether actors truly believe in them is not so relevant (Urfalino 2000, 186).
10. '[A]ccountability ... is vital to democracy and simultaneously a potential threat to it' (March and Olsen 1995, 151).
11. Nevertheless sociogenetic studies of this problem are scant (see the comments in Pierre and Peters 2000, and Papadopoulos 2000).
12. According to Cerny (1999, 17) globalisation further unbalances this public-private mix in decision-making, with public law being increasingly substituted by 'negotiated private law'. Cerny detects some very negative prospects for democratic accountability in these developments. If he is correct in his gloomy forecast, then there may be good reason for populism to remain vigorous in the future.
13. A similar problem is raised by the proliferation of independent regulatory agencies, especially as this change is related to a power shift from the national to the European level (Majone 1995). Decisional competences are awarded to these bodies either in an attempt, of Madisonian inspiration, to promote responsible policy choices through isolation from pressures of electoral majorities, or simply because they are thought to have a monopoly on expertise that would allow them to produce more informed and wiser regulations in complex domains. Potential democratic deficits are thus expected to be offset by legitimacy acquired through efficient decisions favourable to collective well-being.
14. As a specialist on parties puts it:

    > In general, however, while public-policy research has in recent years taught us much about non-party policy communities, it has thrown up little evidence of the way in which party research mechanisms mesh with such communities, and in several countries it is worth asking whether they link up with them closely at all. (Hine 1996, 138–9)

15. As early as the Athenian democracy, leaders could legitimately adopt several positions in their interactions with the *demos*: not only representatives, protectors and counsellors, but also critics and adversaries (Ober 1989, 314–24).
16. The comparison of data on the cantonal level in Switzerland interestingly shows a strong positive correlation between a composite index of social capital and the score of the populist SVP, today the major party in federal politics (index and correlation coefficients computed by Markus Freitag to whom we express our gratitude).
17. When entities come short of a '*Wir-Identität*', then democratisation on populist lines can become dangerous for minorities. Scharpf (1999a) argues on these lines about the effects of a European referendum, that could allow a majority of citizens living in wealthy countries to deny redistributive measures beneficial to European Union regions mainly of the South (and soon of the East). In order to confer legitimacy to decisions, majority rule must be legitimate too (Scharpf 1999b).
18. In a number of Swiss communes the right to award citizenship to foreign residents was shifted (frequently through initiatives by petition) from representative bodies to the electorate. This repeatedly led to a racist selection process in which Italians have no difficulty in obtaining a Swiss passport, but Swiss citizenship is systematically denied to residents from Turkey or the former Yugoslavia.

4
Populism and the Pathology of Representative Politics

Paul Taggart

Introduction

The study of populism is, like the phenomenon itself, limited in scope and duration, and somewhat episodic. It seems that populism acquires a certain intellectual currency at irregular intervals but lacks staying power. In consequence, populism is one of the most widely used but poorly understood political concepts of our time. This is a deficiency because, as I shall argue, it provides us with a useful tool for understanding the pathology of representative politics. Populism is *not* a universal concept that, once unlocked, will enable us to decipher all other political debates, but it is a useful secondary concept that, if used sensitively and systematically, will enable us to understand populist movements, and which will, perhaps more importantly, allow us to understand essential elements in the politics of representation.

The politics of representation, its successes and its shortcomings have a particular resonance for contemporary Europe. Across the Continent, albeit to varying degrees and in various forms, the institutions of liberal representative democracy have become the touchstone for legitimacy. The combination of the 'European project' of greater integration embodied in the European Union and the processes of political and economic transition in Eastern and Central Europe since the early 1990s means that there is a particular resonance to populist reaction to contemporary representative politics in Western, Eastern and Central Europe.

In this chapter I offer a brief account of the literature on populism, expanding on the idea that the conditions are particularly ripe for a reconsideration of the concept of populism in Europe, starting with an overview of the way populism has been studied. This is followed by an outline of the six principal features of populism, and an examination of how these are linked to representative politics in general and to contemporary Europe in particular. Before concluding, I suggest that populism has had some very specific effects on representative politics as well as acting as a bellwether for the latter's health.

The study of populism

There is a tendency for populism to be studied in bursts and considered in very contextual terms, giving rise to a rather disjointed and fractured literature. The surges of interest in populism may have much to do with the political conditions prevailing at the time. For example, with the Cold War in the 1950s, the work of Edward Shils (1956) offered a US perspective, subsequently expanded into a much wider context. This gained further momentum in the 1960s when there was interest in the US in the populism of the libertarian Right and the authoritarianism of McCarthyism (Lipset 1963; Lipset and Raab 1971). In the Latin American case, interest in populism was sparked off by a set of regimes driven by the charismatic leadership of individuals such as Juan Perón in Argentina and Getúlio Vargas in Brazil and promoting a distinct regional path of development. These regimes led to a veritable flurry of conceptualising about populism (Di Tella 1965; Malloy 1977; Germani 1978). With the more recent set of regimes of Menem, Fujimori and Collor combining particular economic doctrines of neoliberalism with strong leadership, there has been a renewed burst of interest in the concept of populism in the region (Conniff 1999). The rise of the Reform Party in Canada in the 1980s and 1990s generated a body of literature that attempts to conceptualise populism in the Canadian context, at times with specific reference to the Canadian populism of Social Credit in the earlier part of the twentieth century (Laycock 1994). It is hardly surprising, then, that we only notice populism when it amounts to a significant political force, leading in turn to a very demand-led consideration, and that this has mitigated against the development of a mature consideration of populism *qua* populism.

What is largely absent is any attempt to synthesise the lessons from the different experiences of populism, and particularly from its wider historical record. The two exceptions are the work by Ionescu and Gellner (1969) based on the 1967 conference at the London School of Economics that brought together leading experts on populism from different parts of the world. But what is immediately apparent from the collection is the difficulty of bringing together ideas to provide a synthetic overview of populism (see also Berlin et al., 1968), the lack of a conclusion, and a single bold attempt to tease out some 'elementary theses' that are generally applicable (Wiles 1969). The other exception is the comprehensive work of Margaret Canovan (1981) which makes an excellent synthesis of disparate sources; it is not so much an attempt to draw out a general conception of populism, as a taxonomy of different types of populism. However, even allowing for these honourable exceptions, populism is a seriously underconceptualised term.

In addition to the fractured nature of work on populism, there is also one glaring absence. It is hard to identify a European literature that deals with populism in the European context. This may be partly due to the impact that the European experience of fascism in the twentieth century (Mazower 1998) has exercised on those focusing on European ideologies and the stability of European political systems, and which still looms large over any consideration of ideologies of the far Right. The shadow has been so great that it has almost entirely occluded any specifically European consideration of populism (with the exceptions of Mény 1998 and Hayward 1996b). This situation becomes all the more anomalous given the fact that certain conditions now prevail (in a European and wider context) that would seem to presage and justify a reinvigorated consideration of populism.

Four factors have resulted in populism coming once more under the lens of European politics. The first is the rise of a 'new populism' on the Right of many liberal-democratic regimes, and a resurgence of interest in the ideologies and activities of the far Right and the associated cluster of new parties located there (Kitschelt and McGann 1995; Taggart 1996; Betz 1994, 1998a). Parties on the far Right have found the combination of neo-fascism with a new populist distrust of governments, parties and elites to be a powerful one and have established themselves in many party systems as protest parties.

The second factor is the collapse of regimes in Eastern and Central Europe in the 1990s which was partly the consequence of the populist mobilisation by social movements, and which has led to the emergence of new political forces in the post-communist era that embody a far more conservative version of populism. It has also meant that those analysts who conceptualised populism in the Latin American context now tend to focus on the transitions in Eastern and Central European societies as a way of understanding the new political forces in Latin America (Di Tella 1997; Weyland 1999b).

The third factor is the sense of a crisis of legitimacy engendered in many liberal-democratic regimes. This has allegedly led to the 'decline' of political parties and to a diffuse sense of popular mistrust of politicians and elites combined with an increasing cartelisation of parties and allegations of corruption (Mair 1997; Mény 1998; Klingemann and Fuchs 1995; Mény and Surel in this volume).

The final factor is the process of European integration entailed in the European Union. This can either be subsumed under the larger process of globalisation or treated as a phenomenon sui generis. Either way, it amounts to a set of structures and processes that have generated new forms of politics, new challenges and new institutional uncertainties that are grist to the populist mill. Together these factors reveal sound empirical grounds for taking populism seriously in Europe.

A common theme in these factors is representative politics and, by implication, *un*-representative politics. In Eastern and Central Europe the process of transition involves, among other things, the construction of representative political institutions and the initiation of processes of representative politics. The issues of a legitimacy crisis and the democratic deficit in the EU are united in highlighting the limitations of structures, processes and the politics of representation. This is particularly important for the Western European states which currently constitute the EU and which portray themselves as the embodiment of stable, legitimate, representative systems of governance. The prospect of an enlarged EU encompassing a swathe of Eastern and Central European democracies in combination with the current Western European membership brings together two very different processes of transition in the experience of representative politics.

The 'new populism' stretches from Western Europe, with the rise of successful forces of the populist far Right in countries such as Austria, France and Italy, beyond Europe to the US, Canada and Australia where new populist politicians such as Ross Perot, Preston Manning and Pauline Hanson have contextualised the new populist critique in more neoliberal or libertarian ideologies (Betz and Immerfall 1998). What unites new populist forces in all these different contexts is that they mount a critique of the systems of politics, as revealed in problems of legitimation, as being unrepresentative.

The study of populism has thus suffered from a rather fractured, demand-led literature. The conditions and problems of contemporary Europe mean that it is important and apposite to reconsider populism in a distinctly European context. Putting these two statements together implies that it is vital that, whilst remaining sensitive to European particularities, we must draw from the widest possible range of sources to identify features, causes and effects of populism. I shall therefore attempt to draw out some features of populism in its most general sense that can then be applied to Europe in particular.

The features of populism

The holy grail of a definition of populism is elusive. Attempts to locate it have foundered, leading commentators along one of three paths. The first is the most frequent, and amounts to the attempt to define populism according to the particular circumstances in which it occurs. This produces work that is strong on depth and on a particular manifestation of populism, but suffers in terms of conceptual development and general applicability. The literature on populism produced in this way is, in effect, a vast array of contextual studies with some rather half-hearted nods to the idea of a general concept of populism (Ionescu and Gellner 1969). The second path is to construct a taxonomy of various types of populism (Canovan 1981). This abandons the idea of a general concept of populism and instead focuses on a comprehensive but variegated consideration of populism. The third path is to offer some sort of ideal-type and, in the process, to identify both the causes and effects of populism (Taggart 2000).

I maintain that populism, as an ideal type, has six principal themes (see Taggart 2000). The first is that populism is hostile to representative politics. This does not mean that it cannot exist where there are no institutions or the ideas of representative politics but that, although potentially ubiquitous in cultural terms or in terms of a political style, it is only under the conditions created by representative politics that it can become a political force or that we can talk about it as a set of ideas. Modernity ('late' or otherwise) ushers in the institutions of representative politics and with those institutions come processes and demands that force populism, insofar as it makes claims, to transform itself from a cultural *leitmotif* into either a fully-fledged political movement or political ideology.

The tension that Mény and Surel (in this volume) identify between representation and constitutionalism as a source of populism is apparent here. Certainly, populists are dissatisfied with the 'horizontal' guarantees of constitutionalism. The security offered by 'rights' (especially individual and minority rights), or the resort to complex legal redress for injustices, are anathema to populists. However, it is not simply that populism calls for greater 'vertical' access of the masses to elites through representation.[1] Populists make a case for a greater linkage of masses to elites which can be realised through processes of direct democracy just as well as through processes of representative politics. Indeed, the very complexity of the processes of representative politics is often a greater source of frustration than constitutionalism for populists. In the way that populists mobilise they often rely on charismatic leadership or at least on centralised political structures. This is clear in the new populist parties, often characterised by both centralised structures and by the pre-eminence of key individuals (Taggart 1995). When we think of the new populists, it is easy to associate this sort of politics with individuals such as Berlusconi, Haider, Le Pen or Bossi. The populist reliance on unusual leaders and structures is not an appeal for *more representative government*; rather, it is a call for *better governance*.

The second theme is that populists tend to identify themselves with a 'heartland' that represents an idealised conception of the community they serve. It is from this territory of the imagination that populists construct 'the people' as the object of their politics. As Canovan (1984) notes, 'the people' is too broad and diffuse a concept to have real meaning as it signifies different things to different populists. This is why it is mistaken to take populists at their words and see 'the people' as the uniting principle of populism. The commitment to 'the people' is in fact a derivative consequence of the explicit commitment to a 'heartland'. Thus, 'the people' are nothing more than the populace of the heartland, and to understand what any populist means by 'the people' we need therefore to understand what they mean by their 'heartland'.

The heartland is a construction of an ideal world but, unlike utopian conceptions, it is constructed retrospectively – being, in essence, a vision derived from the past and projected onto the present. Unlike other ideologies that derive their visions of the future from the key values (such as egalitarianism or communitarianism), populism derives what values it has from its conception of the heartland. It is a diffuse vision, blurred around the edges, and clearly a romanticised and profoundly ahistorical conception, but is no less powerful for that. We see it in political discourse as the resort to 'Middle America' or 'Middle England' as imagined constituencies characterised by moderation, diligence and 'ordinariness'. A shared belief in the virtues of the heartland unites populists.

Examples of heartlands may be derived from the conception of the new populists of a Europe of nations each with a distinct ethnic and cultural homogeneity. There is a strong implied vision of a world 'as it once was' in the rejection of immigration, globalisation and the encroachment of taxation, and the intrusions of the state and its agents as politicians, intellectuals, bureaucrats and boffins. The essence of the heartland is not that of a utopia, but that there was a tried and tested 'good life' before the corruption and distortions of the present.

The term 'heartland' indicates something that is felt rather than reasoned, and something shrouded in imprecision. This means that different positions can implicitly conjure up heartlands that differ from each other, but where the difference can be ascribed to the nature of heartlands rather than to the different starting positions of those advocating them. This ambiguity works in favour of populists because it disguises or ignores what might otherwise be divisions among its constituency. This suits populists who portray themselves as monolithic and untainted by internal conflict, even when the reality is that populism is particularly prone to factionalism. Populists like to perceive themselves as a unified force and the shared sense of the heartland provides them with that unity.

The third theme of populism is its lack of core values. This stems from the importance of heartland, from where core values are derived. The variety of versions of the heartland explains why populism is attached to some very different ideological positions, from the Left to the Right. 'Populist' is frequently used as an epithet or qualifier to another ideological position and this is not coincidental. Mény and Surel, for example, refer to the debate about national-populism in France (in this volume). The attachment of populism to other sets of ideas is indicative of its inherent incompleteness and great flexibility. Populists have been revolutionary, reactionary, left-wing, right-wing, authoritarian and libertarian. This is not indicative of the emptiness of populism as a concept, but, rather, reveals that the empty heart of populism constitutes its inherent weakness and its potential ubiquity. Populism reacts against elites and institutions. The nature of these will vary and the nature of populism varies with them, and the values advocated are derived from sources other than populism.

Notwithstanding this potential political ubiquity, the experience of populism in contemporary Europe is mainly limited to the political Right and is manifest most systematically in the new populism of the New Radical Right (NRR). In this sense, contemporary European mobilised populism lies on the Right of the political spectrum. Less systematically, some Euroscepticism has strong elements of populism. In the EU member states and in accession states in other parts of Europe, Euroscepticism draws its strength from a wide range of political opinions – from the Left-libertarian 'new politics' of some green movements through Communist parties to agrarian parties and conservative parties on and moving back to the populist agenda of the New Radical Right (Taggart 1998; Szczerbiak 2000).

The fourth theme is that populism is a reaction to a sense of extreme crisis. Populism is not the politics of the stable, ordered polity but emerges as an accompaniment to change, crisis and challenge. Although this crisis may stem from a sense of moral decay, it always spills over into a critique of politics and the notion that 'politics as usual' cannot deal with the unusual conditions of crisis. Some of the landmark instances of populist movements occurred in periods of great sociopolitical upheaval, such as pre-revolutionary Russia or post-Civil War America. What is perhaps most important is that populism tends to emerge when there is a strong *sense* of crisis and populists use this to inject a sense of urgency and importance into their message.

Whether there is a crisis of legitimacy in contemporary Europe with mass publics withdrawing support from political institutions is a matter for debate (see Klingemann and Fuchs 1995). What is indisputable, however, is that there is public political debate on the nature of legitimacy, whether in terms of the constitution of the state, the role of political parties, or the nature of corruption in countries such as Germany, Austria, Italy or Belgium. It is these debates that have fired contemporary European populists to champion issues from which to make political capital. The new populists have drawn great sustenance from public debates about legitimacy and much of their support comes from those who feel a mistrust of political institutions and elites.

This leads to the fifth theme that focuses on the self-limiting quality of populism. Populists are reluctantly political insofar as they only mobilise when overcome by a sense of crisis. This explains why they tend to adopt new and different forms of politics, and why it is difficult to sustain populist movements in the long term. The appeal of populists to their constituencies is usually on the basis of their non-political nature and, therefore, as they become institutionalised into politics, they inevitably lose a major part of their popular appeal. Populists often prefer to portray themselves as movements rather than parties, but movements have greater difficulty institutionalising themselves and so this self-portrayal is not without its costs.

Populists have often relied on charismatic leaders so that in the very form of authority, they express a rejection of more bureaucratised, regularised and constrained forms of leadership. This gives populist leaders momentum in the short term but also presents difficulties because the issue of leadership succession becomes fundamentally problematic. Personalising leadership works while the same person is in command, but becomes problematic when authority has to be transferred to a new leader. This is partly why populist movements are so spectacular – they appear, build up support, and are highly visible through charismatic leaders – but the movements often share the same political 'shelf-life' as their leaders.

The final theme is that populists tend to be highly chameleonic. The contextual attributes of populism tend to spill over into the form taken by populism. This is not to say that they hide the 'real' nature of populism, but that populism is de facto constrained by its context. The fact that the study of populism has been dominated by studies of particular movements is partially a consequence of its nature. Because populism is invariably heavily coloured by its context, the similarities over what constitutes populism in different times and places are not always apparent. Deciding what is the 'canon' of populist cases is itself a contentious exercise. The lack of even a shared sense of self-identity on the part of populists makes their identification difficult. Although populist politicians do not necessarily balk at describing themselves as populists, they rarely use that term in their name.

The importance of *specific* versions of a heartland means that each populist movement perceives itself in terms of its own specific features rather than as part of a wider populist phenomenon. Populists mobilise when *their* heartland is threatened, and not merely when *a* heartland is threatened. This means that the context has a key influence in determining what moves and mobilises populists and how they frame their language of frustration.

Illustrating the chameleonic nature of populism, we need not look far to see the context-derived features. Populism assumed the guise of rural radicalism in nineteenth-century America, rural revolutionary romanticism in Tsarist Russia, urban mass movements in twentieth-century Argentina, and now, in contemporary Europe, it has taken the form of the extreme Right. Insofar as it is chameleonic, the study of populism needs to be aware of this as we study it, in order to differentiate between contextual and generic features in any instance of populist mobilisation.

These six features of populism demonstrate how it differs from other ideologies. Its lack of core values, and its self-limitation and chameleonic features, partially explain why populism is so episodic and therefore why, as a subject of study, it is both rather esoteric and difficult. However, taken together, the six features also illustrate why populism is a potential barometer of the health of representative politics. Something as difficult to grasp as populism is analytically hard to deal with, but it is also very easy for it to suddenly appear and transform itself into a significant, albeit short-lived, political force because it draws on deeply embedded and potentially ubiquitous fears about the limitations of representative politics.

Populism as a reaction to representative politics

Certain types of politics tend to emerge around the institutions of liberal representative democracy, insofar as there are some common processes, cycles and even pathologies that can be identified as representative politics. While there are variations in different states and at different times, we can identify a type of politics that shares some important characteristics. The existence of a tension between constitutionalism and representation makes it vitally important to differentiate between the type of politics that occur around constitutionalism from those that occur around representation. Representative politics is built around the 'vertical axis' that links the *demos* to the political elite, primarily focuses on the institutions of representation such as elections, public debate and legislatures, and is comprised of the building blocks of associational politics such as political parties, interest groups and social movements on the one hand, and on elite actions designed to secure the support of the *demos*, such as electioneering, issue articulation and policy implementation on the other. The cycles and processes of representative politics centre on electoral cycles, party politics, public debate, interest intermediation and end up in the processes of public policy-making. Taken together, this means that ideas are put onto the issue agenda, developed, subjected to debate with the implications and alternatives being drawn out, and eventually some ideas are implemented as public policy. Populism has a fundamental ambivalence towards these processes and has in many guises sought to construct alternative processes of direct democracy, radical grass-roots co-operative democracy, or, at the other extreme, authoritarian leadership.

As regards constitutionalism, this focuses on the institutions of the judiciary and is concerned primarily with rights, both individual and minority, and with the rules of the game in which much representative politics such as electoral systems, centre–local relations and executive power occur. We can view constitutional politics as setting the rules of the game in which representative politics take place.

The ambivalence of populism to representative politics can be perceived not only in what populists advocate, but in the way that they mobilise. In what populists advocate, we find a range of alternatives to representative politics ranging from the grass-roots co-operative politics of the American populists in the nineteenth century at the one extreme to the politics of personalised leadership, extending from the centralised structures of new populist parties in Europe to those based on charismatic and sometimes authoritarian leadership (as in the case with Perón in Argentina) on the other. In the mechanisms advocated by populists we often find a predilection for referenda and the tools of direct democracy such as citizen initiatives and recall devices.

One way to regard the relationship between populism and representative politics is to see that representative politics allows populism to embody what is a deeper, more diffuse and perhaps 'primal' political instinct – that of the ruled reacting to their rulers. Populism is forced to articulate a sustained position through the competition of representative politics, but the driving force behind it is not necessarily a sustained one, but is, at root, a rejection of something. The negative drive of populism is apparent in many ways because populists are always much clearer about what they are against than what they are for. The objects of frustration – be they institutions, elites or corruption – invite broad and deeply-held support, but there is more difficulty in developing an alternative. The negativity is embodied in contemporary European populism in the rejection of taxation, clientelism or immigration on the part of the new populists, or by the rejection of the European project by populist Eurosceptics.

If, as I suggest, populism has its roots in a reaction of the ruled to their rulers, it has two implications. The first is that populism is basically both amorphous and diffuse. The manifestations of this feeling may take very different forms. As a vague sense is translated into political actions or political ideas (or both) it will feed into different sets of already held assumptions and into some fundamentally different contexts and will consequently look very different. The structuring effects of different systems of representative politics will thereby give rise to different variants of populism. The second implication is that populism should *not* be regarded as a reaction to modernity. This goes against the grain for many analyses of populism that have portrayed it as a reactionary response to modernisation (such as Lipset 1963). The link between populism and modernity is complex. Modernity allows the conditions for populism to become systematised and therefore to become manifest in populist movements. At the same time, modernity exacerbates the populist sense of frustration against being ruled, by creating complex forms of politics and institutional structures which in turn become targets of populist angst. Modern politics creates the conditions for representative politics and this gives both a target for populists and, at the same time, an avenue for voicing their protest.

Looking at other instances of populist mobilisation, the experience of the People's Party in the United States and of the populist movement that underlay it gives the clearest instance of the link between populism and representative politics. The attempt to bring about a movement that represented the unrepresented, that attacked the established party system as unrepresentative, and which was built up around the idea of grass-roots radicalism and democratic mobilisation, provides us with an example of a movement whose focus constitutes the very process and idea of representation. Hence Goodwyn (1976) depicts the history of the US populists as one of 'democratic promise'. In a broader perspective Michael Kazin's (1995) notion of US populism as a constant thread running through US political history highlights the link between the aspirations of a system of politics founded on the ideal of representation and the politics of populism within that context. The USA provides a rich subsoil for populism because there is no automatic contradiction between the populist hostility to representative politics and the ideals of Americanism. In a sense, the importance and popular legitimacy of constitutionalism provide an anchor that allows American politics to tolerate and even generate populist protest movements and parties.

The importance of leadership is evident in the Latin American experience of populism. The ideas and history of Perón in Argentina are symptomatic of a tendency towards charismatic or personalised leadership. The relationship between leadership and representative politics is complex because of the tension between leading and following mass opinions. We can say that personalised or charismatic leadership runs counter to representative politics because it leads to a reversal of the relationship between the masses and their representatives. With charismatic leadership, followers follow because of who their leaders *are*, whereas in representative politics, leaders are chosen on the basis of who they *represent*. The specifically charismatic nature of populist leadership in some Latin American cases illustrates how far populism can go in pursuit of modes of politics at odds with the mass politics of representation. Perón's highly ambivalent relationship to both party politics and to interest group politics, represented by his centralisation of power around himself and his exclusion of unauthorised labour movements (Page 1983), clearly illustrates the ambivalence to the institutions of representative politics.

The new populism is also ambivalent vis-à-vis representative politics. New populist parties are protest parties. Part of the new populist critique of contemporary politics focuses on the over-representation of minorities. Believing the state to be in league with either organised interests or a liberal elite consensus, new populism attacks contemporary representative politics as dysfunctional. It has a specific critique of the functioning of representative politics together with a diffuse but powerful sense of dissatisfaction with politics. This is embodied both in terms of its ideological stance, but also in the tendency for new populist parties to establish themselves as parties, but as parties with distincly different modes and structures of organisation so as to emphasise their distance from the 'established' parties (Taggart 1996; Betz 1998a).

The instances mentioned demonstrate that the theme of opposition to representative politics runs through some of the major instances of populism. It is under the conditions of representative politics that this is apparent, but we may want to consider the possibility that populism has its roots in a primal anti-political reaction of the ruled against their rulers, and it is only under the conditions of representative politics (as both a set of institutions and a type of politics) that this political instinct can be systematically expressed.

The scale of modern societies, and the concomitant increase in the potential distance between rulers and the ruled, is also a key factor in the emergence of populism, and one which encourages the tendency to abstract the rulers and the ruled. Populism emerges when 'he' becomes 'them'. In a parallel fashion, 'I' becomes 'we' as the people are invoked as a generalised entity subject to the same conditions and frustrations as the individual. The portrayal of elites (at national and supernational levels) as distant, faceless and invidious is an essential part of populism. In contemporary Europe, the denomination of 'Eurocrats', 'party hacks' and 'spin-doctors' is indicative of this trend.

The context of contemporary European politics increases the scope, scale and complexity of representation. Integration through the EU has developed new arenas of politics and extended the potential scope of individual representation. The idea of multi-level governance is symptomatic of the expansion of representative politics at non-national levels both above and below the level of the nation-state. European citizens in the member states have the opportunity to be represented through local, sub-national, national and European elections. Representation is not restricted to these elections as the representation of national governments and ministers at the EU level is also institutionalised in the Council of Ministers and European Councils and, in practice, through the Inter-Governmental Conferences and referenda for treaty ratifications. The quality or effectiveness of this representation is, of course, an important question often framed in terms of the democratic deficit. What is not questionable is that there is more representative politics in contemporary Europe where the process of European integration has expanded the scope of representative politics through introducing new and additional representative processes and institutions in Western Europe while, in Eastern and Central Europe, the transition from communism has led to the introduction of representative politics.

This growth in the scope of representative politics has two effects that potentially promote populism. Firstly, it creates greater complexity and therefore jars with the populist aspiration for simple, direct politics. Complexity, opacity and bureaucracy are part and parcel of the politics of the new Europe but they are also bugbears for populists. Secondly, the new forms of politics engendered in European integration rely on very indirect representation and therefore emphasise the distance between citizens and elites. In short, the quality of representation in these new forms is an easy (and often legitimate) target for populist critiques. The increase in the scope and forms of representative politics in Europe means a quantitative change. Contemporary populism arises out of doubts about the quality of this change.

Populism and its impact on representative politics

The relationship of populism to representative politics is not one-way. Populist movements have some very particular effects on the politics of representative systems. At its simplest, the effect of populism on representative politics is as an indicator of failings, fundamental or otherwise, in the system of politics.

In other ways, populism has some specific effects. The populist rhetorical preoccupation with 'the people' (albeit a very particular conception of 'the people') plays on one of the touchstones of representative democracy. It is not unusual in this. Most movements in representative politics will claim to be 'of the people' in some way. However, in the way that it pits the people explicitly against the elites, populism transforms what would otherwise be a rather bland rallying cry into a potent political weapon. Wielding the weapon of the people, populism, by its very presence in a system of representative politics, creates a context which transforms the relationship between politicians and people. Shils suggests that populism injects politics with an 'inverted egalitarianism' because it 'is tinged with the belief that the people are not just the equal of their rulers; they are actually better than their rulers' (Shils 1956, 101). The extreme form of this is evident in the experience of McCarthyism in the United States, but is also omnipresent in populism through the belief that politicians are synonymous with corruption, while true wisdom and purity resides squarely with the people. This inversion transforms the basis on which institutions of representation claim legitimacy and make claims about public policy.

Populism effectively structures political debate in three ways. It creates a 'politics of simplicity', it reasserts popular sovereignty as a primary value, and it imposes a dichotomy on political debate. In the populist worldview, the politics of simplicity means that politics should embody the wisdom of the ordinary people and therefore should itself be simple and direct. This means that populism, in what it says and in the way that it says it, strives for clarity, directness and simplicity; and it partially succeeds in doing so by the mere expression of this claim. Other parties or movements are forced to reconstitute their positions both in opposition to populist claims but also in imitation of populism's simplistic style. Populism's presence thereby has the effect of delegitimising complex or technical policy initiatives. It forces more established lines of political argument into a defensive posture. It also means that forces opposed to populism are compelled to justify the use of complex representative institutions, such as parties.

An example of how populism employs the politics of simplicity is its attitude to taxes. Populist campaigns frequently target taxation as inherently negative and part of a wider conspiracy to wrest wealth from the productive citizenry for the unproductive and unrepresentative elite. This is evident in the anti-taxation campaigns in the US, and in the campaign of Mogens Glistrup in Denmark in 1973, through to the contemporary new populist party positions. This focus on taxation per se moves the debate away from precisely what taxation should be used for and forces those defending the fiscal *status quo* to defend the very notion of taxation.

Populism also tends to define the vocabulary of political debate. This feature owes much to the spread of democracy as an idea. Given that populism invariably claims to speak in the name of the people (the heartland's population), there is a congruence between these types of claims and the demands of democracy that politics is legitimised insofar as it embodies popular sovereignty. This means that, although populism's commitment to 'the people' is, at best, a vague claim, it is a powerful tool and has the effect of legitimising populist claims. The ambiguity of the term means that it can be used to evoke some very particular constituencies without explicitly excluding others. Populism benefits from the ambiguity in its invocation of the people, allowing it to imply the 'unsayable' without actually having to say it.

Moreover, populist movements have strong exclusionary potential. The anti-immigrant positions of many new populist parties reflect the fact that the ambiguity inherent in their reference to the popular sovereignty of 'the people' is used to define their constituency in exclusionary terms. Populists are often more certain of who they are *not*, than of who they *are*. Contemporary European populists of the Right are certain that they are not the elite (or the corrupt), but they are equally certain that they are not immigrant populations. The confluence of anti-immigrant politics with populist mobilisation is one example of the way that popular sovereignty is invoked to exclude and demonise key societal groups.

The final effect of populism on political debate is that it dichotomises issues, forcing them to be couched in either *pro* or *anti* terms. The tendency towards political dualism inherent in populism is partly the result of an attempt to construct simple politics that allow direct representation, but it is also symptomatic of another way of seeing the polarising of elites and masses as a whole. Both are portrayed as relatively monolithic, and just as populism is reluctant to see divisions between elites because such niceties obscure the fundamental unity of purpose and interest of elites, so they are reluctant to differentiate and divide the people. The broad parameters of the elites and the people are heavily drawn but the detail within those categories is noticeably absent.

If we look at the contemporary debates about European integration, there is evidence of populism in the Eurosceptic position. It becomes evident that this populism polarises the debate into *pro* and *anti* camps and leaves no space for debates about different types of European integration. An example of this is the way in which the discussion on the advantages and disadvantages of joining the Euro have forced the pro-Euro camp in the UK to frame their debate in the much wider terms of the benefits of European integration. The presence of populist Euroscepticism has significantly transformed the terms of the debate.

Populism's framing of the political world in dualist terms, applies to issues as much as to interests. Just as the political world is divided into two competing forces, it makes sense to read off political issues in the same terms. Politics becomes dualised in terms of both the players and the play. This gives us the simple politics of good and bad, of right and wrong. It also explains why populism seems to spill over so easily from the secular to moral fundamentalism with its quasi-religious imagery. In many populist movements, there is a strong overlap between religious imagery and moral fundamentalism. The semi-religious overtones always particularly apparent in the way they mobilise, but invariably in the way the world is presented and in the language of populism. In the battle between good and evil it is always clear to populists on whose side the common people stand.

Finally, in relation to the size of its support, populism has a disproportionate effect on the way representative politics operates. That is partly its strength: it has the effect of changing the way the game of representative politics is played because it is suspicious of the rules themselves. By its very presence, populism introduces an unease about the nature of the process and this may force the more habitual participants into a defensive posture and into changing the way discussion takes place, issues are framed, and constituencies mobilised. This means that populism is potentially damaging for the systems of representative politics within which it mobilises. In one sense, this may be a good thing, as populism can be taken as an indicator of real problems with the system. However, any alternative populism offers is invariably short-lived. The self-limitation of populism means that, practically, it has difficulty in sustaining a movement that develops this critique. The limitations of populism are, however, more than merely practical. The fact that populism is a reaction against representative politics means that it has nothing substantial to offer in its place. The lack of core values means that there is nothing in which to anchor an alternative version of politics. For positive alternatives populism has to turn to the ideologies to which it attaches itself. Populism *qua* populism has little to offer representative politics other than as an indicator of the latter's ill-health.

Conclusion

Representative politics means that a range of political positions can be developed, debated and incorporated into a system of governance. One of the requirements of representative politics is pluralism, in the sense that competition between ideas, groups, parties and individuals is necessary for the institutions to function. Populism has a somewhat different status from other ideologies, being derived from its reaction to the institutions themselves rather than to the debate within those institutions. It is deeply rooted in the processes and practices of representative politics, but only occasionally finds systematic expression. When it does, it does so with dramatic effect.

The irony of populism is that while representative politics is the source of frustration, it is also the means by which populism expresses that frustration and wins support. While populism may be present in a subtle form in non-democratic systems, it is only when there is the opportunity to structure diffuse populist sentiment into political movements or parties, that populism comes into its own. And yet, part of the protest element of populism derives from the sentiment that the very system of representative politics is found wanting. The ambivalence towards representative politics explains the ambivalence towards the institutions of representative politics – political parties and interest groups – and this ambivalence, in turn, explains the difficulty of maintaining populist movements in the long term.

In its most 'extreme' forms, populism may be in danger of spilling over into authoritarianism and moving away from democracy altogether. We see this in the practices of Perónism and in the structures of some new populist parties. Populism therefore tests the tolerance of representative politics. However, it is striking that the 'canonical' cases of populism justify themselves in terms of how far they represent the people (however defined) and have all, with the exception of the Russian *narodniki*, formed parties and contested elections. This demonstrates the resilience of representative forms of politics. That the politically reluctant engage in representative politics despite themselves says something about populism, but says much more about the enduring power of representative politics.

Understanding populism today offers insights into contemporary populist movements, but it also allows us to trace a more generally applicable pathology of representative politics. With 'crises of legitimacy', 'democratic deficits' and the 'decline of parties' there are many conditions that give rise to populist mobilisation and represent the limits to representative politics. Understanding populism for its own sake is one thing, but understanding the link between populism and representative politics gives us a clearer picture of when representative politics weakens or fails and becomes *un*-representative politics.

Note

1. Unlike Mény and Surel, I wish to differentiate constitutionalism as the horizontal dimension of politics rather than seeing it as one of the twin pillars of politics with representation.

5
Populist Democracy vs Party Democracy

Peter Mair

Introduction

In their introduction to this volume, Yves Mény and Yves Surel draw a distinction between 'popular democracy' and 'constitutional democracy', the two pillars on which the legitimacy and effectiveness of democratic regimes rest. The popular democracy pillar is identified with an emphasis on the role of the *demos,* that is, the free association of citizens, the maintenance of free elections, and the freedom of political expression. Popular democracy entails government *by* the people. The constitutional pillar, on the other hand, is identified with an emphasis on the institutional requirements for good governance – the establishment of rules and constraints limiting executive autonomy, the guaranteeing of individual and collective rights, and the maintenance of a system of checks and balances intended to prevent the abuse of power. The constitutional pillar may be associated with the defence of the public good, entailing government *for* the people. For Mény and Surel, an ideal democracy should aim to establish an equilibrium between both pillars.

This distinction between the two pillars of democracy is important in itself, and the belief that both need to be in balance has also become increasingly evident in much contemporary writing on democratic theory. Thus, for example, in what is a sustained and persuasive plea on behalf of what he defines as modern republicanism, Philip Pettit (1997) has outlined a model of governance in which he argues in favour of the benefits of institutional pluralism and deliberation and against a more populist model in which the *demos* rules virtually without constraint. For Pettit, constitutionalism appears to count for *more* than popular democracy. More recently, in an assessment of the legitimacy problems facing modern European governments, both nationally and at the level of the European Union, Fritz Scharpf (1999a) has developed a related argument, urging a much greater reliance on what he sees as output-oriented democracy, with an emphasis on government *for* the people, rather than on input-oriented democracy, with its emphasis on government *by* the people. Indeed, for Scharpf the latter seems increasingly unworkable.

On one level, it may seem ironic that it is precisely during a period in which democracy has finally been seen to emerge triumphant (Hadenius 1997) that so many theorists should now focus so much attention on the apparent need to balance the voice of the *demos*. Little more than a decade ago, the collapse of Communism in Eastern Europe was widely and unequivocally heralded as ensuring the full expression of popular democracy in previously authoritarian regimes. Now, as the century has turned, attention appears to have shifted towards the consideration of how that voice might be restrained. In other words, democracy may be triumphant, but, as Mény and Surel suggest, its popular pillar is increasingly seen to require a constitutionalist curb.

On another level, however, there are at least two compelling reasons why this reasoning seems to find so much contemporary favour. In the first place, as an increasing volume of literature testifies (see for example, Nie et al. 1997; Norris 1999; Pharr and Putnam, 2000b), popular democracy itself now seems that much less robust. Popular engagement in the political process is waning throughout the advanced democracies, with lower levels of electoral participation, declining levels of party membership, and a fading sense of attachment or identification with conventional political alternatives. At the same time, there is ample evidence to suggest that citizens are not only increasingly indifferent towards the electoral process, but also increasingly distrustful of the political leaders that it produces. Indeed, as Dahl (1999, 1; see also Mény and Surel in this volume) has emphasised, we now witness a paradoxical combination of increasingly widespread support for democracy per se on the one hand, and declining confidence in its functioning on the other. Nor is this lack of confidence in the day-to-day functioning of democracy visible only in terms of mass popular attitudes. Distrust or disregard is also evident within the academy, as it were, with some of the recent public policy literature in particular (such as Majone 1996; Blinder 1997) advancing the case for a transfer of key decision-making powers from elected politicians to more politically neutral experts. Part of the problem here is that as government itself has become increasingly depoliticised and routinised, it is seen to require the sorts of skills and knowledge that are more readily associated with professionalism rather than with democracy as such. Those who can win the modern game of elections are not necessarily seen as those best suited to governing our democracies.

Second, and in a related vein, popular democracy may be downgraded in favour of a more constitutional democracy precisely because it no longer appears authoritative.[1] In other words, popular democracy is no longer experienced as the means for settling great struggles between alternative political visions – even should such alternative visions be found to exist.[2] Politics is no longer about groups in society fighting to gain access to government in order to establish their own particular political, social or ideological rules of the game. That period has largely passed. And even had it not passed, the capacity to provide authoritative solutions is in any case constrained by the declining ability of governments to intervene in substance. Whether through globalisation, internationalisation, or even the more local Europeanisation, the capacity of governments to exert political control, and hence the capacity of popular democracy to mandate government action, is now severely limited. Partly in recognition of this new environment, governments in contemporary democracies appear increasingly keen to play down any direct 'hands-on' responsibility, seeing their role instead as that of a facilitator or regulator rather than a controller, or as that of ensuring the conditions in which market solutions can be found rather than as a devisor of those solutions. These conceptions further suggest that the role of government is to enhance the freedom of citizens and so to allow the latter to find their own solutions. The state, in effect, takes a more background position, and this further undermines the relevance of the popular democracy pillar.

But there is also another key reason why these two senses of democracy – the popular and the constitutional – appear to be separating from one another, and why the very idea of attempting a balance or equilibrium has begun to win attention. Put very simply, one of the major reasons why we can now speak plausibly of a distinction between popular and constitutional democracy is that the key institution that once bound these two elements together – the political party – is itself declining in importance. In this sense, it is not only that the two senses of democracy are perceived to be increasingly separated from one another; but that they are also growing apart in practice.

In this chapter I will attempt to fill out this last argument by briefly referring to the major changes that are currently impacting on political parties, and by looking at how these may be undermining the assumptions involved in the traditional conception of party democracy. These changes involve both party identities and the functions that parties perform. I will then go on to discuss how these changes have served to weaken the parties' mediating role and hence how they have also offered an enhanced *scope* for the revival of populism. Two senses of populism are relevant to the discussion here. On the one hand, there is the more conventional sense of populism, conceived as a form of popular protest against the political establishment. On the other hand, there is a more 'respectable' and possibly more relevant sense of populism, understood as a means of linking an increasingly undifferentiated and depoliticised electorate with a largely neutral and non-partisan system of governance. It is on the latter conception of populism, and its practice, that I concentrate.

The erosion of party democracy

Throughout twentieth-century Europe, the linkage between voters and governments under conditions of mass democracy has been organised primarily by party. Voters chose between parties, however loosely defined and organised; representation was channelled through parties; governments were formed by parties, particularly in parliamentary systems; and accountability was assured through parties. As Rudolf Wildenmann (1986, 6) put it, 'party government [was] the crucial agency of institutional legitimisation in democratic ruling organisations, distinguishing the democratic modern state from other types'. This emphasis on party as representative *and* as governor, that is, the emphasis on party democracy, has involved a number of assumptions and beliefs about how modern democracy functioned (see also Katz 1986, 1997). These have included the following assumptions:

- that the link between voters and governments is mediated rather than direct, with the organised political party acting as the principal mediator within the electoral channel;
- that the electorate is characterised by a set of diverse and reasonably enduring interests which more or less compete with one another for the distribution of scarce public resources;
- that these interests are reflected more or less faithfully in the programmes of the parties that compete for electoral support;
- that the governments formed as a result of this process of party competition are more or less partisan, with the winners enjoying

the right to pursue the programme(s) which they themselves have developed and with the losers being obliged to accept that their concerns may be excluded or ignored; hence, in any political solution derived through this process, there are winners and losers.

As is readily apparent, however, it is now increasingly difficult to sustain any of these assumptions. Indeed, given that the partisan character of both representation and government has been subject to significant erosion within contemporary democracies in recent years, it is difficult to characterise modern democracy as party democracy. Two elements are important here: changes in party identity; and changes in the functions which parties can be seen to perform.

Taking party identities first, it is becoming increasingly evident that there has been a significant blurring of the ideological or programmatic identity of at least those parties that inhabit the mainstream of the party system. Parties increasingly share the same voters, and, with the decline in the strength of affective loyalties, they are now even keener to direct their appeals into what had once been the traditional heartlands of their opponents. The result is that the old notions of politics as reflecting social conflict – politics as a 'democratic class struggle' in which the competing parties were seen to represent the political interests of opposing social forces – are now less and less appropriate. At the same time, with more or less all parties becoming available to more or less all voters, the old notions of politics as ideological conflict also ebb away. In addition, as governments and their occupying parties face increasing constraints on their capacity for policy manoeuvre within the modern nation-state, they find themselves more or less obliged to share the same programmes and policies. Although rhetoric and the appeals to differing value systems may well allow voters to distinguish between the parties in any particular government and those in opposition, it is evident that substantive contrasts in the practice of policy are increasingly difficult to discern. Government proceeds by regulation rather than by partisan policy-making. Nor does any party present itself as being very distinctive, in that professional campaigning and marketing techniques have tended to standardise what were once quite particularistic organisational profiles and strategies. These and other shifts in party identity and approach have led to a situation in which voters find it increasingly difficult to detect significant ideological or purposive differences between parties, or to see these differences as being particularly relevant to their own particular needs and situations. In other words, because of the changing relations between parties, as well as changes in the way they present themselves, voters find it less and less easy to think of these parties in traditional representative terms.

The second major element involved here is part of this same process, but is best seen as involving a shift in the balance of the functions traditionally performed by parties in mass democracies. In fact, parties have always been associated with two distinct sets of functions: a set of representative functions, on the one hand, and a set of more procedural or institutional functions, on the other. In recent years, however, and for reasons identified above, the first set has become less meaningful, while the second has acquired more prominence. Thus, for example, as Pizzorno (1981) has argued, the first function classically associated with political parties, that of integrating and mobilising the citizenry, is historically contingent, and is neither necessary nor even possible in fully mobilised democracies. The second function classically associated with parties, involving the articulation and aggregation of interests, is also representative, and is now something that parties increasingly share with, or even cede to, non-party associations and movements, as well as to the media. Indeed, the expression of popular interests and demands now often occurs outside the party world, with the parties increasingly contenting themselves with picking up signals that come from elsewhere. The third classic function, the formulation of public policy, which involves both representative and procedural dimensions, seems also less relevant to contemporary parties, in that policy-making is increasingly devolved to non-partisan commissions and agencies. Taken together, these three elements clearly indicate a devaluation of the representative role normally associated with political parties in mass democracy.

In more narrowly defined procedural terms, on the other hand, we see little sign of devaluation, and possibly even some evidence of a degree of enhancement of the role of party. The classic function of recruitment continues to be important, for example, and as long as parties continue to structure electoral choice, even in the most minimalist sense of the term, it is difficult to imagine this function being bypassed. Certainly, recruitment processes in contemporary parties may now mean casting a much wider net than that originally employed by the classic mass party. Nevertheless, though the pool of talent may now stretch outside the immediate confines of the party, it is still the party that controls much of the access to public office, and in this sense this procedural function not only remains important, but could even be seen to have achieved a greater priority than in the past. The fifth and potentially most important function performed by parties, which is also procedural, concerns the role of parties in the organisation of parliament and government, and here too there is no sign of decay. In systems of parliamentary government, for example, parties are required to form governments, usually through coalition negotiations. Parties are also required to allocate responsibilities in government across the different departments or ministries, and to maintain their governments in office by means of more or less disciplined support within parliament. Moreover, and even beyond conventional systems of parliamentary government, parties also appear necessary for the organisation of legislative procedures, for the functioning of legislative committees, and for day-to-day agreement on the legislative agenda.

Although this assessment of party functions is necessarily brief and over-generalised, it does nonetheless suggest that the representative function of parties is either declining or has been at least partially replaced by other agencies, whereas their procedural or institutional role has been maintained, and may indeed have become more prominent. Just as parties have gradually moved from society to the state (Katz and Mair 1995), so the functions that they perform and are expected to perform have changed from those of a largely *representative* agency to those of a *governing* agency. In other words, and returning to the original distinction at the beginning of this chapter, while parties are proving less relevant in terms of the organisation and functioning of the popular democracy pillar, they continue to play a central role in the organisation and functioning of the constitutional democracy pillar. Moreover, when taken together with changes in party identity, these shifts in party functions clearly reinforce the sense that there has been a substantial weakening of both the partisan and the representative role of political parties and their governments. What is being left in place of this is an increasingly exclusive emphasis on the procedural role of parties as governors.

This also helps explain why the popular and constitutional pillars are not only increasingly perceived to be distinct, but also why they are growing apart in practice. When parties served as *both* representatives *and* governors, it was obviously less easy to sense that the popular pillar functioned separately from the constitutional pillar. Precisely because they proved so important to both, parties bridged, and hence blurred, any boundaries that might otherwise have been seen to exist. As these same parties increasingly fall back on an enhanced procedural role, on the other hand, the popular pillar becomes hollowed out, becoming more inchoate and more problematic. What we see here, in short, is the decline of party democracy, and it is this, above all, which seems to have encouraged the calls to curb the popular pillar.

Two senses of populism

The decline of party democracy has also clearly enhanced the scope for populist solutions. There are at least two senses of populism that are relevant here. The first, and that which has drawn most recent attention among commentators, is populist protest – a substantive if not always coherent programme which seeks to mobilise popular support against established elites and institutions. The second version, by contrast, which is potentially more far-reaching, is populist democracy itself.

The notion of populism as protest, that is, the substantive sense of populism, is familiar in the varied literature on populism (for example, Canovan 1981, 1999; Ionescu and Gellner 1969), and elsewhere in this volume we see a full reflection of the various modes in which this may be interpreted and expressed. As such, I do not intend to consider it at any length. In the context of the decline of party democracy, it is sufficient to draw attention to the populist anti-party sentiment that can now be identified in many contemporary democracies (see, for example, Poguntke and Scarrow 1996; Mudde 1996; Norris 1999), and to the possible link between this emerging protest and the depoliticisation of inter-party relationships. Elsewhere (Mair 1997, 152–4), I have suggested that this populist anti-party sentiment may be at least partly fuelled by a sense that political leaders and their parties are enjoying an increasingly privileged status at the same time as their partisan relevance is seen to be in decline. As party leaderships become increasingly remote from the wider society, and as they also appear increasingly similar to one another in ideological or policy terms, it simply becomes that much easier for populist protestors to rally against the supposed privileges of an undifferentiated political class. As party democracy weakens, therefore, the opportunities for populist protest clearly increase.

For the purposes of this chapter, however, it is perhaps more interesting to work with the second version of populism, focusing more on process and linkage rather than substance, and on what might be seen as an emerging populist democracy. Moreover, used in this latter sense, populism enjoys the potential for the much more pervasive diffusion currently seen in the literature. The process, or linkage, element is, of course, central to almost all definitions of populism, in that all of the discussions in the literature place significant emphasis on the nature of the relationship between a mass of followers and a leader or group of leaders. Over and above this element, however, many of these definitions also entail the more substantive element, thus applying populism only to those parties or movements that advocate a particular political demand or programme. More often than not, contemporary populism, or neopopulism, is associated with the politics of the extreme Right (Betz 1994; Taggart 1995).

Following a more minimalist definition,[3] however, populism may also be seen as integral to a form of democratic governance that operates without an emphasis on party. As indicated above, the first and core element of this minimalist definition posits a relationship between voters and government that is unmediated.[4] In other words, populist democracy primarily tends towards partyless democracy. Representation is no longer adequately assured through traditional processes of party competition (Andeweg 1999) and competing interests are not recognised through competing party programmes. Indeed, populist democracy in this sense does not assume a fundamental clash of interests between different sectors of the electorate: voters are citizens first, and only later, if at all, are they workers, employers, farmers, women, immigrants, or whatever. The people, in this sense, are undifferentiated, and this is the second key element of the minimalist definition of populism employed here. Appeals are directed to the voters at large, or to the people, and not to particular groups that are differentiated by status or belief. An absence of conflict is assumed. Whether formally organised by party or not, the government that emerges in such a democracy therefore has a duty to serve all of the people rather than just some of the people. This, then, is the third and final element of this particular sense of populism: the government serves the national interest, the popular interest, rather than any sectional interest. It serves as an administrator, seeking the best solutions available on the basis of objective criteria, thus rejecting the partisan assumptions involved in conventional conceptions of party democracy and party government.

Seen in these very minimalist terms, this sense of populism may appear to be nothing new. Even beyond the cases most frequently cited in discussions of populism, for example, and most especially in Latin America, such orientations can also be associated with Gaullism in the early years of the French Fifth Republic, with the British Conservative Party even before the halcyon days of Margaret Thatcher, or with the long-term appeals articulated by the dominant Fianna Fáil party in Ireland.[5] But each of these cases may also be associated with a specific substance or programme – a form of 'one-nation conservatism' that was explicitly developed as a partisan strategy in order to counter the appeals of what were posited to be more sectionally-based and, in these particular cases, left-wing opponents. In other words, and in contrast to the more modern variety of populism espoused by New Labour in Britain, for example, these orientations were always explicitly partisan in intent. Whereas populism in the most modern variant is advanced in the context of diminishing the role of parties as such, the populism of this 'one-nation conservatism' was put forward in order to challenge the appeal of particular parties, especially those on the Left, and to enhance the appeal of others.

In fact, the familiar and highly partisan populist appeals of 'one-nation conservatism' do not fit easily with either of the two versions of populism identified above. On the contrary, both substantive populism and populist democracy depend crucially on the erosion of party democracy. The former builds on the declining legitimacy of parties, mobilising protests against the privileges of an apparently self-serving and non-functioning political class. The latter builds more directly on the declining relevance of parties as organisations or intermediaries, and hence works with a notion that democracy can be made to work without the intervention of party. Populism as substance obviously enjoys most scope when popular *distrust* with the political class grows within the electorate, and when popular resentment can be mobilised by challenger parties or movements. Populist democracy, on the other hand, may find its most fertile ground when citizens grow more *indifferent* to democracy, and when popular attitudes are more easily characterised as reflecting both apathy and disengagement. In other words, while substantive populism can threaten established political leaders, this is not necessarily the case for populist democracy. Indeed, populist democracy may actually serve leaders' interests by offering a means of legitimating government within a context of widespread depoliticisation. As I suggest below, this is certainly one plausible reading of the contemporary British case.

In this sense, populist democracy is also potentially more important than substantive populism, particularly in that it now finds the conditions in which it is more likely to be fostered. As noted above, contemporary democracies have already experienced a substantial erosion in the traditional mediating role played by political parties: an erosion in their role as intermediaries between citizens and the state, on the one hand, and as the key linkage mechanism between popular and constitutional democracy, on the other. Parties now manage the state. They no longer prioritise the representation of competing interests. They guarantee procedures rather than mediation. And since, under conditions of party democracy, parties were the only mediating agency between citizens and their governments within the electoral channel, their decline in this respect now suggests that this channel simply becomes that much less mediated. It is this lack of mediation that encourages the resort to populist democracy. In other words, popular democracy, when shorn of the central role played by parties, increasingly nudges towards populist democracy.

At a very general level, therefore, populist democracy may be understood as *popular democracy without parties*. When parties play a central role in structuring collective electoral preferences and political identities, we can anticipate a vibrant and meaningful popular democracy. Moreover, and to recap the earlier discussion, when the electoral role of parties is also complemented by their also enjoying a central role in public office, we can further anticipate a blurring of the boundaries between popular democracy and constitutional democracy, and hence an absence of any real tension between the two. Once the relevance of parties within the electoral channel begins to decline, however, two things follow. First, as noted above, we begin to discern a separation between the popular and constitutional pillars. The parties which once knitted these pillars together no longer enjoy the capacity to legitimate that linkage. Second, as the popular pillar becomes less mediated by party, popular democracy begins to take on the characteristics of populist democracy. There is a fragmentation of once powerful collective electoral identities, there is a blurring of the ideological and organisational distinctions that once defined electoral choice, and, to paraphrase Kornhauser (1959), we see the emergence of a genuinely mass electorate whose relations with the institutions of government are no longer mediated to any significant extent (Hayward 1996a).

More importantly, perhaps, it then follows that the apparent 'tension' which develops between popular and constitutional democracy could well prove transient. Of course, if parties continue to be seen as representatives as well as governors, then they will almost inevitably disappoint, and the result will be tension. Moreover, as long as such tension exists, it will be open to exploitation by neopopulist actors who will point to the failure of the established alternatives to meet traditional expectations. But should the changed position of parties become a more familiar part of the landscape, and should expectations about their role adjust and start to match the changed and less representative reality more closely, then this tension is likely to evaporate. This is also what populist democracy is about, for in populist democracy, understood as a partyless popular democracy, there is no necessary tension between the two pillars. Indeed, one may even argue that populist democracy may in this sense complement constitutional democracy.

Populist democracy in practice: the 'paradox' of New Labour in Britain

Consider the following, extracts from the speech delivered by Tony Blair to the British Labour Party Conference in 1999:[6]

> We know what a 21st century nation needs. A knowledge-based economy. A strong civic society. A confident place in the world ... The challenge is how? The answer is people. The future is people. The liberation of human potential not just as workers but as citizens. Not power to the people but power to each person to make the most of what is within them. People are born with talent and everywhere it is in chains. Look at Britain. Great strengths. Great history. English, the language of the new technology. The national creative genius of the British people. But wasted. The country run far too long on the talents of the few, when the genius of the many lies uncared for, and ignored ... Today it is people...
>
> The old order, those forces of conservatism, for all their language about promoting the individual, and freedom and liberty, they held people back. They kept people down. They stunted people's potential ...
>
> Arrayed against us: the forces of conservatism, the cynics, the elites, the establishment ... On our side, the forces of modernity and justice. Those who believe in a Britain for all the people ...
>
> To every nation a purpose. To every party a cause. And now, at last, party and nation joined in the same cause for the same purpose: to set our people free.

One of the first things this rhetoric reveals is the extent to which a populist language has now become acceptable within what has long been perceived as a decidedly non-populist political culture. Certainly, British political culture remains largely inimical to the mobilisation of neopopulist parties or movements, with anti-establishment appeals from both the extreme Right and the extreme Left proving less successful in the British case than in almost any other Western European polity. On the other hand, the more acceptable face of populism, that associated with populist democracy, is now certainly in full flow, with 'the people', however defined, becoming the key reference point within New Labour rhetoric. Having said this, and however incongruous it may seem, the speech also indicates that even the more substantive notion of populism as protest appears to be making some headway in Britain, albeit sponsored by the very establishment against which such protest might normally be directed. In the last instance, however, this latter sense of populism is unlikely to be sustained, at least within these same governing circles: even within New Labour, the notion of maintaining an anti-establishment rhetoric whilst dominating the key positions within the governing elite will eventually seem implausible. Indeed, it is the more procedural notion of populism, that associated with populist democracy, that is the more important here. This is not only apparent in the current rhetoric, which may well change with time, but rather appears to have guided the overall governing style of New Labour in Britain, and in this sense may well be indicative of the emergence of a more generalised phenomenon. Let us look at this new style more closely.

There are two particular aspects of New Labour's political strategy that are important here. The first is the iron control which is currently exerted by the senior leadership of Labour on both the party organisation on the ground and within the parliamentary party. Within the party on the ground, for example, an exceptionally tight grip is now kept on the selection and nomination of candidates for elections at both the national and sub-national level, with even the recent autonomy afforded to the newly established offices in Scotland, Wales and London being accompanied by massive top-down party intervention in both candidate and leadership selection within these newly devolved arenas. Within Westminster itself, and despite a record and effectively invincible majority, party whips make unprecedented attempts to ensure that all Labour members remain 'on message', and to ensure that the line pursued by the leadership is echoed throughout the parliamentary party ranks. Meanwhile the core leadership has taken on an increasing burden of decision-making, avoiding the use of cabinet meetings and delegating to ministers the freedom to administer rather than to make key policy choices. This is a system of 'one party, one voice', with the words used by that voice coming only from the top.

The second aspect which is relevant here is the increased reliance on plebiscitarian techniques of winning support. Crucially, all of the key reforms instituted by this present New Labour leadership have been preceded by plebiscites – within the party itself, where the leadership position has on occasion been endorsed by a 95 per cent majority; and, at the level of the political system, in each of the regions for which devolution is proposed. Even the introduction of direct elections for the mayor of London was preceded by a plebiscite, as will be any attempt to devolve a regional level of government within England.

The two strategies are related, insofar as both can be read as the intention to eliminate the autonomous impact of party. The crucial actor is now government, while the crucial legitimator is now the people writ large. In this new political strategy, it is government that still proposes, but it is now the people, rather than parliament or the parties as such, that dispose.[7] The link between the two is unmediated, and it is here that we see contemporary Britain entering the realm of populist democracy.

But there is more to it than this: for coupled with this developing political strategy there has been a major programme of constitutional reform. Indeed, after just one term in office, New Labour has done more than any other British government in recent history to transform what has been an exceptionally strong tradition of majoritarian democracy. The various changes in this regard are already well-known, and together they add up to what almost amounts to a constitutional revolution: the massive process of decentralisation which has followed from the devolution of government to Scotland and Wales; the incorporation of the European Convention of Human Rights into British law, thus setting an immediate and important judicial constraint on parliamentary sovereignty; the adoption of proportional representation for elections to the newly devolved regional parliaments as well as in elections to the European Parliament; the establishment of a commission on electoral reform to examine possible alternatives to the plurality system for Westminster elections; the introduction of a directly elected mayor in London, with the prospect of expanding this system to other cities and regions in the future; and the abolition of voting rights for hereditary peers in the House of Lords, with the probability that the Upper House will eventually be transformed into a directly or indirectly elected chamber. In addition, New Labour has also proved sufficiently non-partisan to stretch across to other parties, inviting the Liberals to take part in a key cabinet committee on constitutional reform, and appointing senior figures from both the Liberal and

Conservative parties to head official commissions on changes in policing, the electoral system, and the House of Lords. Whereas the United Kingdom originally provided the paradigmatic case for majoritarian democracy in Lijphart's (1984) well-known typology, under New Labour, and on almost every one of the features identified by Lijphart, with the crucial exception of legislature-executive relations within Westminster itself, it has now moved quite markedly in the direction of consensus democracy.

What we see here, in fact, and this is the reason why it is such an interesting case, is a unique but potentially generalisable combination of an anti-party political strategy, on the one hand, and an enhanced commitment to institutional pluralism, on the other. From one perspective, of course, the combination seems almost paradoxical. Indeed, this is precisely the view taken by David Marquand (1999, 240–1), who notes that although Tony Blair and his colleagues,

> [h]ave imposed a Prussian discipline on their own followers, exceeding anything attempted by any previous Labour leadership ... the logic [of their constitutional reforms] is pluralistic, and the end product will be a series of checks and balances at variance with the tacit assumptions of the democratic-collectivist tradition.

From another perspective, however, the combination may seem to make a lot of sense. In other words, if we accept that the political strategy has not been developed as a means of strengthening party and partisanship, but rather as a means of taking party and partisanship out of the equation, the apparent paradox disappears. Indeed, seen in this light, both the political strategy and the constitutional strategy are wholly compatible with one another. The key point is that neither is driven by a partisan impulse. By exerting total control over their own members and representatives, the Labour leaders in government effectively substitute themselves for the party as a whole, thus denying the party writ large a separate or autonomous voice. This also leaves the leadership free to reach across in an effort to incorporate other parties or elements of other parties into a loose and potentially less partisan governing coalition. Indeed, and quite predictably in the light of the proportional electoral systems that have been adopted there, the administrations in both Scotland and Wales are now both constituted by Labour-Liberal Democrat coalitions. Taking party out of the equation also makes it that much easier to think in terms of institutional pluralism and the wider territorial dispersal of power, while the evasion of party and partisan interest allows consideration of electoral reform, even when this might seem to run counter to party self-interest. Successful parties rarely change the rules of the game when these have already guaranteed them victory. When party itself no longer matters, however, the rules may be changed quite easily.

That New Labour should be striving for a non-partisan style of governance is hardly surprising. The rhetoric is also non-partisan: 'Party and nation joined in the same cause for the same purpose: to set our people free.' Moreover, the governing programme itself – the so-called 'Third Way' – is also deliberately couched in non-partisan terms, being presented as a new synthesis which rises above the traditional divisions of Left and Right, and which can unite all sides behind an objectively validated approach to which there is no real alternative (see Giddens 1998). As Marquand (1999, 227) notes: 'Moral and ideological arguments for the Third Way are unnecessary; it does not have to be defended against alternative visions of the future, based on different moral and ideological premises. There is only one future, and resistance to it is spitting in the wind.'

In short, the paradox of Blairism only becomes apparent when the internal party strategy of New Labour is read as an attempt to strengthen the party, and hence as a partisan strategy. If it is read as an attempt to use leadership control in order to evade party, and as a non-partisan strategy, then the picture as a whole makes more sense. These are non-partisan leaders with a non-partisan programme running a non-partisan government in the interests of the people as a whole. This is, in short, *partyless* democracy (Mair 2000). And it is here that the story comes back to populist democracy: populism as a form of governing in which party is sidelined or disappears; where the people are undifferentiated, and in which a more or less 'neutral' government attempts to serve the interests of all.

There are two features of this new form of populist democracy which need to be borne in mind, however. First, although I suggest that the shift towards this form of populist democracy is now most easily visible in the British case, the logic suggests that it may well become much more pervasive. As the representative and partisan identities of parties in general become eroded, the appeal of populist democracy will inevitably be strengthened. Moreover, especially at the European level of government, it is likely that it will be this British-style combination of populist democracy and enhanced constitutionalism that will predominate. Indeed, since the only real alternative to populist democracy is party democracy, and since party democracy finds great difficulty in operating at the European level, it is virtually inevitable that it will be the populist conception that will win through, albeit tempered, and necessarily so, by a stricter and more transparent system of institutional checks and balances. This may also be the logical consequence of Scharpf's notion of 'output-oriented democracy'.

Second, it is also therefore important to recognise from the British case that populist democracy is compatible with constitutional democracy. Indeed, if enhanced constitutional democracy is facilitated, or even required, once party and partisanship are taken out of the equation, then it can be argued that populist democracy is also required as the means by which the practice of this partyless constitutional democracy is ultimately legitimised. Constitutional democracy sees good governance emerging from a renewed system of checks and balances, in which majorities are constrained by prior principle, on the one hand, and by the dispersal of decision-making across a variety of institutions, on the other. This is precisely the direction in which New Labour is currently taking the UK. But, at least as practised in the British case, there is also a strong populist component, insofar as democratic accountability is also assured by the introduction of plebiscitary elements. In the absence of party, these seem almost inevitable. In this sense 'the people' also have an important role as one of the final elements in the overall system of checks and balances. The choice is therefore not between populist democracy, on the one hand, and constitutionalism, on the other – indeed, both are enhanced as the hold of party is eroded – but between an emerging populist democracy and a more traditional party democracy, a choice where the odds seem increasingly stacked against the latter.

Notes

1. This argument is also suggested by Schedler (1997, 10–12).
2. As Perry Anderson (2000, 17) noted recently:

> Ideologically, the novelty of the present situation stands out in historical view. It can be put like this. For the first time since the Reformation, there are no longer any significant oppositions – that is, systematic rival outlooks – within the thought-world of the West; and scarcely any on a world-scale either... Whatever limitations persist to its practice, neoliberalism as a set of principles rules undivided across the globe: the most successful ideology in world history.

3. Although the minimalist definition used here comes close to that discussed by Margaret Canovan under the heading 'political populism', her use of this latter term includes an important substantive component in that she speaks of a 'tension' that 'looms large' between leaders and followers (Canovan 1981, 8–16). As used here, populist democracy does not necessarily involve any such tension. Both Worsley (1969) and Weyland (1999b) offer very complete overviews of the variety of conceptual definitions that have been applied to populism.
4. Note here the distinction made by Kornhauser (1959),

   > [A] pluralist society supports a *liberal democracy*, whereas a mass society supports a *populist democracy* ... In liberal democracy the mode of access [to power] tends to be controlled by institutional procedures and intermediate associations, whereas in populist democracy the mode of access tends to be more direct and unrestrained [i.e. unmediated] (Kornhauser, 1959, 131).

5. As one former leader of the latter put it – in a way that could probably just as easily have been echoed by De Gaulle, Macmillan, or even Thatcher – 'representative as it is of all the people – and I mean all sections of the people – farmers, workers, businessmen and employers... Fianna Fáil is in a unique position to produce and put into effect the policies best suited to the needs of the Irish people' (Lynch 1969, 1).
6. The full text of the speech can be found on the *Guardian* website of 30 September 1999; see: http://www.newsunlimited.co.uk/lab99.
7. The emphasis on the need for popular approval of constitutional reform is stressed particularly by Lord Irvine, the current British Lord Chancellor, who co-ordinates the reform programme as a whole (Lecture by Lord Irvine on Britain's constitutional reform agenda, Leiden University, 22 October 1999). For a lengthier discussion of the New Labour strategy, from which the following section of the chapter is drawn, see Mair (2000).

Part II
Identifying Country Variations

6
The United States: Populism as Political Strategy

Alan Ware

Introduction

> You're everywhere and nowhere baby, that's where you're at (opening line of the song, *Hi Ho Silver Lining*)

Unless discussion is focused specifically on the People's Party of the late nineteenth century, American populism proves to be a curiously elusive subject. From one perspective, many aspects of American politics can be described, broadly, as populist in character. However, once particular instances of alleged populism are subjected to analysis, it appears that much that might otherwise be identified as populist can be incorporated within some other tradition of politics in the United States. Populism is everywhere, and nowhere. In trying to understand this, perhaps the best starting point is the concept of populism itself.

There are three main points to note about populism, particularly in its relationship to democracy. First, there are important links between the idea of populism and the idea of democracy, but the two concepts are not the same. Democracy within a nation-state is founded on the idea that, ultimately, government is justified by reference to the preferences and/or the interests of the citizens of that state. However, the practice of democracy in anything other than the level of small communities necessitates a variety of devices – most notably the election of political representatives – that makes any link between citizens' preferences and public policy largely indirect. Thus, even in a state comprising only the most enthusiastic of democrats, there would be many aspects of public policy where decisions would not correspond directly with the structure of preferences evident among the citizens, were some means of discovering such preferences available. In other words, the 'fit' between citizens' preferences (such as they are) and public policy is a loose one, and democrats accept this as one of the consequences of scale in collectivities any larger than a small village or neighbourhood. By contrast, unlike many other kinds of democrats, and most certainly those whom Riker (1982) called 'liberals', populists refuse to accept the legitimacy of a loose fit between citizens' preferences and public policy. Populism prioritises the opinions of people over anything else; that a policy proves acceptable eventually to most citizens, or promotes their interests but is not a policy they want, is an insufficient basis for political legitimacy. What matters for the populist are overt opinions and demands emanating from within the body of citizens; in the terminology of Barry (1965, 180–2) they prioritise 'wants-for-policies' rather than 'wants-for-results'.

Of course, real-world populist leaders do not necessarily promote policy objectives and policies that their followers, let alone anyone else, actually want. However, a justification is characteristically populist only if it refers to the alleged views of 'the people'. Populists therefore seek to remove from elected politicians much of the autonomy granted to them by proponents of representative government. In doing so, populism is diametrically opposed, of course, to Burkean notions of representative government; populists deny the legitimacy of a system in which representatives decide which policies will promote the interests of the people unconstrained by anything save for the need to be re-elected periodically (Haskell 2000). For the populist, the representative is likely to be subject to influence from various elites, and, according to populists, one result of this is that political representatives have a strong tendency to pursue policies which run counter to those actually wanted by the people.

Secondly, democratic theorists often disagree as to whose interests and views should be taken into account in a democratic process, those who are citizens *strictu sensu*, or should participation in the political process be extended to all those affected by a decision? Consequently, when democrats refer to 'the people', it may well be unclear who is being included. With populists the problem of inclusion is even greater. While populism nearly always justifies political action by reference to 'the people', in practical politics this reference group is often a considerably smaller body than either the citizenry or, for example, everyone residing within the boundaries of the polity. For many populists 'the people' are a core subsection of the inhabitants of a country (possibly a majority of them), and these are the individuals whose opinions and demands are the ones that populists believe should really count. To put it crudely: populists often do not mean 'everyone' when they speak of the people.

The third point about populism is that, as a force in practical politics, its adherents may be considered 'democrats with attitude'. That is, for a populist, the core group in a society – the people – are in opposition to elites whose actions frustrate the implementation of the popular will. Riker's point (1982, 338) that '[W]hat the people want cannot be social policy simply because we do not and cannot know what the people want' is one that populists scarcely ever address. Of course, many populists are not really democrats at all; they merely claim to be voicing what 'the people' want but do little or nothing to facilitate popular input into their own political activity. Consequently, populism can merge easily with an authoritarian style of politics. However, even when there is a democratic element to it, populism as a practical creed is confrontational – it seeks to oppose the minority that is preventing the demands of 'the people' from being realised.

What then provokes such a confrontation? The answer varies depending upon how democratic a regime is, but in liberal democracies populism often arises when constitutional procedures seemingly frustrate democratic input to the policy-making process. As rights protected by law increase in a society, so processes that were once widely accepted as democratic may appear to be counter-majoritarian in practice. Populist movements can mobilise such mass frustrations against elites who seem to be exploiting constitutional protection in opposition to the views of 'the people'. However, this account of populist mobilisation does not fit easily with the American experience. On the one hand, a rigorous set of constitutional checks was built into the political system from its foundation in 1787, while on the other hand, from the Jacksonian era onwards, there was an extensive set of democratic institutions that fostered popular participation. This is not a context in which one may expect populism to thrive and yet by the end of the 1880s a major populist movement based on farmers had emerged, a movement that was to culminate in the formation of the People's Party in 1891. How do we explain the growth of this populist phenomenon?

Essentially the problem with American democracy was that its decentralisation provided popular access to the relevant decision-making arenas only so long as the most important aspects of politics were local. Once the scale of American economic enterprises changed – especially following the rise of the railways – widespread popular access to local politics mattered less; to check the power of these economic interests would have meant mobilising political resources against them on a massive scale and at a national level. For all its democratic elements, the American political system could provide few checks against concentrations of economic power once such interests started to appear. By the end of the Civil War both major parties had been penetrated at the state level and also in Congress by 'big business', with the railways in the vanguard, and this penetration appeared to be growing. If the normal democratic system was not working, *ab*normal politics would have to be the weapon used by those who were the victims of business policies, and it was this that led to the rise of a populist movement in late nineteenth century America.

Given that decentralisation in the American political system was a structural factor that persisted, one may expect major populist movements to have been a recurring feature in American politics throughout the twentieth century. However, this was not the case. Instead, populist demands and populist rhetoric started to permeate mainstream politics. Populism became a political strategy deployed by a wide range of politicians. This chapter is concerned with two aspects of the transformation of populism in America from political movement to political strategy. In the following section I argue that this change was made possible by the fact that populism resembles a number of mainstream political values, conflicts, and traditions in America, so that making a distinct separation between populist appeals and appeals to these other values and traditions is often difficult. Not only, therefore, is populism difficult to disentangle from other kinds of political activity in the United States, but, in addition, it lacks much of the anti-regime character evident in other countries. The 'confrontational element' is often, though not always, muted. This is followed by an examination of the deployment of 'populism-as-strategy'. It concurs with Kazin's (1995, 3) point about populism in America, that it has been 'employed ... as a flexible form of persuasion'. The argument made in this chapter, however, is that, although 'populism-as-strategy' was evident in American politics long before the mid-twentieth century, the weakening of party structures after the 1960s has enabled that strategy to play a more prominent role in national politics.

How populism merges with other political values in the United States

In examining how different values, conflicts and traditions in America relate to populism we will begin with the idea of an American nation and its construction.

Nation-building in America

America has been, perhaps, the most successful example of nation-building in the nineteenth and twentieth centuries. In 1787 the United States consisted of 13 former colonies, each of which had been governed separately; until the War of Independence few of its inhabitants regarded themselves as Americans. Moreover, even among the white, English-speaking population, there was a distinct clash of cultures, centred mainly around the issue of religion (Phillips 1999). Between the War of Independence and the Civil War major efforts were made by America's political elites to create a widespread popular commitment to the idea of 'America', a movement that could not be completed until the Civil War had foreclosed any idea that a rival political system could exist on 'American' territory. An American identity was being forged, and with it came supposedly distinctive American ways of conducting affairs, as well as distinctive American activities, including re-invented sports, such as baseball.

The re-founding of the nation in the Civil War strengthened the idealisation of 'the American', and it was further bolstered during mass immigration from continental Europe in the six decades following the Civil War. Towards the end of that period a determined effort at 'Americanisation' was made with respect to these immigrants (King 2000). Consequently, the idea that anyone who is American should hold certain values, and cherish certain symbols, is long established, and this is held to justify legal action against those who show disrespect for those values and symbols. One of the more recent manifestations of this phenomenon is the controversy over flag-burning. In 1999, the House of Representatives voted overwhelmingly once again (305–124) to pass a constitutional amendment that would permit federal laws against the desecration of the American flag.

Moreover, just as there are 'American' values, so correspondingly there are 'un-American' values, that is, values supposedly incompatible with the former. Notoriously, the name of the congressional committee established to investigate, first, fascist, and, later, Communist, activity in the United States was the Un-American Activities Committee. Whereas in Britain an 'Un-British Activities Committee' would be conceived only in the mind of the political satirist, in the United States the idea of something being 'un-American' emanates naturally from the way in which the idea of 'the American' has been cultivated for generations. However, this ideal of 'the American way' and of 'the American' has little real content. The point has been made well by Foley (1991, 227–8):

> What keeps Americans together in the diversity of their ideas is their belief in, and usage of, a largely unexamined amalgam of values authenticated by American experience. This problem of accessible and amenable American experience promotes a peculiarly American approach to ideas, in which choices between conflicting values are evaded in favour of conflicting constructions of an absorbent American past. In this way, theoretically opposed values are not reconciled, so much as passed over in practice as being mutually inclusive by virtue of being drawn from a common core of American ingredients.

This inherent vagueness about the components of a national tradition means that, more than would be the case in other countries, appeals to the tradition are couched not in terms of what the tradition supposedly comprises, but of what a large body of people *say* it is. That is, advancing a particular version of the American tradition is justified by reference to the numbers of people allegedly supporting that position. It is not so much a question of 'feel the weight of the argument' as 'feel the weight of the persons who take this position'. The similarity of this line of reasoning to populism should be evident, and, it should be noted, furthermore, that it was precisely this kind of tyranny by majority opinion that worried De Tocqueville in his observations of American society in the early 1830s.

Disputes as to who 'the people' are

One of the ways in which textbooks on American politics often mislead students is to claim that there has been a dominant political tradition in the US, from the time of the American Revolution, and that tradition is liberalism. In reality, there was no single tradition in America, rather there have always been conflicting sets of values, and disputes about them continue (Smith 1993). One of the main respects in which Americans disagreed was over how inclusive American society should be. At one extreme were those who adhered to the sort of view encapsulated in Emma Lazarus's poem on the Statue of Liberty: 'Give me your tired, your poor, Your huddled masses yearning to breathe free, The wretched refuse of your teeming shore, Send these, the homeless, tempest tossed, to me.' Given this view, anyone could come to the USA, and become American if they wanted to; all that was required was a commitment to living a free life. Being American consisted in little more than living that life within the boundaries of the USA, and the American people were those persons within its boundaries who did so.

At the other extreme were those who saw being American primarily as associated with being a member of a particular racial or ethnic group, or leading a lifestyle that conformed to a particular socioreligious tradition. On this view, widely held even at the beginning of the Republic, the American people were not the sum of those living within the US borders. The Jeffersonian vision of America, which remained strong until the end of the nineteenth century, saw the United States as a rural country populated by independent farmers. Those who subscribed to Jeffersonianism identified the American people with its farmers. Another subset of the population long identified as constituting 'the people' has been its white population, so that African-Americans, native Americans, Latinos and others were occupants of American territory, but did not really constitute part of its 'people'. Thus, their opinions and political demands would not count in the same way as those of 'the people'. Moreover, even being a white Anglo-Saxon Protestant might not be sufficient to be 'an American'; those held to follow certain lifestyles (such as, today, being gay, or being 'secular humanists') have also been deemed not to be full members of the community, and hence not truly part of the American people. Equally, those who were critical of American society, or who criticised actions of the government undertaken on behalf of the 'nation', may be seen in a similar light, and be commanded: 'America: Love it or Leave it'.

The importance of this tradition of political exclusion for populism is that the populist notion of a core group in society who really constitute 'the people' has been a central component of American political ideas since the time of the Revolution. In that sense, populist notions are not at the fringes of American political society, challenging aspects of that society, but appear instead to be at its very centre.

Anti-governmentalism

It was suggested earlier in this chapter that populists are 'democrats with attitude'; in appealing to 'the people' populists seek to mobilise against elites. In many circumstances these elites are regarded by populists as having produced their supposed achievements through their control of government. As a result, a common theme in populist movements is to wrest control of government from the elites and to place it in the hands of 'the people'. In the case of the United States this creates difficulties in identifying populist movements and tendencies because throughout its history there has been a strong tradition of anti-governmentalism. Separating truly populist appeals from anti-governmentalism is not always straightforward, and can produce misleading conclusions, to the effect that populism is so pervasive in the United States that there is little else *but* populism.

Hostility to government, and especially centralised government, had its origins in the conflicts between colonial authorities and colonists in the years leading up to 1776. It was reinforced not merely by the experience of the War of Independence, but also by the rise of Jeffersonianism two decades or so later. Along with the Jeffersonian vision of the United States being a land of farmers went a view that governments should intervene as little as possible in the affairs of the people. The intense conflict in the 1790s between the Jeffersonians and their Federalist rivals, who favoured a more activist federal government, was resolved, finally, after Jefferson's election to the presidency in 1800. Jeffersonianism then remained the dominant political tradition until after the Civil War. By the end of the nineteenth century, though, farmers were among the social groups that wanted to utilise the power of government to regulate economic monopolies and cartels. However, even after this time, the idea that government activity should be restricted remained an influential one. Thus, in the twentieth century, and despite the change in the role of government effected during the New Deal, distrust of government remained a powerful sentiment that politicians could seek to mobilise. It became particularly easy to do so in the decades following the Great Society programmes and the Vietnam War, both of which, in different ways, were perceived as failures of government. From the early 1970s public opinion surveys revealed a declining trust in government and in politicians, a trend that continued until the end of the century, apart from a partial reversal at the beginning of the 1980s. This period also witnessed major voter revolts against current levels of taxation, beginning with the well-known initiative referendum on local property taxes, Proposition 13, in California in 1978.

For obvious reasons, politicians running 'against government', irrespective of whether they are attacking incumbents and the interests they support, advocating the reduction of taxes, or whatever, tend to invoke the support of 'the people' in doing so. But does this necessarily mean that such movements are inherently populist, or exclusively populist? Not surprisingly, populist rhetoric may often conceal the politics of self-interest on the part of fairly prosperous social groups. Often those who have spearheaded tax-cutting initiative referenda in the states have been middle-class individuals who stood to benefit personally from a reduction in the particular tax in question. Even when couched in populist, or quasi-populist language, attacks on government taxes and expenditures are often themselves as much about the politics of special interests as any other political conflicts in America (Smith 1998). The anti-governmental tradition in the USA means that it is relatively easy to garner support for such movements, but usually self-interest plays a key part in explaining why a movement starts, and flourishes. The slogan of 'government versus people' provides a useful camouflage for what is actually a conflict between different sections of society, rather than one between an elite and a broadly-defined mass public.

Egalitarianism

There is also an egalitarian element to populism: it is anti-elitist. It involves appeals to the supposedly common opinions of a large aggregation of persons, that is 'the people'. Their opinions are held to be at least as valuable as those who regard themselves as having superior claims to be heeded, because they are wealthy, or well-educated, for instance. However, while some left-wing populists might also advocate more rigorously egalitarian principles, not all populists support economic redistribution in favour of the many. Nor do they necessarily favour political procedures that systematically reveal the actual preferences of the individuals who constitute 'the people'; often populist leaders simply impute views to this aggregate that may correspond imperfectly with the known views of the population. Nevertheless, allowing for these qualifications, populism essentially involves a kind of egalitarian view of society rather than a hierarchical one. In societies where egalitarian views compete with widely-held hierarchical positions, populism, even in its more right-wing forms, at least appears to contain an element of egalitarianism. In the United States, though, some forms of egalitarianism enjoyed a broad level of acceptance from the founding of the nation, and, certainly, by the Jacksonian era outright anti-egalitarianism was a fringe political belief. As Foley (1991, 149) notes, '[T]he formal dedication to equality in the very act of American independence bequeathed a potent vein of egalitarian intent to the stated principles and purposes of American society itself.' The main dispute in America concerned the kind of egalitarianism that should be pursued, and how conflicts with other political principles should be resolved (Ellis 1993, chapter 3).

In a society where some version of egalitarian principles have been widely accepted, it has been both easier and simultaneously more difficult for populism to become a legitimate form of political action. It has been easier in the sense that populists have not had to overcome the opposition of persons who staunchly defend their position in a hierarchical society, and who are therefore unwilling to listen to populist arguments or to heed its symbols. On the other hand, populism has found itself competing with so many different kinds of egalitarian appeals that it has tended to become merged with them. Nearly all politicians in the United States make reference to what they say the people want, because the legitimacy of enacting public policies that people want is so widely accepted. Consequently, populist appeals in the USA are much less distinctive than in many other parts of the world because populism has rivals in the form of various other egalitarian or quasi-egalitarian beliefs.

Populist values are similar to those that form part of the mainstream of American politics. For that reason, and unlike socialism, it has been unusual for their opponents to portray populist movements and populist appeals as being in conflict with the American political system. Furthermore, while American populism may be *anti-governmental* it has rarely been *anti-regime*. That is, the constitutional order established in 1787 has rarely been challenged by populists. In this respect, American populism differs from populism in many other countries where rejection of the current regime has been an important element of bids for popular support by populist leaders. Nevertheless, American populists have often been at the forefront of calls for institutional reform. For instance, leaders of the People's Party in the 1890s were among those campaigning for the introduction of various devices of direct democracy, including the initiative referendum and recall elections.

In this last respect American populists may appear to be similar to populists elsewhere. However, in the United States support for instruments of direct democracy differs in two crucial respects. In the first place, not all of those who argued in favour of such devices in the period between the 1890s and 1920s – that is, during the era in which many states introduced them – were populists. Support for direct democracy was far more wide-ranging. Advocates of such reforms included Progressives, such as Charles Merriam. By no stretch of the imagination could the views of the Merriem, the founder of modern American political science, be described as populist, but at the 1920–2 Illinois Constitutional Convention he advocated the adoption of the initiative referendum (Pegram 1992, 209). For these kinds of reformers, the point of direct democracy was not to bypass representative government, in order to promote the 'wants-for-policies' of the people, but to act as a check on representative institutions that could be, and had been, corrupted, and for which other kinds of reforms might not be wholly adequate. For many Progressives the justification for direct legislation was that it reinforced representative democracy, and not that it was a substitute for it.

Secondly, during the twentieth century, populists in America lost some of their faith in the practice of direct democracy. These devices did not always appear to constrain the elites and restore power to the people. Instead, they could be the means by which elites could protect their own interests: it appeared that money was often more decisive in changing public opinion during initiative referenda campaigns than it was in campaigns for elective office (Broder 2000; for an alternative argument, see Gerber 1999). It was possible to effect huge shifts in public opinion simply by outspending the opposition, especially when the issue being legislated was not one on which voters had entrenched, and deeply-held, views. Thus, unlike populists in countries with little experience of direct democracy, those in America often turned away from it as a guarantor of the 'people's will'. Populists now looked for devices to make it difficult for legislators to act as Burkean-style representatives. In the 1990s the device on which they often fixed their attention was that of term-limits. During that decade several state legislatures, including California's, became subjected to term-limits, a device that had earlier been deployed on political executives, including the Presidency and many state governors (Carey et al., 2000). The populist justification for term-limits was that restricting the length of political careers in a legislature would make it less likely that political representatives would move away from the attitudes of 'the people'. Nevertheless, as with direct democracy, term-limits were not promoted solely by those with populist views. Orthodox Republicans also championed them because they seemed to present a means of breaking the long-standing Democratic dominance in state legislatures and in the Congress. By the end of the decade enthusiasm within the Republican Party for term-limits was noticeably reduced, partly because they now controlled Congress and many other legislatures.

The argument developed here is that, in contrast to other countries, populism in the United States has not stood apart from mainstream political values and traditions, nor have its solutions for institutional restructuring been distinctive. Having said that, the manifestation of populism has not been the same at different periods of American history. In particular, while a major populist movement developed at the end of the nineteenth century, no such movements were evident at the national level of politics in the twentieth century. Instead, populism developed into a strategy that could be adopted by individual politicians and by parties alike. 'Populism-as-strategy' was made more possible by major changes in the nature, and operation, of American parties, and it is to this that we now turn.

Populism as a political strategy

In the 1830s competitive, well-organised, but decentralised, parties emerged throughout the United States. For nearly six decades America was, in Silbey's (1991) words, 'a political nation'; it was the era that McCormick (1986) has described as 'the party period'. Not only was politics organised around the notion of party, but parties penetrated deep into society, with many (white) American males having a direct stake in the results of elections and the subsequent distribution of spoils. However, the party system was not a perfect mechanism for channelling political demands; indeed, in the pre-Civil War era it was effective precisely because one of the major sources of division between Americans – slavery and its expansion – cut across lines of division between the parties. After the Civil War the role of the major parties as channels for demands from within American society was also restricted because large economic interests, most notably those concerned with the railways, used parties as a means to further their own ends. Because these interests were so influential in the two parties, those who were affected adversely by them had, in part, to move outside the party arena to mobilise opposition. Farmers in the South and West of the United States were the main groups affected by policies such as high railway shipping rates, and in the second half of the 1880s a major protest movement centred on this issue was formed. The movement culminated in the formation of a separate political party, the People's Party, in 1891.

This was a classic populist movement. It used appeals to 'the people' which it identified largely with farmers, and it sought to reduce the power of economic elites whom, it was believed, had taken control of political decision-making. Having obtained more than 8 per cent of the vote in the presidential election of 1892, the People's Party immediately found itself in crisis with the onset of the economic depression in 1893, and the party's electoral advance was largely halted by 1894 (McMath 1993, chapter 6). In 1896 it fused with the Democratic Party for the presidential election. After the defeat that year of the 'shared' candidate, William Jennings Bryan, the People's Party drifted into political oblivion. More significantly, its passing marked the last occasion on which a widespread populist movement was mobilised in the United States. For all the circumstances favouring support for populist values in America, the country did not sustain such a movement again. What happened?

One of the main factors limiting the potential for populist movements was the nature, structure and operation of the major political parties. Furthermore, changes in the party system in the twentieth century, at both the state and the national level, had an enormous impact on the potential for the mobilisation of populist movements.

America's constitutional arrangements had always made the states a more fertile arena for populism than national politics. Fewer resources and less co-ordination were needed to elect public officials, enact laws, or amend a state constitution than were required for such activity at the national level. Thus, while the national polity was more like a European state, in being protected by constitutionalism from populist assaults, individual states arguably remained far more open to populist campaigns than would be possible in Europe. Whether such campaigns actually developed depended on the particular political cultures of the states. For example, populist appeals were not part of the political tradition of New England. The situation in much of the South, and in some parts of the West, was very different. From the late nineteenth century, and with the collapse of party competition there, populism in the South became an aspect of intra-party politics, rather than being manifested in movements outside the parties. Thus, in some Southern states, such as Louisiana, the nomination for the Democratic Party from those years onwards became a battleground between populist-style politicians and opponents defending the status quo, and also between different populists. (It was largely absent, though, from a few ex-Confederate states, such as Virginia.) Louisiana's Huey Long was probably the best known of this style of politician, but he was far from being its only practitioner.

During the six or seven decades after the 1890s, Southern populism often went hand-in-hand with demagoguery and race-baiting. Although it is tempting to draw comparisons between this and the racial politics of contemporary Europe, it must be remembered that not all Southern populists were demagogues nor did all 'play the race card' against their opponents. The gradual demise of populism in the South came with economic growth and diversification in the region from the 1960s onwards. Accompanying this economic transformation was political realignment, a process not completed until the 1990s. Two-party competition tended to squeeze old-style populism between the orthodox economic conservatism of the Republicans and the need of Democrats to build broad coalitions in opposition to the 'Grand Old Party'. As the South became fully integrated into the economic and political mainstream of the country, so the remaining aspects of truly populist politics in America tended to disappear. However, it is worth remembering that it is only recently, in the 1990s, that these changes have been completed.

While the continuing economic backwardness of the South until the 1960s made it a region that might have formed the backbone of a national populist movement had party competitiveness not been eliminated there, at the same time the West became ever less a colony of Eastern capitalism. Greater diversification of the economies of the Western states, together with the effects of a nationwide full-employment economy after 1941, made it more difficult for politicians to claim that the West's socioeconomic problems were caused by elites based in the East. Although populist rhetoric in political discourse continued to be a feature of some Western politicians, the West declined as the potential breeding ground for a national populist movement.

In any case, at the national level the potential for populist mobilisation had always been weakened by the dominance of two major parties, the experience of 1892 notwithstanding. The strength of the two-party system, drawing on institutional factors such as presidentialism, had many consequences for American politics, including the failure of a major socialist party to develop in the US. The two-party system strangled other movements and would-be parties because only the two major parties could compete effectively for the highest offices. It was much more difficult than in the European parliamentary democracies for small or medium-sized parties to sustain themselves in the long term; too often a vote for such parties would appear to be a wasted vote. To be successful in the United States a new party had to make an electoral breakthrough of such proportions that only one new party in American history (the Republicans) has been able to achieve it to date. Arguably the absence of a large socialist party deprived populism of a rival that could have helped sustain it, by providing it with an opponent that it could 'confront' vigorously. However, the more significant point is that both socialism and populism were victims of factors that operated against the development of more than two parties in the United States.

Moreover, the major parties have been sufficiently flexible to be able to act in ways that have undermined the distinctive political appeals of other political groupings. Thus, following the success of the People's Party in 1892, the two major parties started to embrace populist arguments and rhetoric in their presidential election campaigns. John Gerring's 1998 analysis of presidential speeches, addresses, and party platforms, is illuminating in this regard. Within his overall argument, that, in fact, competition between America's parties has been ideological, he contends that since the 1890s both the Democratic and Republican parties have had phases when the appeal to voters has been populist in tone. Thus, he characterises the years 1896–1948 as the 'Populist Epoch' for the Democrats, while, from the 1920s onwards, the Republicans turned to populist rhetoric in which appeals were made to such diminutive figures as 'the little man' and 'the little taxpayer' up against the actions of government (Gerring 1998, 196 and 144).

Nevertheless, while Gerring is correct to alert us to the early use of populist discourse in the national campaigns of the two major parties, there is a danger of overstating the point, and thereby missing a more recent change in the use of populism in national politics. This change occurred in the 1960s and early 1970s, and was prompted largely by the transformation of the presidential nomination process. Before that time the nomination of both parties was controlled by party elites, through their control of state delegations to the National Conventions. Of course, nominations were contested fiercely because of disagreement among those elites. However, the views of most party activists counted only indirectly in the process, and candidates who had demonstrated popularity in the presidential primary elections – such as Estes Kefauver in 1952 – might well find themselves passed over for selection. With this form of nomination there was limited scope for candidates to make direct appeals to their party's voters, and, consequently, there was little opportunity for populist campaigning by would-be candidates at the nomination stage. Because of this, and because also of the need for parties to continue to appeal to a broad range of voters, a campaign could not become too populist without running the risk of alienating those party elites who found a populist style unattractive.

Obviously, third-party candidates were less affected by this consideration because of the more limited potential of their electoral support. Of the major presidential campaigns in the first 70 years of the twentieth century, the most populist in style was that of George Wallace in

1968; expanding on his race-based appeal in the South, Wallace sought to mobilise the 'little man' in the North as well. Television had transformed the opportunities for an individual politician running under a third-party banner to use populist appeals as a main plank of his or her campaign, and Wallace was the first third-party candidate to take advantage of this new technology. Because third-party campaigns – whether populist or not – are difficult to launch, well-supported campaigns of this kind have remained infrequent. For this reason, it is the populist strategies within the two major parties that remain the more interesting phenomenon. Consequently, Wallace's significance as a populist in the second half of the twentieth century may lie less in his 1968 campaign than in his bid for the Democratic nomination in 1972. Between 1968 and 1972 the Democratic Party changed its rules for nominating candidates, with the result that many states switched to the use of presidential primary elections. (Even more were to do so by 1976.) Power in the nominating process moved from party elites to the candidates themselves. Political styles that would have been futile in earlier years could now be tried in serious bids for a party's nomination. In 1972 Wallace's brand of populism was deployed in contesting the nomination of a major political party, and while he did not win the Democratic nomination, he had a major impact on the style of the campaign.

With the candidates now the dominant actors in the nomination process, the successful nominees were in a better position to control the campaigns at the general election. The party organisations very much became junior partners in this process. The effect of this was to remove some of the earlier barriers to populist appeals in national election campaigns. Of course, the need to attract a wide coalition of voters still placed some limits on the use of populism, but, overall, the pressures to restrict populist messages were less than they had been. Populism could come more to the forefront of political campaigns. It has become a strategy that candidates of the two major parties, and the parties themselves, can adopt, as and when they see fit. Invoking the alleged opinions of 'the people' depends on there being some evidence that the opinions of party elites and the mass public coincide. When it becomes apparent that they conflict, not only may the language of elites be changed, but the politicians may then turn actively on 'the people' for failing to support the 'correct' ideals. Nowhere was this more apparent than in the ultimately failed love affair between Republican politicians and 'the people' from the late 1960s to the end of the impeachment proceedings against President Clinton in 1999.

For the most part during the twentieth century, and excluding Joseph McCarthy, few prominent Republicans had gone beyond the sort of populist appeals discussed by Gerring (1998) and sought to build up support for themselves on the idea of 'the people's' views being the foundation of political legitimacy. Between 1933 and the mid-1960s, Republicans were torn between trying to transform public opinion fundamentally – as with the Goldwater campaign of 1964 – or merely trying to offer a bland, and more conservative, alternative to the Democratic agenda. The Vietnam War and the Great Society programmes provided an opportunity to break that mould, with an appeal to 'the people' whose views were not being heard.

On the one hand, the erstwhile Democrats who formed the core of opposition to the war – against the policies of their own President – could be branded as disloyal to the American nation. On the other hand, the Democrats could also be portrayed as having diverged from the views of most Americans in introducing major domestic programmes which, it was alleged, mainly benefited minorities, especially racial minorities. In the Nixon years, therefore, the notion of the 'silent majority' – the majority of Americans who, allegedly, did not wish to withdraw from Vietnam without a military victory, and who did not support the great expansion of federally funded social programmes – became prominent. For nearly three decades, under Nixon, Reagan and others, this idea that the Republicans were in tune with the views of the people, and reflected them much more closely than the Democrats, became a key part of political campaigning. Republicans believed that they detected within 'the people' views that they shared and which they could claim to represent. In part, they could justify their faith in this alleged close relationship with the people because of their predominant position in presidential elections between 1968 and 1992, a period during which the Democrats won only once, in 1976. (That is, precisely when the Democrat Jimmy Carter ran his 'anti-Washington establishment' election campaign.) That the Republicans had less success in controlling Congress could be written off as the result of the impact of factors, such as incumbency, which perpetuated Democratic majorities that did not reflect popular sentiment.

During the 1990s this belief among many Republicans that they, rather than the Democrats, now stood for what the people wanted took a more dangerous turn. Many on the Right refused to accept that the Democrat, Bill Clinton, really had a popular mandate in 1992, partly because of the low share of the vote he had achieved in a three-way contest. This perception of the Republican position was reinforced by their mid-term election victory in 1994, following which

House Speaker, Newt Gingrich, sought to impose his 'mandate', the 'Contract with America', on the American political system. As Garry Wills (1996) observed: 'It would be hard to overstate the audacity of the Contract with America. No one had ever before tried to create a national mandate from congressional elections.'

Despite the Clinton victory in 1996, and the reduced Republican majority in the House after that election, the belief that Clinton somehow lacked legitimacy persisted, and the impeachment over his affair with Monica Lewinsky became the vehicle for pursuing him. The problem was that, as the impeachment hearings continued, it became evident that the main thrust of public opinion was no longer with the Republicans. Irrespective of their attitude towards Clinton's behaviour over the matter, a large majority of Americans did not want him impeached – a reality confirmed by the results in the 1998 mid-term elections. Surprisingly for the president who had been in office for six years, these elections actually produced an in creased number of sears for his party in the House of Representatives.)

Having so long portrayed themselves as the party that reflected what the people wanted, many Republicans now rejected popular opinion as the source of political legitimacy; a party that had essentially emphasised its links with popular sentiments had now become one that sought to detach itself from the people. As Joan Didion (1999) has shown, a common reaction to the failed attempt to impeach Clinton was to blame 'the people' for that failure. Consequently, by 1999, the Republican Party had come full circle in its relationship with 'the people'; 30 years of being the party that supposedly reflected the views of the 'average American' had ended in a divorce from the public. This is a good example of how populist appeals by politicians in contemporary America do not so much reflect a commitment to the value of the wants and opinions of 'the people', as form part of an overall political strategy. So long as the views of the people do not appear to be incompatible with those of a party politician they can be used to justify political action. However, when it becomes evident that the views of the people do not conform with key political beliefs held by politicians, reverence for the public's views is abandoned – and, indeed, they may even be held up to ridicule. By the end of the twentieth century the populist language of the Nixon and Reagan era had given way to a Republican view that was essentially elitist and characterised by the sort of attitude towards 'the people' that Alexander Hamilton would have found acceptable two hundred years earlier.

Conclusion

In recent years the United States has not experienced the sort of upsurge of right-wing populist movements seen in a number of European democracies. The reason for this lies partly in the fact that populism meshes so well with several political values and traditions that have long been central in American politics. In that sense, populism in America appears less to be the politics of outsiders who are seeking a voice for themselves and, instead, it forms one aspect of the political mainstream. Moreover, populism has become one component of the rhetoric deployed by politicians in the major parties, and has thereby become a strategy that may be deployed against their opponents. Its full use as a strategy has been made possible by the weakening of party control over the nomination process and the rise of candidate-centred politics in recent decades. However, long before the 1970s, America's constitutional structure, and the nature of its party system, tended to work against the emergence of populist *movements* except within particular states, mainly in the South. At the same time, it had facilitated the use of populism by individual politicians who sought to win election under the label of a major political party. Populists may well conclude that in America the elite have even taken over the populists' distinctive means of conducting politics. Populism is everywhere in American politics, but nowhere in particular.

7
Populism Italian Style

Marco Tarchi

A phenomenon with deep roots

Analyses of the neopopulist wave that swept through a growing number of European countries from the mid-1980s onwards often emphasise its novelty and link it to some of the great social transformations that have, throughout history, brought the relationship of trust between citizens, political parties and representative institutions into a state of crisis. Among causes mentioned are shifts in the traditional cleavages outlined by Lipset and Rokkan (1967), the crumbling away of large-scale heavy industries and the consequent weakening of class ties, the opening up of borders and loss of relevance for nation-states, the growth of new forms of production linked to territory, to families or even single individuals, the financialisation of the economy, and globalisation, which favours competition without frontiers, and massive shifts in population from poorer to richer countries. It is frequently stressed that all these processes taken together have created a new, accelerated phase of modernisation which, by overthrowing consolidated social hierarchies, political loyalties and cultural traditions, have opened up a gap between 'winners' and 'losers' in the globalised society (Kriesi 1999). Among the 'losers' this process has sown the seeds of a psychological condition marked by resentment, delusion and disenchantment on which populist parties can capitalise (Betz 1994), by stirring up and directing protest against the political classes who are held responsible for the situation.

By placing the phenomenon in this context we avoid obscuring it or misrepresenting it through inappropriate references to past, and only marginally related, experiences – fascism or national socialism – and highlight some key characteristics that preclude its inclusion in the category of the traditional extreme right (Ignazi 1992; Mény and Surel 2000). The assertion that the success enjoyed by populist parties throughout Europe today depends on a series of contingent circumstances is, as all the empirical analyses of individual national cases show, correct (Betz and Immerfall 1998), but this does not mean that the political trend they manifest is devoid of a history or a tradition. The passion for genealogy can indeed cause errors of perspective in the study of politics and suggest hazardous analogies. In this sense, the work of those who – while seeking to give an unambiguous meaning to the polyvalent concept of 'populism', which incorporates elements of political style, discursive strategy and ideological content – have been careful to keep its practical application to non-homogeneous geographical and chronological contexts distinct, is worth noting (Ionescu and Gellner 1969; Canovan 1981; Incisa di Camerana 2000). An examination of yesterday's populism may, however, if conducred unpolemically and with an eye to the similarities and differences, help explain the diffusion, limitations and features of today's populism. It may, for instance, explain why many scholars, especially at the outset, compared the political and electoral progress of the French *Front national* to that of the movement led by Pierre Poujade,[1] trying to interpret both successes in terms of psychological and cultural tendencies of an alleged '*France profonde*' (Fonvieille Alquier 1984).

In the Italian case, we can better understand the explosion of populist-type attitudes and arguments that marked the political transition of the 1990s, sparked off by the political corruption trials referred to collectively as 'Tangentopoli' or 'Bribesville', by looking to the past. For it is in Italy that we find the prototype of contemporary European populism in the shape of the *Fronte dell'Uomo Qualunque* (The Common Man's Front, UQ). Launched on the back of a highly successful weekly, *L'Uomo Qualunque*, which had been founded in late 1944 in the liberated zone of a country where the Centre and North were still in the throes of civil war, the UQ was the first prominent manifestation of the psychological climate of hostility that spread – or was conserved – among citizens in the closing years of the fascist regime, especially after the start of the war. Like all similar movements that followed, it was led by an exuberant, autocratic figure, the Neapolitan journalist and playwright, Guglielmo Giannini. This man became the interpreter of the mood widespread in broad sectors of the petit bourgeoisie, exhausted by the sufferings it had undergone in the war and disappointed by the prospectes of peace, which seemed to offer the return to power of much of the same ruling class whose uncertainties and errors had brought about the collapse of democracy in 1922. The increasingly massive circulation of the weekly *L'Uomo Qualunque*, and the initial electoral success of its founder when he decided to go into politics, were due to the positive reception to the typically populist positions upheld by Giannini. 'Qualunquismo' presented itself as the voice of ordinary people, those excluded from the division of power, fed up with greedy and corrupt politicians, indifferent to ideologies they saw as a mere cover for elite ambitions for domination, sceptical of any programme and mistrustful of electoral promises they expected to be systematically broken by those elected. Declaring its aversion to both fascism and anti-fascism, to the monarchist, clerical or conservative Right and to the Republican, Socialist or Communist Left, the UQ focused on the unbridgeable gap between the people on the one hand – united in their desire to be 'left in peace', and to get on with life in the wake of the bloody passions that had for years divided the peninsula – and the professional politicians on the other (Setta 1995a). Giannini's rhetoric counterposed the idea of a government made up of technicians and neutral administrators competent in public affairs to that of the hegemony of the 'parasites' and their natural allies, the plutocrats. It is this extreme simplification of politics and the offer of 'easy, ready-made solutions', identified 50 years later by analysts as pivots of the argumentative structure, that allows us to place Le Pen and Tapie (Saussez 1992), Bossi and Berlusconi, Haider, Blocher, De Winters, Glistrups and the leader of the Rumanian Populists, Tudor, in the same family. It is precisely this simplification which was used as an effective instrument to gain consensus by the UQ in 1945.

After the 5.3 per cent of the vote and 30 seats won in the elections to the Constituent Assembly in June 1946, and the victories in local administrative elections in the South later that year, a combination of international and internal factors, together with strategic errors directly attributable to Giannini, limited the UQ's subsequent chances of electoral success. Over half a century later, an examination of 'qualunquismo' reveals the populist potential of Italian politics. On the one hand, it highlighted the profound mistrust of political parties, accused of factionalism and insensitivity to the national interest, and of the divided, inconclusive parliament that the 'nationalisation of the masses' attempted by the fascist regime had, despite partial failures, left as a heritage to the ordinary man. On the other hand, it allows us to understand how the frontal attack on the entire political class in the name of efficiency, honesty and practical common sense can gain consensus in an area that cuts across the left/right division. It was, for example, no coincidence that in seeking allies to enable him to translate votes into effective political influence Giannini oscillated between the Christian Democrat, De Gasperi, and the Communist, Togliatti, via the Liberal Party with which he presented joint lists at the 1948 general elections. Moreover, this composite aggregation that deliberately refused to call itself a party (the 'part' divides, the 'front' unifies – significantly the same formula adopted by Communists and Socialists to emphasise their electoral union), for the first time expressed a protest which, for all its anti-political radicalism, was not aimed at overthrowing the rules of the democratic game. In start contrast to the rise of fascism in the aftermath of the First World War, the UQ did not propose overthrowing the representative principle that constitutes the basis of liberal democracy, but rebalancing it in favour of the theoretical bearers of power. The 'qualunquist' complaints of the omnipotence of the parties, the arrogance of the public bureaucracy, and state interference in citizens' daily lives, particularly in the form of heavy fiscal pressure, were not covers for some aspiration to authoritarian restoration, but aimed at claiming the right of the people to set the limit beyond which their representatives ought not to push; that is, to bind them to respect the mandate temporarily bestowed on them via the ballot box. The fact that these demands were demagogically proclaimed by just one man, Giannini, who in articles or at meetings arrogated to himself the exclusive role of protecting the masses,[2] only reinforces the linkage between the UQ and the ideal type of populist political formation as we know it today. And although one cannot assert that Italian populism in the 1990s is the child of 'qualunquismo', there are undoubtedly many similarities of form and substance between the one and the other that should not be ignored (Setta 1995b).

The dissatisfied society

Although the *Fronte dell'Uomo Qualunque* faded out of the picture after its flare-up in the late 1940s, the grounds for its ephemeral success did not disappear. Distrust of elected representatives, of the institutions, and of the state has permeated the history of republican Italy, and with it the potential consensus available to populist movements and leaders. Italian democracy was born with a chronic legitimation deficit because of the mass-level consequences of 20 years of authoritarian political socialisation and the lack of an adequately prepared political elite educated in the values of pluralism,[3] and aroused little enthusiasm among the population. Surveys carried out in the 1950s and 1960s show that the prevalent sentiments in public opinion in relation to the political system were distrust and resentment at politicians and governments. The state was regarded as distant and inaccessible. The relationship between Italians and politics is thus historically characterised by alienation, detachment and negative feelings (Luzzatto Fegiz 1956, 1966; Almond and Verba 1963; La Palombara 1965; Guidorossi 1984). The fact that this protest potential was not expressed in open forms of opposition to the system, at least until the late 1960s, was basically because the legitimacy deficit of the political system had partly been filled by three factors: the strong control the parties exercised over civil society thanks to their penetration of the public institutions, starting with the economic ones; clientelism and corruption which, through the practice of the 'exchange vote', kept individuals and family groups tied to the parties; and the explicit support that an institution with a high level of civil prestige, like the Roman Catholic Church, gave governments in the context of the Cold War. The equilibrium thus guaranteed lasted until the early 1990s, but was inherently unstable. Italian society continued to be dissatisfied with both its representatives and its rulers and surveys carried out in European Community countries after 1972 reveal these misgivings regarding transparency and legal conformity. Eurobarometer reports rates of dissatisfaction with the functioning of democracy in Italy which are almost twice those in other countries, with percentages close to 90 per cent, and never falling below 70 per cent, and in particular reports an almost identical gap with the European figures throughout the twenty-year period, 1973–93 (Morlino and Tarchi 1996). Combining these figures with data from other research on Italian political culture, one finds that this dissatisfaction is not accompanied by a nostalgia for authoritarianism, and is spread among individuals with a range of differing political convictions – centrist voters are almost as disenchanted as voters for extreme parties – and is of an increasingly more pragmatic and less ideological nature. That is, it is associated with the poor opinion Italians have of how the political class responds to their demands and expectations; it is caused by the sensation that parties and parliamentarians are indifferent to the need for better public services, for a fairer tax system, and for honesty and transparency in public administration.

In the early 1990s the populist wind was blowing fiercely through all sectors of Italian politics. The judicial whirlwind sparked off in February 1992 by the start of the Milan prosecutors' enquiries has been an important chapter in the process of progressive growth of populism within Italian politics. What became known as the 'Mani pulite' or 'Clean Hands' operation upholds the validity of the arguments of those who for years had been accusing the parties and institutions of acting on the basis of a logic of defending illegitimate, particularist interests, in complete disregard for the aspirations of the people they were bound to serve. It also revealed that corruption was endemic throughout the political class. The proportions of the scandal were enormous: in the first year of the legislature that began with the 1992 elections, seven ministers in office were compelled to resign after being served with writs for judicial proceedings concerning them, while requests for authorisations to proceed against Members of Parliament reached the impressive figure of 540 (Ricolfi 1993). Not surprisingly, the percentage of those believing that parties are not necessary to democracy, which was estimated at 38 per cent in 1991 (Betz 1994, 49), shot up.

At the mass level, the psychological shift from anti-establishment protest to the cultivation of anti-political feeling was now a fait accompli thanks to the mediation effected by 'justicialism' (*giustizialismo*): that is, the state of mind where sizeable sections of the general public believe that in order to save Italy from the virus of corruption it was necessary for the instruments of criminal justice to substitute those of representative politics. It is significant that the newspapers and television defined those expressing this conviction, and systematically mobilised in favour of the magistrates' powers of enquiry whenever it was perceived to be threatened by government measures of amnesty or pardon, as the 'fax people'. By labelling the tens of thousands who sent messages of solidarity to the judges, encouraging them to continue the job of 'disinfection' as 'the people', the latter not only became the virtual interpreters of the entire citizenry, but counterposed them frontally with the very institutions that were the object of their criticisms. Without the support of this 'people', the acts of governments, parliaments and other figures holding important public appointments lost legitimacy. The 'fax people', with their ostentatious justicialism, simultaneously represented the triumph of the street over the palace, a rejection of the mediation that is at the basis of representative democracy, and a promotion of the media – written, audio-visual or telematic – as the authentic voice of the popular will, authorised to organise daily plebiscites to judge the actions of those on whom 'the people' had provisionally conferred their mandate whilst in the polling booth.

The *Lega Nord*: populism as a social movement

The revival of populist issues in Italian society was thus the outcome of a protracted erosion of representative democracy, marked by the end of international and domestic bipolarism, and topped by the 'Tangentopoli' scandals and the 'Mani pulite' investigations. Its translation into effective tools of political competition was the work of one party in particular, the *Lega Nord* (Northern League), which in 1989 unified and co-ordinated the activity of a series of local autonomist groupings that had developed in the North, especially in the Veneto and Lombardy (Diamanti 1993), and led them to play a leading part in the transition phase that changed the face of the Italian party system.

The factors accounting for its emergence, forms of expressions, style of action, leadership and organisational characteristics, the themes it exploited to generate consensus and the strategies adopted in the various stages of its growth from a small marginal group to a party of government all tend to make the *Lega* emerge as the ideal type of the embodiment of populism. It was born on the initiative of a few outsiders from a variety of ideological backgrounds, and had always remained on the margins of conventional manifestations of politics. When the *Lega* did enter the political arena it did so because it had been pushed to enter by the desire to assert those values believed to be rooted in the collective historical memory, but which were neglected or even ridiculed by the political elite. The message expressed in the first *Lega* manifestos and documents was summary, basic and aimed at the man in the street; it appealed to local identity as the basis for reconstructing homogeneous, solid, secure communities free of class discrimination, and with clear, undisputed acknowledgement of a number of interests (and values) common to all their members. The proposal to revive the various Northern dialects as means of daily communication and to make their use legal in institutional contexts, from administrative offices to local council chambers, was designed to emphasise the links that ensure solidarity amongst ordinary people, and at the same time indicated their distance from the 'legal country' (*pays légal*) of the elites. When this claim was dropped, the attempt to create a unitary local popular consciousness found other instruments: slogans stressing a strong aversion to the exploiting centralised state, and, above all, an original, exclusive use of rhetoric that soon became a distinct trademark.

Language is an essential tool for asserting the specific nature of the *Lega Nord*. It is the key to the winning formula that the movement adopted in the late 1980s, regionalist populism (Biorcio 1991). Drawing on the modes of thought and speech of ordinary people, proved an immediate success, and the sole tactic able to give people who differed in social condition, education, habits and cultural traditions the sensation – or illusion – of belonging to a single national, if not indeed ethnic, aggregate. That aggregate was the Lombard, Veneto or Piedmontese 'people', exalted by *Lega* propaganda in the first years of the movement's activity and subsequently transformed according to strategic requirements to become first 'the people of the North', and then 'the people of Padania'. Using direct, crude, sarcastic expressions, and not infrequently violent in its polemics, the *Lega* broke the symbolic codes to which voters had been accustomed by the traditional political forces, broke through the barrier of ideologies and made the appeal for a return to genuine communitarian traditions – away from planetary horizons to concentrate on the prime needs of territory, family and work – more credible. While the politicos' jargon is a synonym for hypocrisy and division, and bureaucratic verbiage gives an impression of abstractness and remoteness from the real problems of everyday life, the language used by *Lega* leaders is that of common sense, as spoken at home, in the bar, or in the street among friends: the language that unites, homogenises and allows frank communication. The fact that the main person speaking on public occasions is the man who personifies the movement – Umberto Bossi – is manifest proof of the leader's availability to openness to a direct relationship with the people. As Bossi repeats on every possible occasion, the *Lega* is not just popular but also and especially of the *common* people.

The choice of a more 'vernacular' language helps reinforce the theme presented in the *Lega*'s propaganda – that is, the rejection of intellectual, political and cultural mediation, mistrust of representation, and the demand for autonomy in local communities (Poggio 1994). Although the *Lega* had always pushed to enter regular politics via parliament and the local authorities, it also proposed itself as the expression of a popular will that refuses to be expressed solely in rational forms through formal procedures, and which instead seeks channels of manifestation located beyond the institutional context that value emotions and affective social ties. The movement's charismatic nature (Tarchi 1998, 1999) lends itself to this role: in his personal appeal to the people, Bossi presents himself as a catalyst who perceives and articulates citizens' needs thanks to his direct relationship with them (Biorcio 1991/92), and who unites them and commits himself to promoting them in the places where decisions of public interest are taken.

Like all populist movements, the *Lega* delights in giving its enemies a name and a face, making them the objects of incessant polemical argument. Given that 'the people of the North' lack a single clear, ethnic or linguistic base that would make their specific nature undeniable, they are instead defined negatively, that is, by contrast with a hostile environment which determines their nature. The *Lega* has taken on the task of informing Italians about these negative forces. In the first place there are the parties, the parasites par excellence. 'Partitocracy' is to blame for the detachment that has grown up between citizen and state, and of the latter's incapacity to supply adequate responses to the problems generated by modernisation, first and foremost the imbalance between North and South. Now that the initial ethnonationalist phase is over, the criticism levelled at the Italian state by the *Lega* no longer relates so much to the legitimacy of its historical process of formation as to the inefficiency that marks it, its oligarchic degeneration, its yielding to the 'strong powers': the parties, the supranational bureaucracies such as the European Union, and, above all, high finance and big industry. Big business is in fact identified as a particularly dangerous enemy of the people, as a factor dividing the popular community because of the logic of exploitation that typifies it. It is the interests of big business, protected by the parties, that constitute the greatest threat to the cohesion of the popular community addressed by the *Lega*: the mass introduction of 'outsiders' into the regions of Northern Italy, bringing a culture radically different from the one that had, in the course of time, laid the foundations for a common Northern identity.

In their first years of activity the various 'Leagues' displayed their hostility to these outsiders by targeting Southern Italians, referred to by the movements' press as '*terroni*' (an expression widespread among the middle and lower strata of the population), and portrayed as 'good-for-nothings' refusing to take on the mentality and traditions of their host environment. Those were the years when, by formulating the equation between Mafia and establishment, Bossi struck simultaneously at the South and at the partitocracy. Subsequently, *Lega* polemic shifted to immigrants from poor countries, whose cheap labour competes (unfairly) with autochthonous workers, making the dream of preserving the idealised original unitary character of 'the people of the North' ever more utopian. As the phenomenon spread, its media visibility grew and its social fallout became more acute, opposition to immigration from the Third World and Eastern Europe became the *leitmotiv* of *Lega* publicity campaigns, forcing the movement to intensify contacts with other parties in the neopopulist family, first and foremost Haider's FPÖ. This does not, however, make it a single-issue movement. Defence of the cultural integrity of the Northern regions against the risks of 'invasion' from outside is constantly combined with other themes: the denunciation of cosmopolitanism is accompanied by an emphasis on the value of territorial roots, but also by the polemic against any power not legitimised by popular consensus, foremost among them that of money.

In the early 1990s the *Lega* attempted to move into the political space left vacant by the shift in the basic party-oriented cleavages and the consequent weakening of related subcultural loyalties generated and fed by that system. It did so by drafting a programme where liberalism and populism were mixed, but where the second element in the formula was always predominant. The *Lega* presented itself as a populist movement of protest and identity (Taguieff 1995): it claimed to be fighting to liberate the Northern communities from the evils that afflicted them from within, and at the same time seeking to preserve them from the potential corrosion of external aggression. The people at whom its propaganda is targeted constitutes a unitary entity in which class distinctions have no relevance.[4] At the same time it is also a genuine entity, healthy, natural, and exempt from the vices that contaminate the ruling classes. In other words, *Lega* propaganda seeks to interpret in line with an organicist paradigm – as a community more than as a society, using the distinction proposed by Tönnies (1991) – the collectivity it is concerned with, and to forcibly emphasise its unitary nature by downplaying the social and cultural fault lines that run through it.

In order to root this vision in public opinion, the *Lega* followed two parallel tracks. On the one hand, there was a commitment to inventing a cultural tradition to unify 'the people of the North'. On the other, there was an endeavour to neutralise the conflicts running horizontally through Northern society, by stressing instead the vertical confrontation with the Italian state.

In 1996, the first of these lines of strategy peaked in the claim for an identity for Padania, the macro-region of the Centre-North extending as far as Tuscany in the South and Umbria in the South-East. It formally proclaimed the independence of Padania in a mass public ceremony lasting three days and mobilising all *Lega* members and sympathisers. It created a shadow government of the North (called, in order once again to stress their originality, the *'governo-sole'* or 'sun cabinet', i.e. not a 'shadow cabinet'). It established a Padanian phantom parliament through self-organised 'elections' carried out by setting up voting stands in the principal squares of mainly Northern localities. It organised regular propaganda days, called 'Padania days', to emphasise the main themes tackled in its programme. It also created a large number of 'Padanian' occupational, cultural, sporting, recreational and voluntary work associations, designed to compete with those of the Italian state. It founded a Padanian National Guard to act as stewards assisting the police, and to help the population in cases of emergency or natural disaster. The limited practical results obtained by many of these initiatives nonetheless highlighted the limitations of such an endeavour, which now survives almost exclusively for internal use in the party press, to reinforce party members' identification.

The other strategic option taken has been more successful: it is to downsize the relevance of the cultural and economic differences among the various 'Padanian' regions and provinces in the eyes of the Northern Italian public, by stressing the external dangers that may threaten the entire population of the North, and the need to unify to withstand any such a threat. The polemics initiated by the *Lega*, against state centralism, against the skewed application of welfare policies in favour of the South, against the unfair tax system,[5] against public television, against governments' permissive immigration policies, and more recently against the negative economic consequences of globalisation and the threat of an Islamicisation of the Roman Catholic religious identity of Italians have all been expressions of this strategy. In the unfavourable conditions after 1994 which witnessed the entry into politics of a formidable competitor, Berlusconi, the *Lega*'s insistence on this line of action committed Bossi's party to holding on to and strengthening an autonomous political space which is hard for opponents to encroach on. This defence, albeit small, enabled the *Lega* to replace that part of the middle-class electorate that had voted for them in 1992/3 but subsequently defected to *Forza Italia*, by more lower-class support. The outcome of this change in electoral support was that in 1996 made the *Lega* the preferred party of workers in the regions of Northern Italy. The similarity with what had occurred in

France with the *Front national* and in Austria with the FPÖ was indeed striking.

The myth of civil society from Berlusconi to Di Pietro

With the success of the *Lega* in the early 1990s, the term 'populism' returned to the Italian political lexicon, but in analyses of Bossi's party, journalists often prefer to talk of 'qualunquismo', referring to a model which has deeper roots in the national collective memory. What hallowed the fortune of this word in political communication was Silvio Berlusconi's decision in December 1993 to found the party, *Forza Italia* (Go Italy!). This party enabled him to win the elections the following March and to transform himself in only four months from entrepreneur and telecommunications magnate into prime minister. As head of party and of government Berlusconi was given a hostile press by opponents and labelled a populist with the deliberate intention of disqualifying him. The term was often used interchangeably with the adjective 'Perónist' in order to stress the demagogic nature of his personality and habits, with the result that he refused to accept the epithet and systematically returned it to the sender. However, even those who have analysed the Milanese businessman's political activity from a scientific rather than evaluative viewpoint, have found many points of similarity with the typical features of populism, although in *Forza Italia* it never takes the form of a spontaneous social movement as was the case with the *Lega*, but principally that of a style deliberately chosen to supply answers to the political demands that have emerged in Italian society after the collapse of the pre-existing party system.

Despite being various judicial enquiries pending into his business activities, and though his polemics against 'interference' by the judiciary in politics have been repeated and bitter, Berlusconi largely owes his 1994 success to the consequences of the actions of the judges whose investigations brought the widespread political corruption in the public administration to the notice of the public. By proving or alleging the grave responsibilities of many public figures for offences committed at the expense of the state, the judiciary effectively helped sow the seeds of populism: discredit for the governing political parties, and those who when in opposition had shared their modus operandi, and a distrust of politics per se, now seen by many as an area in need of radical purging. Being a newcomer to politics became an advantage, and in the case of well-known public figures a potential claim to aspire to a front-line role in the hoped-for renewal of Italian politics. This created another crucial precondition for the success of populist policies: the feeling of impending regeneration. The search was on for new people able to redeem the country's good name and well equipped with the credentials of technical ability, character and honesty. It was held that these qualities were not to be found among professional politicians. In 1993, when the first direct elections of mayors were held, the hunt was again on for new faces to present as candidates, as alternatives to the old faces of the party machines. Particularly in the Northern cities the new local administrations fielded businessmen, technical officials or intellectuals whose slogan, quite apart from professed political convictions, could be summarised in one and the same imperative: limit party influence in running the cities, and give credit to professional skill in choosing independent councillors.

This apotheosis of amateurism should have favoured the *Lega*, but instead the latter paid the price for lacking a party elite capable of handling the administrative tasks that the great electoral advance was thrusting on the movement. As a relatively fledgling movement with a still underdeveloped organisation the *Lega* found it hard to recruit people of sufficient ability and experience. Moreover, the sheer radicalism of some of the positions espoused by Bossi, together with his authoritarian style of running the party, expelling and denigrating anyone casting doubt on the validity of his viewpoints or decisions, made many sympathisers with suitable technical/administrative qualifications diffident about committing themselves in politics. Despite its credibility and value as an instrument of protest, in moderate circles the *Lega* was not considered capable of taking on the tasks of government – a handicap that penalised it in the big cities of the North. Only in Milan did its candidate win the city elections for mayor. It was this *impasse* that fostered the ideal conditions for Silvio Berlusconi's entry into politics. He was able to present himself to anti-Left voters as the 'man of providence' who had entered the lists at precisely the right time to prevent the country's government ending up in the hands of the ex-communists.

Before running the risk of going into politics personally, Berlusconi used a survey company with links to his enterprise structure, Diakron, to carry out opinion polls to discover precisely what expectations were most strongly held by his potential supporters. The style with which he presented himself to the public therefore left no room for improvisation or chance, the choice of tones and populist themes was cut to fit the available electoral market share. Nonetheless, the public figure of

Berlusconi and the mentality and image that have accompanied it from the outset are characterised by a number of significant features that enabled him to adopt the role without too much difficulty. He is the archetypal self-made man who has not cut his ties with his social hinterland, and who, despite his enormous wealth, tries to seem like the man in the street: more able, more fortunate, but of the same mettle. 'I am one of you' is the phrase he frequently adopts in dialogue with the public. The charisma his supporters rapidly acknowledge in him is not natural, but situational (Dobry 1992); it is based not on a halo of personal qualities, but on his followers' desire to imitate, fed by an efficient alternation of demagogic attitudes, that simultaneously narrow his distance from rank-and-file followers, and claims to assume the indispensable role as leader, that reinstate it. Paternalist and reassuring, Berlusconi proclaims himself as the interpreter and defender of the popular will, but his ideal rostrum is not a soapbox at a public meeting but the small screen of television – as the owner of the three most-watched private networks, he knows the medium to perfection. His model is not that of the mob orator, but the proprietor of a firm trying to straighten out the accounts, to distribute responsibilities and to guarantee the collaboration of all his employees.

When launched, *Forza Italia* embodied this model in its organisation. It was a party endowed with flexible, 'light' structures, consisting essentially of employees of one of the firms owned by the leader, Publitalia. *Forza Italia* had no articulated hierarchy, and depended heavily on publicity campaigns and image. Populism emerges as the basic feature in the programmes and communicative style of *Forza Italia*, even if often expressed in soft tones, and mainly taking an anti-politics line. Berlusconi never misses a chance to declare that *Forza Italia*, its leading figures, its candidates and its leader are temporarily 'lent' to politics from the world of work, to which they will return once they have finished their task of saving the country from the risk of a left-wing government. Whenever the opportunity arises, Berlusconi declares that his opponents (D'Alema and Rutelli) have always 'lived off politics', making careers as party officials, without ever demonstrating they could do anything else. To complete the picture, Berlusconi's speeches are rich with references to the rhetoric of the 'ordinary people' 'forgotten' or 'abandoned' (Canovan 1993, 55) by the political parties and left-wing trade unions. Berlusconi claims that the latter have abandoned the 'losers' in order to protect those who have 'made it', the insiders, whereas, as the slogan printed alongside Berlusconi's smiling face on the giant posters which plastered Italian cities in the run-up to the 2001 elections reminds us, 'helping those left behind is a moral duty'.

This anti-political, paternalistic attitude has led to talk of a plebiscitary populism that exploits cultural stereotypes of the Left – all power to 'the people', the intrinsic value of the 'new', the force of *vox populi* – and some classical arguments by the advocates of direct democracy in favour of a conservative project that de facto limits citizens' decisional capacity (Revelli 1996). If the polls report a low level of consensus for the government, this is enough for the leader of *Forza Italia* to declare that the government is de facto delegitimised and to call vociferously for its replacement. This reasoning may equally well be applied to the Parliament or the Head of State. Survey findings are thus the only authentic 'voice of the people' in an era of telematic communication, and thanks to continuous updates offer that snapshot of the citizens' will that elections held only every four or five years simply cannot guarantee. Moreover, the surveys reflect and multiply individual opinions, another feature making them an ideal instrument for reaffirming Berlusconi's notion of 'the people' as a collective entity whose voice – made up of as many different tones as the individuals that constitute it – can be harmonised and made unitary only by the godlike action of an interpreter designated by the consensus of the masses.

Thanks to his communicative skills and organisational resources, Berlusconi has managed to interpret the message of plebiscitary populism that spread through Italy in the wake of 'Tangentopoli' with unequalled efficiency. But there is no lack of competition. If the *Lega* is handicapped by a territorial basis confined to Northern Italy, and *Alleanza Nazionale*, the heir to the MSI and with an organicist, plebiscitary culture in its genes that particularly fitted it for the part, is hesitant to play the populist card openly in order not to compromise the image of moderation that enabled it to return to the political game, there are others that are prepared to challenge *Forza Italia* on its own ground. This is starting to happen, albeit with some hesitation, with the Centre-Left coalition of the *Ulivo*, whose prime ministerial candidate in the 2001 elections, Rutelli, not by chance an ex-member and ex-leader of the *Partito Radicale* and therefore a pupil of Pannella, has displayed increasing signs of having adapted to his opponent's style. But the chief embodiment of the populist alternative to the *Forza Italia* leader is probably Antonio Di Pietro. The most famous of the judges in the pool of Milan prosecutors that first revealed the corruption of Italian politics, he certainly has the credentials to play this part: he is the recognised champion of the fight against partitocracy, and can claim to have contributed through his own actions decisively to sinking the First Republic. His use of direct language, which is – not unlike Bossi's, but with a Southern rather than a Northern tone – immediate and forceful, full of dialectical inflections and grammatical solecisms, brings him into harmony with the popular mood. He has an aversion for the formal rules of institutional politics and upholds the need for reforms to give value to people at the expense of political parties.[6] A presidentialist, committed to support for referenda and a paladin of direct democracy, Di Pietro is also indifferent to the distinction between the Right (which initially acclaimed his action as a magistrate, to the point that Berlusconi offered him a ministerial post in his government, but was turned down), and the Left (under whose banner he was elected senator), accusing both of artificially dividing society, which ought instead, in his opinion to be divided into the honest and the dishonest. His movement, the newly-founded *'L'Italia dei valori'*, tries to recreate the psychological climate of the years of 'Tangentopoli', to set themes of illegality at the centre of political discourse, and to incite a new, strong anti-partitocratic reaction among ordinary people. Yet he lacks the essential ingredient for the success of populist recipes: a serious economic and/or moral system crisis such as that which occurred in the early 1990s. Without this key precondition he failed in his attempts to obtain the 4 per cent of the vote that would have enabled him, along with other candidates elected on his ticket, to engage in across-the-board opposition in Parliament. His attempt is nonetheless indicative of a psychological climate that continues to offer opportunities to those political entrepreneurs who have made the fight against the establishment and the claim to exclusive power for the people their *pièce de résistance*.

Conclusion

Populism has left a deep and visible mark in the 55 years of republican Italy. Only twice, with the *Fronte dell'Uomo Qualunque* in the mid-1940s, and the *Lega Nord* forty years later, did it take the form of a *social movement*, i.e. an expression of political and cultural tendencies rooted in society and able to guarantee mass support, and in both cases expansion was limited by strategic errors by the leadership and competition from conservative forces. By contrast, its influence as a *political style* has been much more constant. Probably because of the fascist heritage, some of its inspirational themes, such as the distrust of political parties and the political class in general, the desire for an organic reshaping of society beyond 'artificial' ideological or class oppositions, faith in the personal virtues of individual leaders rather than in the soundness or applicability of their programmes – have all generated a resounding response from the Italian public, and have even influenced the style of propaganda and actions of the big parties. As of the late 1960s, growing dissatisfaction with the functioning of democracy and the malfunctioning of the public administration prepared the ground for populism, but the system resisted the pressure of such discontent thanks to the ties constituted by the bipolar East–West confrontation internationally, and a consolidated clientelist, and as from the 1970s consociative, system domestically.

When these ties began to relax, the populist political style resurfaced and was used with the twofold aim of delegitimising the representative institutions and those who embodied them, and simultaneously legitimising other political parties claiming to be more representative (Pombeni 2000). The Radicals' anti-partitocracy campaign, with its continual promotion of referenda as a way to put pressure 'on the palace from the street' and with its direct polemics against the Constitutional Court and the Parliament, marked a first stage in this process. The electoral and organisational growth of the *Lega* constituted a later, more mature phase: for the first and only time, populism took on the shape not just of a vehicle of protest, but also a factor of identity and a stimulus to political mobilisation aimed at changing the regime, albeit within limits demarcated by the democratic principle. The *Lega* gave expression to the opposition to the 'centralist' state in the name of the ordinary people's right to reappropriate the government of public affairs. It did so by seeking to weld the rebellious mood of the petit and middle bourgeoisie in the North with the charismatic personality of its leader Bossi, by working towards the model of a united popular community cemented by local traditions and immune to contagion by outside elements (immigrants from Southern Italy or from abroad, the parasitic mentality of the 'Rome parties'). 'Tangentopoli' marked a further, decisive turning point. The polemic against the institutions reached its peak along with the discrediting of the parties, and the populist argot became the current language of Italian politics for a period of at least two years. The myth of civil society favoured a comprehensive turnover in the political class, and disseminated hostility towards the establishment that spread on the Right, on the Left and even in the Centre. The revival of the extreme Right and its resemblance with the *Front national*, the birth of the tele-populism of the 'electronic marketplaces', the justicialism of La Rete, the temptation to make judges into rehabilitators of public life, the severe criticism levelled at the parliamentary system by President Cossiga, Segni's presidentialist campaigns, and the anxious search for local government candidates not 'compromised' by politics, were all symptoms of this evolution. Yet the person who derived the greatest advantage was Silvio Berlusconi, who exploited the fact he was an outsider to political life and the success he has achieved as an entrepreneur to mobilise the unpolitical and the orphans of the moderate parties in his own favour. His populism has no ideological flavour or ethnic backdrop, but abounds in promises of regeneration and demands for an *union sacrée* to snatch Italy from the abyss that the old political class, especially the Left, was hastening it towards. It is not a conviction but a communicative style, that drags in its wake a series of significant cultural stereotypes: the sovereignty of public opinion over the institutions, the faith in the miraculous virtues of the man who devotes himself to the good of the people, plebiscitarianism, the superiority of society and the economy over politics, the right of the individual citizens to impose a mandate on representatives and revoke it whenever they feel betrayed or misunderstood by sending a message to the rulers through the percentages in an opinion survey.

The telecratic, paternalist rhetoric of Berlusconi is indicative of Italian populism's many-faceted nature and capacity for self-renewal. It now appears to be confirmed as the communicative code of a political season that is far from over. Many have now appropriated its style, and in part its content. The Right displays at least three different versions of populism, which are not as compatible as the alliance among the parties that are its expression – *Forza Italia*, *Alleanza Nazionale* and *Lega Nord* – might lead one to think. The Left bears a more than superficial stigma for this, probably destined to become still more manifest in their attempts to compensate for their electoral defeat. Di Pietro embodies another potential model, located 'beyond Right and Left', and other potential imitators are looming on the horizon. The convergence around populist themes and argumentative styles in Italian politics in the year 2001 makes one suspect that what was previously considered a pathology of representative democratic systems may well become an inherent physiological element of such systems, and one to which both voters and political scientists will have to get accustomed, whether they want to or not.

Notes

1. They also indicated Jean-Marie Le Pen's experience as a Poujadiste deputy in the 1950s.
2. Whose virtues he exalted in a book entitled *Folla: seimila anni di lotta contro la tirannide* (*The Crowd: Six Thousand Years of Struggle against Tyranny*), published a few months after the end of the fascist experience (Giannini 1945).
3. Many of the leading figures in the anti-fascist parties had long lived in exile, in prison, or in one way or another outside the country's political life.
4. Those who have highlighted this feature have often cited the foundation programme of the *Lega Lombarda* (Lombard League), which asserts that common belonging to Lombardy, the fact of being Lombards, must prevail over all other social, economic, cultural or religious differences among individuals resident in the Region.
5. On several occasions tax strikes were threatened.
6. He has proposed, among other things, to cut the number of parliamentarians from the present 945 (Chamber and Senate) to 300.

8
Populism in the French Party System

Yves Surel

Introduction

In recent years populism has reappeared in France in two distinct ways. First, it has re-emerged as a defamatory term applied to those individual political actors or groups characterised by demagogic rhetoric and the indictment of the traditional political elites. Thus, the leader of the *Front national* Jean-Marie Le Pen was immediately and systematically referred to as a populist, particularly because of his tendency to criticise the regime and traditional politicians. Secondly, in the 1995 presidential campaign the term was applied to the hitherto mainstream politician Jacques Chirac. Interestingly, this use of populism as a 'disqualificatory' label (Taguieff 1997) is in marked contrast with the understanding of the word in other contexts or other frameworks, particularly in the United States, where populism often constitutes a common reference point for a large number of different politicians and parties (see Kazin 1995; Hertzke 1993).

In this chapter which considers the contemporary French situation, we shall try to show why and how populism has been revived and revitalised in recent years. The general hypothesis presented here rests on the idea that the instrumentalisation of populism as a referent has brought about a redistribution of political resources within the French party system. Having pointed out the structural and cyclical conditions that favour this renewal of populism, we shall then try to show how and by whom populism has been used as an 'effective' discourse-related and ideological resource – that is, one capable of enlarging the electoral audience, during the 1990s. Understood in this sense, populism could be mobilised by a multiplicity of political actors with very different ideological and party origins.

The conditions for the (re-)emergence of populism in France

If we accept that populism does indeed constitute one of the determining tensions inherent in any democratic system, it is hardly surprising to find that the French case reveals issues and institutional factors that testify to the existence of populism. From this perspective the most concrete set of factors are the constitutional provisions themselves, many of which have the specific objective of enshrining the populist features of the system. Article 2 of the 1958 Constitution which established the Fifth Republic states that 'its principle is: government of the people, by the people and for the people', whilst Article 3 enshrines the idea that 'national sovereignty belongs to the people, who exercise it through their representatives and through referendums'.

Over and above the founding constitutional principles, we can demonstrate that certain specific historical and political factors have acted as vehicles for the emergence or revival of populist themes and discourse. From this perspective, the Fifth Republic is a political system marked by its origins, that is, the collapse of the parliamentary system under the Fourth Republic, and the ideals of its creators, chiefly those of General de Gaulle (Gaïti 1998; François 1996). The collapse of the Fourth Republic is associated with challenging the parliamentary logic and the dysfunctionalities of the party system as factors responsible for governmental instability and inefficiency, in line with the criticisms commonly made at the time. By contrast, de Gaulle's return to power is associated with his personal legitimacy, and in particular his 'immediate' and genuine link with the people. In the words of the General, 'I am a man on my own. I am not to be confused with any party … in short, I am a man who belongs to no one, and to everyone'.[1]

Whilst it would be simplistic to conclude that General de Gaulle's approach was resolutely populist – it involved first and foremost a personal syncretism, with no real basic tendency or lasting legacy – it is nonetheless clear that his mistrust of the parliamentary system and contempt for political parties were important features underlying his particular notion of political institutions, and that, consequently, they constitute key structural features of the Fifth Republic.

The practice of the regime set up by de Gaulle made a deep and lasting impression on French political life, and reveals the extent to which his rejection of the Fourth Republic transformed the conception of politics, colouring it with a populist emphasis. Throughout his presidency, de Gaulle made great use of referenda, not only to reassert his own legitimacy (which sometimes lent the referenda the air of plebiscites), but also because of his deep-rooted belief that it should be the sovereign people who should decide in the last instance. The 1962 crisis arising from a clash between de Gaulle, then President of the Republic, and the French Parliament is entirely symptomatic of this.

Apart from the 1962 crisis, what persists in the French political system today is the special position of the President of the Republic. As guardian of the institutions and representative of the nation, he is supposed to enjoy a favoured relationship with the people. Since his legitimacy derives from the people, it is to them that he must turn when his responsibility is called into question. This is why, in 1969 de Gaulle acted on a negative referendum result by immediately tendering his resignation. By contrast, Chirac asserted the principle of his institutional immunity in order to reject a summons served on him by a judge in connection with an investigation of obscure financial dealings in Paris, where he was mayor from 1977 to 1995.

In parallel, the recent developments in the French party system have also brought about a revival of this logic and of the normative schemas associated with the idea of populism. There are four tendencies that should systematically be stressed, particularly because they appear to occupy a predominant place in the French context: (i) the shift in ideological and party alignments; (ii) the crisis of the traditional political groupings; (iii) the increased personalisation of public life; and (iv) the ambiguous but marked role of the media in changing the rules of the political game.

The first factor – the shift in ideological and party alignments – touches on hypotheses and arguments which are increasingly familiar in the literature (Kitschelt and McGann 1995; Mair 1993; Kriesi 1998; Boy and Mayer, 1997). Without going into detail, the idea is starting to gain credence that the cleavage structure highlighted by Lipset and Rokkan (1967) is currently undergoing a disalignment that breaks the frozen cleavages inherited from the nineteenth century. According to Kitschelt and McGann (1995), post-industrial capitalism lies at the origin of a new sociopolitical cleavage, characterised by a polarisation around a libertarian Left favouring redistribution, and a liberal and authoritarian Right favouring a sociopolitical status quo. These dynamics of polarisation, which appear to contradict the classical cleavages, are explained by the combination of two series of determining factors. First, the changing labour-market status of individuals, particularly given exposure to the processes of globalisation and the transnational relations associated with it, mean that the old faultlines organised around class membership are becoming increasingly blurred. Secondly, the individual's cultural orientation, which is in turn conditioned by the degree of exposure to the dynamics of communication, has undergone a process of polarisation between universalist and egalitarian approaches generated by exposure to communication dynamics on the one hand, and particularist or authoritarian ones on the other. Taking these features into account, Kitschelt proposes that the relevant cleavage structure is at present operating around two lines of polarisation: one marking the dominant cleavage inherited from the nineteenth century, namely the class cleavage, and the other being the libertarian/authoritarian opposition nurtured by post-industrial capitalism. Thus, according to Kitschelt, the axis structuring party systems in Europe has shifted, and now derives from more complex dynamics than the Left/Right opposition organised around class conflicts. In this new system, the Left has a tendency to evolve in a libertarian direction, following the shift in axis of the party systems, as the various coalitions between Social Democrats and Greens in Europe would seem to indicate. By contrast, the Right is presumed to be evolving towards more systematically authoritarian positions, as indicated by the division of the *Rassemblement pour la République* (RPR) in France between a liberal, Europhile tendency and a statist/national one, which even led to the formation of a dissident party, the *Rassemblement pour la France* (RPF), on the initiative of Charles Pasqua.

Kitschelt regards this rotation of the axis of European party systems as the chief explanatory factor for the emergence of new extreme Right parties with heavily populist overtones. The New Radical Right (NRR) parties, a term Kitschelt finds better suited to the present situation, thus correspond to groupings typified by a mixed electoral base, founded on a capitalist-authoritarian type of normative orientation. These parties are populist in the sense that they challenge the legitimacy of the current leaders and existing political systems, enabling them to tap a very broad stratum of electoral support, but their specific characteristic, in relation to, for instance, traditional fascism, lies in their claim to promote more balanced and/or traditional economic dynamics, in contrast to the critique traditionally levelled at the capitalist economy by fascist ideology.

These features, which are characteristic of the structural changes taking place in all western countries, are also relevant in France. The main Left/Right cleavage has long constituted the central positioning axis for parties, and the most powerful identification factor for the electorate. However, in the early 1980s, two political formations, the Greens and the National Front (*Front national,* FN), began to disturb what was sometimes referred to as the quadripolar party system, with the Socialist Party and Communist Party (*Parti Socialiste Français, Parti Communiste Français*) on the Left, a centrist grouping (*l'Union pour la Démocratie Française*, the Union for French Democracy, UDF), and the Gaullist movement on the Right. The emergence of these new parties and their repeated electoral successes indeed contributed to the realignment of the party system. The complex links between Greens and Socialists tended to complicate the relatively stable relationship between Communists and Socialists, while the non-alliance strategy adopted in relation to the FN by the Right generated multiple splits in both chief groupings, which in turn began to electorally penalise the parties of the traditional Right. On either side of the party system, the Greens and the FN sought new ways of 'doing politics', and often criticised traditional politicians and political organisations. In order to open up a space within the party system, these 'new' formations, essentially the Greens and the NRR parties, rejected the chief actors, practices and logic of representative democracy. Ipso facto, these actors tended to mobilise populist discourses and issues, calling for the revival of 'genuine' democratic mechanisms, albeit at times in very different but structurally similar ways. These processes could also be observed in many other European countries. In the case of Austria, for instance, Patrick Hassenteufel has shown that the Greens, like the FPÖ, used populist normative schemas, challenging the traditional elites and political formations, Social Democratic and Christian Democratic, that had shared power for years (Hassenteufel 1991). This parallelism does not mean that the Greens and the NRR parties developed similar modes of action and issues, but that their respective claims – participatory democracy on the one hand and nationalist renewal on the other – turned on the accusatory discourse of populism in the sense that they mobilised criticism against the political elite, re-evaluated 'the people' as the constitutive principle of the system, and called for a return to 'authentic' democracy.

For the FN, more specifically, this hypothesis of reshaping the electoral and party alignments is consistent with the idea of 'Left lepenism' and 'worker lepenism' developed by Pascal Perrineau (1997) and Nonna Mayer (1999). For these two authors one of the most remarkable phenomena associated with the FN vote is undoubtedly the increasing support by a sizeable section of the working class for the FN, and for Jean-Marie Le Pen in particular. As Nonna Mayer writes, the bulk of recent studies show that the FN

> [a]ttacks not the periphery of the group but its core, the elements most integrated in this milieu ... It can therefore, ... be called a class vote, in the course at least among younger people of taking on the privileged place the Communist Party held twenty years ago. And it is indeed in class terms ... by opposing the working-class to that of the 'bosses' and the well-off, those below to those above, that working class voters justify their vote for Jean-Marie Le Pen in 1995 [the presidential elections]. (Mayer 1999, 114)

This disalignment and change in cleavage structure is accompanied by a questioning of some political figures and traditional practices that sometimes leads to talk of a 'crisis of representation'. Given their intimate association with the structure of western representative democracies, the political parties in France today give the impression of having been overtaken by an alternative logic of mobilisation and representation. In this sense a growing number of financial scandals, together with the widespread involvement of traditional politicians and parties in corruption cases, mark a shift in public perception which has brought about a questioning of the role traditionally ascribed to political parties. In France in particular, the uncovering of financial scandals in the 1990s revealed concealed yet generally well-known practices that had hitherto been tacitly accepted (Mény 1992; Pujas and Rhodes 1999).

Since then, the 'traditional' parties have disappeared or been reformed whilst others, in particular the French Communist Party, have seen their electoral support shrink. Some formations have, for instance, broken up, especially on the French Right, for reasons that have as much to do with the weakening of ideological references as with the evaluation of personal strategies. In parallel, new political organisations have appeared, capturing voters, shaking up the 'old crony' system, and 'liberating' the traditional ideological vote by offering alternatives often of a sectoral or cyclical nature. These single-issue parties rarely last long on the French political scene, but have nonetheless helped shake up established positions and prepared the ground for populist themes. Thus, the Hunting, Fishing, Nature and Tradition movement (*Chasse, Pêche, Nature et Tradition*, CPNT) in France has enjoyed repeated electoral successes, especially in European elections, by attacking directives regulating hunting practices, and the absence of genuine democratic control in the European context (Traïni 2000).

One measure of these changes is the growth in the level of electoral volatility. Although still disputed,[2] particularly because it makes any empirical validation difficult, this idea of increased volatility is relevant in the French case, as we have seen with the phenomenon of 'Left lepenism' or 'worker lepenism'. Furthermore, these shifts in voting are all the more meaningful since the level of participation in elections has been steadily falling for some years. If we examine, for example, the last two general elections in France, we can see that the electoral coalitions that won power never obtained more than about a third of the potential vote.

Another recent phenomenon which has strengthened the potential for the emergence of populist themes is the personalisation of political life. A variety of factors have been advanced to explain the increasing emphasis on the person as the determining feature in electoral choice, and, more generally, in the logic of political identification. The weakening of the traditional cleavages, the decline of the main political ideologies,and the growing influence of the media in public life have all contributed to this process of personalisation in France, as elsewhere in Western Europe and beyond. In particular, personal leadership charisma as a mode of obtaining legitimacy is growing in importance, to the detriment of other modes.

In conclusion, one should cite a final set of factors that favour the emergence or re-evaluation of populist dynamics with the 'mediaisation' of political life – the increasing role of the written, spoken and televised press in structuring and disseminating a given political logic. In a certain sense one form of mediation is thus driving out another insofar as the media is replacing the political parties both as a mechanism for selecting the political class and as an instrument for mobilising public opinion, or for setting the political agenda (Neveu 1997).

All of these factors exert a differing force and differentiated weight on the French party system. Leaving aside potentially unfruitful attempts at research into the causes of populism, the fact that these different features strengthen or restore the populist logic inherent in the French political system has been a prevalent phenomenon of the 1980s and 1990s. The last two decades have been marked by more frequent alternations in government (five in less than twenty years, whereas the first 21 years of the Fifth Republic were dominated by the Right), by the growing convergence of governing-party programmes, and by a strengthening of external pressures, whether from European integration or economic globalisation. All these institutional and cyclical factors have thus facilitated the opening up of a political opportunity structure (Kitschelt 1986) favouring the re-emergence or revival of populism in France.

The rhetorical and ideological mobilisation of populism

The first form of the re-emergence of populism in France is primarily related to instrumentalisation of populist rhetorical and ideological elements by leaders or political organisations who associate them with an entire range of normative systems. Thus, the hunters' movement, organised around the CPNT, mobilises a populist discursive and ideological repertoire. An extract from a text written by Jean Saint-Josse, one of the leaders of the movement, throws some light onto this phenomenon. In attacking the successive changes made to French legislation designed to bring it into line with European directives on hunting, he states that

> [f]aced with such a masquerade of democracy, will French men and women, hunters and country people, at long last understand the double language of the political class? Only one solution presents itself to us: the bad, unfair, wicked laws must be changed. To amend them, we have to change the people, and that means putting up candidates for election. We have to move beyond traditional political cleavages and do everything to organise the CPNT into a vast assemblage, which if it is to be strong must go beyond the framework of hunting and bring together all those men and women who want identities and differences to be respected ... Let us organise on the ground; we are neighbours, we are the people, and let us give ... a lesson in good sense to a political class that has no other concerns than to keep or regain power.[3]

The demand for the protection of traditional social practices thus drifts into a rejection of elites and the celebration of popular common sense, the only issue able to function as a legitimate reference for all political action. The party that has most directly and lastingly participated in this redistribution of rhetorical and normative resources, however, remains the FN. Since its initial electoral successes in the 1980s (Birenbaum 1992; Mayer and Perrineau 1996), the FN has stood out as the movement most firmly tied to populist themes and rhetoric. This capturing of resources by the FN has been a powerful engine in the transformation of the cleavage structure and alignment and the positioning logic within the French party system.

Strictly speaking, this use of a populist repertoire is not new in France, especially in the case of extreme Right movements. The last significant instance of the use of such a repertoire was the success, albeit ephemeral, of the *Mouvement Poujade* in the late 1950s – one of its members was Jean-Marie Le Pen. The FN's specificity thus lies elsewhere, in its unprecedented capacity to play on the different meanings of the term 'the people' – that is, to consider the people both in the social sense ('the people against the grandees', Birnbaum 1979), and the political sense ('the people betrayed by its elites'), thus legitimising a nationalist and racist repertoire (see Taguieff in Mayer and Perrineau 1996).

Playing on the idea of a gap between political actors and institutions on the one hand and the people on the other, the FN and its leaders have thus become the spokesmen for an allegedly authentic conception of democracy. Because of this their rhetoric contains constant reminders that the people are the constitutive principle of the system. For instance, Bruno Mégret, delegate-general of the FN before the 1999 split, was able to render the democratic ideal as follows:

> Of the people, by the people, for the people; in France, the people are sovereign. It is from them that power proceeds, they decide their destiny, and it is for them that our rulers act. That is at any rate the principle of sovereignty in our nation, that is the deep meaning of the Republican institution, those are the foundations of democracy in France. Far from being a mere constitutional mechanism defined by holding elections, it is, over and above this legal implementation, the well-nigh sacred expression of the legitimacy that comes from the people. (Mégret 1997)

This reminder of the people's legitimacy acts on the negative diagnosis of current modes of representation: since representation does not function perfectly in practice, it must be reformed, or even eliminated, in order to make way for mechanisms of direct democracy. Underlying this critical statement we find the conviction that the present situation is an example of an 'asymmetry of civic principles' (MacRae in Gellner and Ionescu 1969). Faced by a conspiracy of the elites, the people must win back the pre-eminence due to them by reactivating the moral and political principles that are the cornerstones of social relations and political governance. This presumed asymmetry thus leads to a response channelled by the populist movements in the direction of 'inverse inegalitarianism' which is, in the words of Jack Hayward, based on 'mass self-esteem ... encouraged by an "inverse inegalitarianism" in which the people are not just the equals of the rulers; they are in fact better than the rulers' (Hayward 1996b).

In order for this conviction to become reality, one must, for instance, ensure that representation manages to incarnate the people in the broadest and most accurate sense. 'Accepted' representation thus rejects all distance, and all geographical, social, or even physical (that is, racial) dissimilarity between the people and their representatives. In the last instance, however, it is perhaps the ideal of 'resemblance' highlighted by Bernard Manin (1995) in considering the slow genesis of representative government that is the driving force and distinct feature of this 'populist' perception of representation mobilised by the FN.

This conception, based on a necessary homology between representatives and those represented, is one of the constants in populist discourse. For the FN leader Jean-Marie Le Pen, it was his own personal trajectory that legitimised him as a suitable representative of the people. In his speech at the Joan of Arc day organised by the FN on 1 May 1997 we find the following self-portrait which lays claim to the 'popular' nature of the extreme Right party's leader:

> A grandson of peasants and sailors who in the first half of the century worked for ... people, as did my grandfather Le Pen, from the age of five, fifteen hours a day, seven days a week, brought up their children with no family allowances or hope of a pension, and went off from time to time to die in war, I knew from childhood the hardship of their condition. I am the son of a father who died for France, who left at the age of thirteen to go round the Horn before the mast, and a mother who had to leave school at twelve to bring up her brothers and sisters. Having personally known some of the roughest trades, including bearing arms, I have walked hand-in-hand with human misery, and am able ... let me tell you, to understand working people and their humble but heartrending problems.[4]

Since resemblance prevails over all other criteria, it thus establishes the legitimacy of the FN leader and his claim to stand as the 'authentic' representative of the people.

The populist normative schemas and the related repertoire of discourse are clearly not the exclusive or sole ideological property of the FN. Like a good many previous extreme Right movements, the FN is primarily a nationalist party, whose success in the 1980s can also be explained by its capacity to transform itself into a single-issue party by stressing the immigration issue. In 1997 Bruno Mégret thus claimed that

> [d]emocracy cannot ... be achieved with a mere collection of individuals with no ties among them, still less with a juxtaposition of

> different ethnic groups, or ones with incompatible cultural references. To grow and develop, it needs the crucible of an authentic people, that is, a community of men and women who recognise themselves mutually as being close to each other in language, culture, faith, blood and history. (Mégret 1997)

Democracy is thus seen here not as the voluntary association of equal individuals asserting the sovereignty of the community, but rather as the exercise of power on the part of the people understood as a pre-existing conception of the people, founded on ties of blood, history and language. Here, the authenticity of the people is the nation, and populism, in this narrow 'cultural' sense, is a vehicle for claims and issues that are first and foremost nationalist. The linkage of the sovereign people and the national people, the latter understood as the *Volk*, thus highlights the specific feature of a movement whose distinct characteristics are only imperfectly rendered by the term 'populist'.

Populist strategies?

Contemporary populism in France also appears to be a repertoire for what are purely strategic discourse and demands. In some cases adopting populist discourse allows repositioning to take place within the party system and the creation of distancing from competing parties and leaders. The most typical example in contemporary France is the 1995 presidential campaign where Chirac pursued the strategy of embracing a number of populist themes and ideas in order to create a space within the party system and to establish himself as the alternative candidate. It was essentially the political context of the times that compelled Jacques Chirac to 'shift' along the axis of the party system to mark his difference and establish his legitimacy. Anxious not to relapse into the 'clash of the executives' that had characterised the period of cohabitation between 1986 and 1988 and which was regarded by Chirac and his camp as one of the reasons for his defeat in the 1988 presidential election, when the conservative coalition won the general elections in 1993 Chirac chose not to stand again as Prime Minister. Faced with the steady rise in popularity of the then Prime Minister, Édouard Balladur, who had gradually managed to present himself as the conservative candidate with best chance of winning and of securing support from the UDF and part of the RPR, Chirac found himself marginalised. Extremely unfavourable opinion polls a few months before the election induced a total change in his campaign strategy. Blocked on the conservative side, Jacques Chirac presented himself as the candidate for twofold alternation: from the Socialist Party, still represented in power by François Mitterrand, and from his own camp, in power since 1993. This change of direction led him to seek popular support around such themes as the 'social fracture', but especially by systematically mobilising typically populist elements of discourse and ideas.

Thus, one of the recurrent themes in Jacques Chirac's campaign for the 1995 presidential election was based on the belief that a gap had gradually opened up between the people and their political representatives. Taking up one of the central themes of populist discourse to set himself up as the candidate for this 'twofold alternation', Chirac was able to argue the case that

> [t]he people are aware they have not been taken into account in the thinking of the hierarchies that are supposed to lead them. Hence their rejection of a system completely detached from the realities ... The people have become the forgotten in a democracy of image and appearance: that is the primary cause of the French sickness. (Chirac 1994, 39)

Against these elites who have been criticised, then, it is politicians regarded as closest to the people who should be called on to govern.

> If I have these last two years chosen to keep away from the glitter of the Republic, if I have taken the risk, sometimes, of a certain solitude, it is because I wanted to turn towards the French, not towards power. For one cannot improvise oneself into a candidate; it is a serious step, the mysterious meeting of a man, a people, and a moment of history. (Chirac 1994, 29)

To restore the contact, it is thus best to turn aside from the traditional channels of communication and analytical instruments: 'in these last years I have sought to listen to the French, to understand them, in other ways than through books, opinion polls and statistics'.[5] The logical conclusion is therefore that as candidate Chirac could state that 'The Republic is the power of the citizens, power to the people. I am thus taking my objective as giving the French back control of their fate'.[6]

It is, therefore, clear that the presidential campaign waged by Jacques Chirac in 1995 adopted a stance and had a normative undertone that were essentially populist. All the fundamental features identified here were mobilised: the reminder of popular sovereignty 'in the last instance', contrasting with the sometimes widespread feeling that the choice of Édouard Balladur was a matter for the political and economic elite; the indictment of traditional political practices and the inability of the political elite to solve the 'real' problems (the famous 'social fracture'); and the desire to return to a more traditional, 'happier' France, associated particularly with the economic growth of the 1960s. Other factors operated in Chirac's favour – in particular the absence of any credible competitors on the Left at the time – and may help account for an initially unlikely success. The main reason for his election appears, however, to be related to this transitory exploitation of the discourse and normative schemas of populism.

Apart from the case of Jacques Chirac, there are other more general reasons to account for the strategic weight of populist discourses and ideas within the French party system. In this respect, Andreas Schedler has suggested the existence of a special positioning of populist figures within the party system, which locates them on its edge, between violent and 'legitimist' challenging of the current system (Schedler 1996; see also Poguntke 1996; Ignazi 1996). Schedler suggests that contemporary populist parties are typified by their attempts to mount a generalised challenge to the government parties, and, more generally, the holders of positions of power in various social domains, without openly questioning democratic ideals or institutions. He goes on to define contemporary populism as the set of political formations or actors determined in terms of their opposition to the elites ('anti-political-establishment opposition'), while differing from anti-system parties in their ability to assimilate the traditional political logic, particularly by taking part in all types of electoral activity. The FN as a party built essentially on its ability to criticise the traditional parties whilst legitimising its actions by ever-wider participation in all national or local electoral consultations is a case in point (see Birenbaum 1992). The anti-establishment discourse places itself on the margins of the party system, seen as corrupt and deviating from democratic ideals, whilst presenting an alternative that will follow the 'normal' logic of democratic competition.

Extending his argument, Schedler suggests that the position of populist parties in contemporary Europe is determined by a combined dynamics that can be represented in the form of a triangle (see Figure 8.1).

Populism, thus conceived, rests on two related dynamics. Classically, populism is the constant recall of the determining nature of the people

Figure 8.1 The 'anti-political' triangle according to Schedler

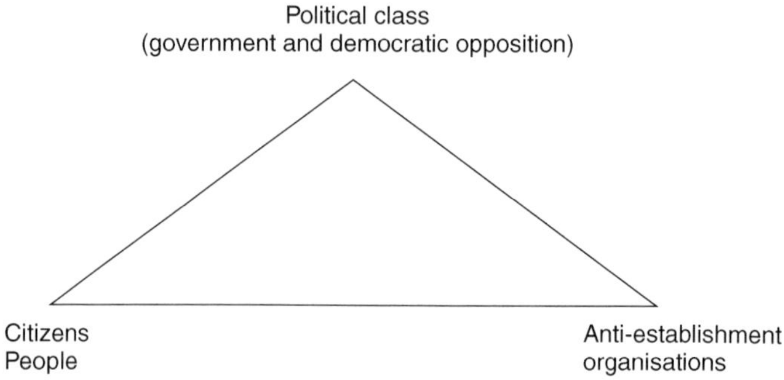

in the logic of politics – that is, that the sovereign people are the sole bearer of legitimacy in a political community based on democratic principles that the populist organisations claim to represent. Secondly – and this is what distinguishes populists from anti-system parties – this stress on the people is accompanied by a critique of the implementation of popular political supremacy by the elites, who are accused of having betrayed the ideals and modes of legitimation and organisation of the political community.

Political figures who employ populist discourse and normative schemas have accordingly a dual role in the party system in the most classical sense: they constantly recall the democratic foundations of the system, whilst simultaneously highlighting deviation from the original ideals brought about by the actions of those in power, especially the government parties. Populist parties are in a sense characterised by a dual hybridisation: they are part of the system and simultaneously challenge its shortcomings; they recall the primacy of the people over the elites, whilst portraying themselves as the only 'authentically' representative political formations.

This analysis of the party system has proved extremely useful, especially when employed in combination with hypotheses regarding the unfreezing of cleavages. We can argue that the shift in the axis structuring the party systems associated with recent socioeconomic changes has led to the relative marginalisation of some social groups. Thus, artisans or shopkeepers are increasingly being challenged by the development of distribution circuits which they are unable to join, withstand or adapt to. But, as a series of analyses show (see in particular, the studies by Perrineau and Mayer on the FN electorate), these are the socioeconomic strata that constitute the earliest and longest-lasting support for organisations and figures promoting the 'populist repertoire'. By combining these two sets of factors we can hypothesise that this marginalisation of social strata who feel overtaken by recent socioeconomic developments has prompted a re-evaluation of populist rhetorical elements and normative schemas. These have the specific 'function' of keeping within (or on the margin of) the party system those individuals or groups who tend to move away from it by adopting a passive attitude to political participation (with growing abstention being its chief manifestation), or else a provocative or challenging attitude that may go as far as the violent expression of discontent with the whole social and political system. In a sense the mobilisation of this more or less socially and politically excluded electorate (both in the working class and in certain sections of the middle classes, or within the petit bourgeoisie) is the result of the (re)constitution of a political supply adjusted to new demand generated by the shift in the structural axis of the party system. The distinctive brand of this political offering would, then, be the more or less periodic use of populist discourse and its normative resources.

This hypothesis would appear to be confirmed in the French case. Thus, one of the original features of the FN was its ability to maintain a certain ambiguity as to its positions, objectives and methods. At times ultra-legalist, attacking existing elites for corrupting the French political system, the party has also often played on alternative repertoires, including violent action. The existence of paramilitary structures and youth organisations, and the ambivalence that has always surrounded its relations with violent small groupings, particularly the neo-Nazi skinheads, attest to its hybrid position in the political spectrum. Neither a government party nor an anti-democratic party, the FN draws support from individuals and groups who are already marginalised, or, more often, who are in the process of becoming marginalised.

There are, however, undeniable limits to these hypotheses. The use of discourse-related and ideological elements of a populist nature is indeed highly variable depending on the actors and contexts involved. Thus, a few months after his election it became clear that Jacques Chirac had returned to the 'normal' practice of political action, marked by the sort of pragmatic management conservatism that has undoubtedly been one of the few constants in his political career. Moreover, the systematic and repeated use of this type of resource often helps to strengthen or sustain the marginality of figures who mobilise this populist 'stock'. Here the example of the FN is indicative: the 1999 split in the FN was primarily generated by a leadership crisis and a division over the strategy to follow. Against the party's dominant orientation, Bruno Mégret and his supporters proposed a strategy of 'normalisation' in the form of alliances with the parties of the classical Right whilst leaving the populist 'tinsel' aside. Indeed, the consistent mobilisation of populist resources may well be a barrier to genuine integration into the party system.

It is nonetheless the case that these resources have undergone a major and lasting revival in the 1980s and 1990s, for the structural reasons mentioned here, but also at specific turning points, such as the 1995 presidential elections. From this perspective, the best proof of the sense of efficacy that these populist rhetorical and ideological elements give can be found in the first feeble signs of the campaign for the 2002 presidential elections. In a recent visit to the West of France to prepare his candidacy, Jacques Chirac declared that what was now needed was to bring in a new sort of 'governance', close to 'the deep-down France', in order to break with what he described as 'a democracy detached from the realities of life, given over to ideologies and the spirit of party'.[7] Why, indeed, abandon a winning formula?

Notes

1. Press conference on 19 May 1958, cited in Gaïti (1998, 64).
2. Especially in the work of Bartolini and Mair (1990), who demonstrate the remarkable permanence of the electoral publics of the main European parties throughout the twentieth century.
3. Available on the movement's website at www.cnpt.asso.fr.
4. Speech by Jean-Marie Le Pen, 1 May 1997, FN's website at www.front-nat.fr.
5. Speech by Jacques Chirac, Pelouse de Bagatelle, 29 April 1995.
6. Speech by Jacques Chirac, Porte de Versailles, Friday 17 February 1995.
7. Cited in a Reuters dispatch dated 5 April 2001.

9

Evil or the 'Engine of Democracy'? Populism and Party Competition in Austria

Wolfgang C. Müller

Introduction

The international attention received by Austria in recent years has mainly been due to the spectacular rise of the Freedom Party (FPÖ), which began in 1986, when Jörg Haider was elected party leader.[1] A party which had virtually been written off in the early 1980s, it became the second strongest party in terms of votes in 1999 (having won 415 votes more than the People's Party, ÖVP). In terms of seats won, it is now on equal terms with the ÖVP, and even 'within striking distance' of the Social Democrats (SPÖ) (Table 9.1).

Whilst spectacular, the FPÖ's success would not have received so much attention had it been a 'normal', that is, 'coalitionable' mainstream party. Instead, it has been classified as 'anti-cartel', 'radical Right populist', or 'extreme Right' by academic observers (Katz and

Table 9.1 FPÖ electoral results 1983–99 (Austrian and European Parliament)

	1983	*1986*	*1990*	*1994*	*1995**	*1996***	*1999***	*1999*
% votes	5.0	9.7	16.7	22.5	21.9	*27.5*	*23.4*	26.9
% seats	6.6	9.8	18.0	23.0	21.9	*28.6*	*23.8*	28.4
Seats (N = 183; *N = 21*)	12	18	33	42	41	*6*	*5*	52
Difference SPÖ–FPÖ (in seats)	+78	+62	+47	+23	+30	±0	+2	+13
Difference ÖVP–FPÖ (in seats)	+69	+59	+27	+10	+11	+1	+2	±0

* Including the results of the partial repetition of the elections in October 1996.
** These figures represent the two direct elections to the European Parliament, the first of which was held when Austria joined the EU.

Mair 1995; Kitschelt and McGann 1995; Betz 1994), and has been the most successful of the Western European parties grouped under any of these labels. European politicians have largely shared these negative evaluations of the FPÖ, and in 2000 the leaders of the other 14 EU member states reacted negatively to its participation in the Austrian government by declaring, in an unprecedented attempt to intervene in the domestic politics of a fellow member state, that bilateral relations with Austria would remain solely at the technical level as long as the FPÖ participated in government or did not change its nature. These so-called 'sanctions' proved counterproductive in many ways and eventually the 'EU-14', as they became known, invited three wise men nominated by the president of the European Court of Human Rights – Martti Ahtisaari, Jochen Frowein and Marcelino Oreja – to prepare a report on the Austrian government's commitment to key common European values and the evolution of the political nature of the FPÖ. This report, published in September 2000, led to the lifting of sanctions, provided a generally positive evaluation of the government, but characterised the FPÖ as a 'right-wing populist party with extremist expressions [*sic*]'.

The FPÖ has always rejected the 'extreme Right' label and refrained from co-operating with parties classified as extreme Right, such as the *Front national* in France or the *Vlaams Blok* in Belgium. It has been more ambiguous in its response when labelled 'populist' as, in contrast to 'extreme Right' or 'protest', the term does not undermine its electoral appeal. Party chairman Haider, for instance, has accepted the term 'radical' in the sense of being thorough and going to the roots of issues, and 'rightist' by granting that the FPÖ is certainly not a party of the Left. He has also claimed that 'populist' could be aquated with popular, or 'with the people', clearly a good thing in a democracy. Although the FPÖ has never used the term 'populist' when referring to itself, since 1986 it has always claimed to be 'different' from the cartel parties or '*Altparteien*' as they are called in FPÖ terminology.

The FPÖ has not only been popular in terms of the absolute number of voters it has attracted, but also by virtue of the fact that votes have been drawn from a wide spectrum of Austrian society. The FPÖ has thus managed to make substantial inroads into all of the traditional core groups of the SPÖ and the ÖVP electorate (see Table 9.2).

Populism, as understood in this volume, focuses first on the built-in tension between the popular will and constitutional democracy, and second on the means of populist mobilisation. In this chapter I will address these topics by asking: why has the FPÖ been so successful in

Table 9.2 Changes in voting behaviour of SPÖ and ÖVP traditional core groups, 1983–99

	1983	*1986*	*1990*	*1994*	*1995*	*1999*	*Change*[1]
Trained blue-collar workers							
SPÖ share (%)	60	66		44	40	31	–29
FPÖ share (%)	2	11	25	33	35	48	+46
Untrained blue-collar workers							
SPÖ share (%)	63	59		52	43	40	–23
FPÖ share (%)	4	8		24	33	45	+41
Farmers							
ÖVP share (%)		93	85	73	72	87	(–6)
FPÖ share (%)	4	5	9	15	18	10	+6
Self-employed and professions							
ÖVP share (%)		60	51	40	39	41	(–19)
FPÖ share (%)	4	15	21	30	28	33	+29

Note:
1. Figures in parentheses do not cover the whole 1986–99 period and therefore can only be compared in their tendency with the other figures.
Source: Plasser, Ulram, and Sommer (2000, 466–7).

elections? Can the factors accounting for its success be can summarised under the heading of 'populism'? And, if so, does populism conflict with liberal democracy? This calls for an examination of the demands made by the FPÖ and the strategies employed to put these issues across. As Mény and Surel point out, populist mobilisation concentrates on the vertical dimension of political conflict, between the rulers and the ruled. The Austrian tradition of elite bargaining, in the form of grand coalitions and corporatism, constitutes a particularly suitable target for populist mobilisation and hence will be considered briefly before turning to the FPÖ's behaviour.

The context: cartel politics

The rise of the FPÖ cannot be considered in isolation from the structure of party competition in Austria. During the period covered by this research (1986–2000), the duopoly of the SPÖ and the ÖVP held executive office, enjoyed the spoils of government, and made the relevant policy decisions within the 'grand coalition', usually in close co-operation with the major interest groups in Austria. The post-war consensus among these two major political parties can be considered as a real-world approximation to the party system at the cartelisation stage. As Katz and Mair (1995, 24) have suggested, the cartel party 'inevitably generates its own opposition'. A number of features made the SPÖ and ÖVP easy targets. To begin with, their coalition did not minimise policy distance (Müller and Jenny 2000), so that many voters who supported the government parties were dissatisfied with the policy sacrifices produced by this constellation. All too often, policy inertia occurred, and even when the SPÖ and ÖVP did manage to hammer out a compromise, its components were already discredited by earlier public debate between the coalition parties. Secondly, many voters viewed the 'permanent' coalition between the two traditional major parties as lacking in accountability and hence of being incapable of responding appropriately to the demands of voters. Thirdly, the SPÖ and ÖVP proved easy targets because of their perceived record of patronage (Müller 1989; Kitschelt 2000). In reality, even in the heyday of patronage politics in the 1950s, only a minority of citizens had benefited directly. Recognising the potential dangers of a clientelist strategy, the SPÖ and ÖVP have since reduced this appeal, but they cannot credibly deny that they still exercise patronage. Thus, citizens whose claims to public goods and services are not satisfied may interpret this as giving preferential treatment to the government parties' clienteles rather than their own objective needs. finally, the government parties constitute easy targets with respect to allegations of the abuse of power in the way suggested by the cartel party thesis. For example, the FPÖ has accused the SPÖ and ÖVP of manipulating its mass media coverage.

Mass media and media logic

In his interpretation of the changes in political representation, Bernard Manin (1997) has argued that since the 1970s party democracy has been replaced by 'audience' democracy where electoral competition centres on the question of who will become chief executive. Parties have been replaced by the mass media as the main channels of communication and these are 'for the most part politically neutral' (Manin 1997, 228). Indeed, television has become the main source of political information for more than two-thirds of Austrians (Plasser 1997, 469). Given the predominance of public television in Austria, party influence over the most important channels has not ceased. According to the cartel party thesis of Katz and Mair (1995), cartel parties – the SPÖ and ÖVP – should be in an advantageous position, whereas the anti-cartel FPÖ should encounter an alien media environment. The party has indeed made this claim and has often accused the public broadcasting corporation and some weekly magazines of belonging to a 'hunting party' out to shoot the FPÖ. The loud claims of unfair treatment on the part of the FPÖ are designed to force the public broadcasting corporation into providing a stage for the major anti-cartel party. The extent to which this strategy works will depend on the FPÖ's communication ability on television. However, the effect of journalistic intervention between the 'sender' and the 'receiver' of a message is minimal in live interviews – particularly during the face-to-face debates which have become frequent events during campaigns since 1994 – compared to that in the printed media.

In this context, changes in the media go far beyond the decline of the party press and the rise of television as a medium of political communication. Public broadcasting corporations increasingly face competition from private channels. Even when the market share of private channels is comparatively modest, public channels have to meet this competition if they are to maintain their leading position. Although the competition between public and private channels mainly takes place on entertainment programmes, it also has an impact on political news. Indeed, the entertainment value of political news has become much more important. This is also true for the print media, in particular weekly or monthly publications. Entertainment value may be generated not only by new political positions, but also by new faces and the non-political activities of politicians. The number of television performances by a party leader or representative depends on their capacity to provoke 'media events', and even small parties not belonging to the cartel can maximise their media presence if they are capable of doing so.

However, not all media events are manufactured or fit with the strategy of the relevant party. Intra-party conflicts, for instance, are likely to catch the media's attention, but rarely benefit the party. Thus, a high degree of control not only over the party's decisions, but also of the flows of communication leaving the party, constitute a competitive advantage, as long as it does not create the image of democratic centralism of Communist parties. Mr Haider has been remarkably successful in controlling his own party and streamlining its communication output.

The requirements of television and the need to 'dramatise' press reports lead to the increasing personalisation of politics, which in turn tends to equalise the parties' chances in competition. It is no longer a match between the SPÖ against the FPÖ, but of Vranitzky vs. Haider, where the personal qualities and media appearances of individual politicians take precedence over party programmes (Plasser 1997). This new media logic constitutes a particularly friendly environment for a natural communicator such as Mr Haider.

Issue competition

An 'available' electorate not politically socialised to support one specific party exclusively, and an 'open' media system, are preconditions for changes in the party system, but the realisation of these changes is conditioned by change in the issue agenda. In the words of Sartori (1968, 23), '[T]here can be no consumers without political entrepreneurs', and it is to the issue competition approach that I now turn.

According to the theory of issue competition, party alignments form around a specific issue agenda and related party commitments. These remain stable as long as the issue agenda or, more precisely, its underlying dimensions (cleavages) and party commitments remain unchanged (Carmines 1991). Losing parties therefore turn to new issues to improve their position. If these new issues split the voter alliances supporting the winning party (or parties), while uniting the electorate of the losing party, they may produce change in the party system. If successful, the introduction of new issues 'produces a new majority coalition composed of the old minority and the proportion of the old majority that likes the new alternative better' (Riker 1986, 1).

However, very few issues are strong enough and Riker (1986, 1) has ascribed an 'artistic creativity of the highest order' to those politicians who 'invent the right kind of new alternative'. In practice, many new issues are simply organic extensions of old issues, and may help reinforce existing conflicts and thereby consolidate existing electoral alliances (Carmines and Stimson 1993, 156). Moreover, even if a party does manage to find an issue which is not already 'owned' by another party, this does not necessarily guarantee an impact on existing electoral alliances, since 'the vast majority of new issue proposals are bound to fail, striking an unresponsive chord in the mass public and leaving the current majority party's coalition intact' (Carmines and Stimson 1993, 154).

The introduction of a new issue is probably as much opinion-formation as agenda-setting. Recent research in public opinion suggests that citizens do not as a rule have fixed issue positions from the outset (Zaller 1992). While they may relate new issues to the values they hold, these values are often inconsistent and, consequently, have a considerable degree of leeway. In the words of Stimson (1995, 183), '[E]ach citizen has a range of views, depending on which consideration is consulted, not a single fixed one, and that range tends to be large.' According to the directional theory of voting, parties are rewarded by the voter 'for taking a clear and deeply committed stand to an issue the voter slightly favours' (Rabinowitz and Macdonald 1989, 94). Parties which take more intense stands than their competitors but 'avoid stands so extreme that voters reject them as irresponsible' will benefit (Hinich and Munger 1997, 187–8). Those citizens who generally favour this *direction* will credit the party, as long as its demands are not perceived as extremist. Parties which express only partial or lukewarm support will not be credited for this. Opposition parties in particular are likely to profit from taking strong positions in this respect (Merrill and Grofman 1997).

Producing a 'responsive chord among the mass public' is not only a function of the intrinsic quality of an issue, but also depends critically on the communicative ability of the politicians promoting it, and both friends and foes consider Mr Haider to be one of the most gifted, and least constrained, communicators in contemporary Austrian history.

Issue competition and elections

According to the theory of issue competition, only two factors help explain changes in party support: new voters and new issues (Carmines 1991, 70–2). With regard to new voters, generational change has been by far the most important source of change in the composition of the Austrian electorate. The new generations of voters differ from the older generations. In particular, those who reached voting age since the mid-1980s have turned their backs on the traditional parties and are more likely to vote for new parties (such as the Greens and the Liberal Forum), or radically transformed parties (such as the FPÖ) (see Table 9.3). The SPÖ and ÖVP enjoy a considerable lead among the older generations, even at the end of the time series, but this lead diminishes from cohort to cohort and from election to election. The younger generation were not responsible for the gains made by the SPÖ and ÖVP in 1995. Quite the reverse, the older the generation, the greater the tendency to support the two mainstream parties.

With regard to new issues, how do these make their way onto the political agenda? I offer three complementary explanations (see Carmines and Stimson 1993): objective changes in the agenda; the break-up of internal contradictions and imbalances in existing voter alliances; and the strategic behaviour of politicians and parties.

Table 9.3 Aggregated differences in the voting behaviour of age cohorts, 1986–99 (Advantage [+] or disadvantage [-] of SPÖ + ÖVP compared with FPÖ + Greens + Liberal Forum)

Age cohorts	*1986*	*1990*	*1994*	*1995*	*1999*
18–29	+44	+18	±0	–4	–10
30–44	+60	+44	+14	+22	+14
45–59	+80	+60	+34	+44	+37
60+	+78	+80	+48	+56	+47

Source: Plasser, Ulram, and Seeber (1996, 185); Plasser, Ulram, and Sommer (2000, 469).

Objective changes: new problems

Objective changes in the problems affecting a society or political system may occur in the form of 'shocks' or more incrementally (Carmines and Stimson 1993, 155). Since the mid-1980s Austria has experienced several such objective changes. Whilst not exhaustive, the following list includes the key developments.

The end of full employment

Since the early 1980s Austria no longer enjoys full employment and, although still not at the level of other European countries, unemployment has been rising constantly until 1999. Moreover, the perceived risk of unemployment has increased more than unemployment itself.

Economic adjustment shocks

Previously sheltered sectors, such as the food industry, suffered an adjustment shock after Austria's accession to the European Union. A similar impact was experienced after the collapse of Communism in Central and Eastern Europe, with the result that some goods and services were available in those countries for a third of the price in Austria, producing negative effects for some economic sectors and regions. The record number of bankruptcies in the 1990s is partly a result of these adjustment shocks. There is no doubt that, on the whole, Austria will benefit from the intensification of economic exchange with its western and eastern neighbours. However, there will be losers as well as winners once the balance sheet is drawn. Enlargement of the European Union is likely to multiply these effects. Thus, enlargement is considered more of a threat than an opportunity by large sections of the population. The economic fears produced by such shocks are not confined to blue-collar and white-collar workers, but are also felt by the self-employed, businessmen, and farmers.

Immigration

Austria has been a target country for sizeable flows of immigration since the early 1980s. The number of legal immigrants in the resident population – particularly from the former Yugoslavia, Turkey and Eastern Europe – rose from less than 300 000 in the early 1980s to over 700 000 in 1993 (Faßmann 1995, 403). In addition, there is an unknown number of illegal immigrants. The entry of economic migrants was strictly limited at a later stage and the numbers seeking political asylum was reduced by new laws. However, over 70 000 Bosnian refugees, the majority of whom did not return home, constitute a major new group of immigrants. By Western European standards, Austria has one of the largest shares of foreign nationals in its resident population. The figure stood at 9.1 per cent in 1997 – second only to Luxembourg – most of whom live in parts of Vienna. Moreover, due to a more transparent and objective allocation process, immigrants entering Austria during earlier waves of immigration, and who have since become Austrian citizens, have been allocated council housing in the last few years. The heavy immigrant presence in certain parts of the city and the coexistence of Austrian-born nationals and immigrants have led to latent cultural conflict. According to a survey reported by Lebhart and Münz in 1998, 77 per cent of Austrians thought that foreign citizens had not adapted sufficiently to the Austrian way of life (1998, 22–3).[2]

The breaking through of internal contradictions and imbalances in voter alliances

Each electoral alliance contains within it the germs of its own destruction. It remains stable as long as the voters are mainly concerned with a specific issue or set of issues, despite the fact that they disagree on many others. Once the issues which have been decisive in the formation of a specific electoral alliance lose importance and those issues over which there is no agreement gain importance, the voter alliance disintegrates. In other words, each new issue which reaches the political agenda may cause the end of an electoral alliance (Riker 1982, 208–12). The old electoral alliances around the traditional Austrian parties contain a number of potential contradictions, some of which have been the focus of academic concern. In the present context we can distinguish between sectoral and social-issue conflicts.

Sectoral conflicts

Kitschelt and McGann (1995) argued that the classic economic conflict between labour and capital has increasingly been replaced or moulded into a conflict between two economic sectors, one open to international competition, largely the private sector, and the other protected from it, that is, largely the public sector. Members of the protected sector continue to be inclined towards welfarism, whereas members of the sector open to international competition are required to remain competitive and are becoming increasingly sympathetic to neoliberal policies and the reduction of costly welfare programmes. There is indeed a tendency towards such a split in the Austrian electorate (Plasser, Ulram, and Seeber 1996, 191).

Social-issue conflicts

Austrian society has been characterised by the emergence or increasing salience of specific cultural conflicts, over gender, the environment, and immigration expressed by interest groups, new social movements, and political parties, and where the traditional voter alliances of the SPÖ and ÖVP are anything but concordant.

The strategic behaviour of politicians and parties

What can the new issue producers offer their political 'consumers'? In the second half of the 1980s and 1990s new producers with policies which differ fundamentally from those of the FPÖ have emerged, such as the Greens (in parliament since 1986), and the Liberal Forum (an FPÖ splinter). Although their policies have not proved nearly as popular as those of the FPÖ, they still attract a sizeable minority. For the SPÖ and ÖVP this means being squeezed between the FPÖ on the one hand, and the Greens and Liberals on the other, with little room for manoeuvre. Of all Austrian political parties, it is the FPÖ that has made the greatest change in the content of its electoral manifestos. This took place in 1986, after Haider became party leader (Luther 1997), since which time the FPÖ has concentrated on the following issues during campaigns and other attempts to appeal to the public.

Political class

Since 1986 the critique of the political class has been a constant feature of FPÖ propaganda. In a country with a high degree of disillusion with politicians and parties, such issues are welcomed by the electorate (Müller et al., 1999, 208). However, it is critical that the party articulating this issue manages to avoid being affected by disillusion itself. In this respect, the FPÖ, in its capacity as an opposition party and a party not belonging to the traditional power cartel of the Second Republic, enjoys a good starting position. This is reinforced by the party's hard work and remarkable communicative performance: the FPÖ has uncovered real and alleged scandals or privileges; it has called itself a 'movement' and temporarily removed the negatively charged word 'party' from its name,[3] and on one occasion even refrained from accepting some of the party subsidies to which it was entitled. In general, it has claimed to be unlike the 'old parties', and the FPÖ leader's occasional claim to be the 'Robin Hood' of politics – taking from the rich to give to the poor – has become the party's biggest communication asset.

In more substantive terms, the FPÖ claims that politicians in other parties have lost touch with the people and are not responsive to the needs of the 'little man'. It criticises the high salaries of professional politicians and the accumulation of (paid) positions in the public sector by intermediary-level politicians of the major political parties.

The direct democratic instrument of the (consultative) people's initiative has been an effective means through which the FPÖ has placed issues on the agenda (Müller 1998, 1999). The FPÖ has also frequently demanded the use of other instruments of direct democracy which require a parliamentary majority. At all levels of government it has repeatedly demanded referenda on particular issues, including the introduction of the Euro currency and, more recently, EU enlargement. Concomitantly, the FPÖ as a governing party has also suggested holding a consultative referendum on the sanctions of the EU-14, thus stretching both the constitutionality (this instrument refers to matters of Austrian legislation), and practical application of the instrument. The FPÖ also agreed with the ÖVP during the coalition negotiations to introduce a proper 'people's initiative', that is, to hold a binding referendum at the behest of 15 per cent of the voters. (This constitutional reform, however, would require a two-thirds majority and hence the support of the SPÖ which had always rejected such an idea.)

Immigration

Since the fall of the Iron Curtain, the 'foreigner issue' has occupied a prominent place on the FPÖ's agenda. The party takes a very restrictive position with regard to asylum rights and, in particular, the rules governing immigration and residence rights for foreigners. The FPÖ claims that new immigrants compete with Austrians, or with already integrated immigrants in the labour market. In short, immigration increases unemployment and drives up housing prices. More important than these economic arguments, however, are the cultural ones. The FPÖ stresses the potential conflict between different cultures and claims that too many foreigners constitute a danger to Austrian culture. In the most drastic formulation, Andreas Mölzer, currently Mr Haider's cultural adviser, declared that Austria runs the risk of '*Umvolkung*' – that is, the impairment of its ethnic stock, and the FPÖ claims that Austria has gone too far in this direction and has called for a '*Recht auf Heimat*' for Austrian nationals. The party links the foreigner question to issues such as the abuse of welfare provisions and crime. It claims, for instance, that child benefits are paid for nonexistent children in Turkey, that foreigners make their living by having very large families (thus Austria is paying for 'breeding-out' Austrians), and that many foreigners (in particular, asylum-seekers) are criminals and that those who are caught do not receive adequate treatment (including deportation) (see, for example, Kräh 1996, 219–32). All these issues are new in party competition. They are cohesive for the FPÖ's voter alliance and split traditional voter alliances of the SPÖ and ÖVP.

European integration

Traditionally, the FPÖ has been the party with the most positive stance on European integration and Austrian accession to the EU. Since 1991, however, its position has been negative. The FPÖ campaigned against EU membership and was the only party to reject the single currency. Although the FPÖ does not demand withdrawal from the EU, it wants to shift competences from the EU back to the national level and is opposed to enlargement for the next two decades (a policy it pursues by tying enlargement to conditions that are unlikely to be met earlier by the countries of Central and Eastern Europe). The issue of European integration is a new issue in the sense that it was not relevant for party competition at the mass level before the second half of the 1980s. In all cases – membership, currency, EU reform, and enlargement – the electoral alliances of *all* parties, including the FPÖ, are split. However, the share of those with a negative attitude towards European integration has always been considerably higher than the number of FPÖ supporters (Plasser and Ulram 1994). Thus, the probability that the FPÖ will gain votes from stressing these issues tends to outstrip the electoral risks thus incurred.

Church issues and the issue of the Austrian nation

In the 1990s, the FPÖ has attempted to distance itself from the anti-clerical tradition of the German-national political camp (*Lager*) and to appeal to the conservative wing of the Roman Catholic Church. Due to the choices and decisions made by Pope John Paul II, the Austrian Roman Catholic Church is deeply split, both at the mass level and within the hierarchy. For a while the FPÖ sided publicly with the conservative wing of the Austrian church (while the ÖVP, the traditional party of the Roman Catholics, has tried to maintain a low profile). In its 1998 party programme, the FPÖ welcomed 'a church which fights for its values'. However, the close relation with the conservative wing of the Roman Catholic Church does not appeal to the hedonistic and working-class supporters of the FPÖ. Pushing this image into the background, after some strong signals to the conservative Roman Catholic constituency, is probably the most electorally viable strategy. The FPÖ also attempted to relinquish the ideological ballast at the core of its traditional identity, its German-national orientation. In 1995, party chairman Haider announced that the party would no longer keep up this German-national sentiment. As a party of a million Austrians, for the vast majority of whom the concept of the Austrian nation is self-evident, the FPÖ can no longer hold up the German-national banner (Luther 1997, 298). Anti-clericalism and German-nationalism are traditions that potentially undermine the cohesion of the FPÖ's new electoral alliance and constitute barriers to its growth. However, this electoral logic is not unanimously accepted within the FPÖ and the resistance of some individuals and organisations has caused a modest amount of negative publicity for the FPÖ.

Welfare policy

Until 1999 the FPÖ did not pay much attention to welfare policy. To the extent that it figured in the FPÖ's propaganda, it concentrated on the exploitation of the welfare state by 'social parasites' implying that, once the latter had been identified and their welfare benefits removed, the welfare state would be saved. A partial exception was the FPÖ's model for pension reform which was, however, sufficiently vague not to disturb pro-welfarism voters, and during the 1999 campaign, the party even demanded constitutional protection for existing pension rights. In 1999 the FPÖ invented a new welfare benefit, the 'children's cheque' (the *Kinderscheck* or child allowance payable to mothers for each child). The FPÖ made this cheque its most prominent demand in the highly successful *Land* election campaign in Carinthia (which resulted in Mr Haider becoming governor), and in the general election campaign. This idea was transferred to the federal level, despite the fact that it had not been implemented at the *Land* level.

Taxation

Since the mid-1990s, the FPÖ has promoted a model of radical tax reform, introducing a flat-rate system at a uniform rate of 23 per cent. While the proposal is generally considered unworkable by the other parties and experts, it constitutes a strong stand suggested by the directional theory of voting.

What, then, are the results of the FPÖ's efforts to find new and relevant issues and to assume electorally viable positions with regard to old issues? Table 9.4 shows that the FPÖ has managed to become the 'owner' of several new issues. Since 1990, it has had a competitive advantage *vis-à-vis* the SPÖ and ÖVP with regard to immigration policy, and since 1993, it also championed the issues of 'the prevention of wasted public resources' and 'the fight against corruption and privilege'. But just how important are these issues? Austrians are still mainly concerned with the 'bread-and-butter' issues of jobs and pensions. However, on average two of the FPÖ issues have been placed among the top five in the 1990s. The 'foreigner' issue made its appearance among the top five issues in 1993, but subsequently became less important, largely due to the policy responses of the government parties. In 1992, the government parties enacted a package of laws which addressed various aspects of immigration, and which to some extent pre-empted the FPÖ agenda (Wolfgruber 1994). The government parties have since maintained this course, for instance by the reform of the law regulating access to citizenship in 1998. Naturally, the FPÖ has tried to revitalise the issue using the strategic angle of EU enlargement. As the only remaining anti-EU party, the FPÖ is in a good position to exploit misgivings about the EU. Austria borders a minimum of three East – Central European countries which are likely to be included in the first wave of new accessions. According to the FPÖ's scenario, this will lead to another wave of immigration. However, the FPÖ did not really push this issue during the 1999 campaign with the exception being Vienna, where most concrete immigration problems occur and where the Freedom Party faced competition from a new party, The Independents (DU, *Die Unabhängigen*), which made immigration one of its key campaign issues.

Finally, how important are these issues and their underlying cleavages when it comes to elections? Table 9.5 reports the responses to exit polls

Table 9 4 Issue competence of the FPÖ, 1990–98 (In response to the question: 'Could you please tell me for each of the following items, which of the parties – the SPÖ, ÖVP, FPÖ, Greens, or LF – will be all the more likely to work hard in ... ')

Issue area	*Policy competence (%)*						*Policy competence ranking*					
	1990	*1993*	*1995*	*1996*	*1997*	*1998*	*1990*	*1993*	*1995*	*1996*	*1997*	*1998*
Fighting corruption	11	35	33	39	44	24	3	1	1	1	1	1
To get control of the 'foreigners' question'	23	32	38	40	44	32	1	1	1	1	1	1
Prevent the waste of public money	16	23	29	35	35	20	2	1	1	1	1	1
Fighting crime	n.a.	18	18	18	20	12	n.a.	3	3	3	3	3

Source: Müller, Plasser, and Ulram 1999, updated.

Table 9.5 Motives of FPÖ voters, 1990–99 (as % of FPÖ voters)

	1990	*1994*	*1995*	*1999*	*Mean 1990–99*
Only the FPÖ seriously combats scandals and privileges*	62	68	79	65	69
The FPÖ takes the right position in the foreigners' question**	39	49	51	47	47
The personality of Jörg Haider	42	39	38	40	40
To teach the coalition parties a lesson	44	39	32	36	38
The FPÖ best represents my interests	26	34	34	48	36
The FPÖ is the lesser evil compared to the other parties	18	18	19	Not asked	18
The FPÖ combats the power of the parties and for more citizen rights	Not asked	45	Not asked	Not asked	45
The FPÖ strive to be economical and combat the abuse of welfare	Not asked	Not asked	52	Not asked	52
The FPÖ brings the 'wind of change'	Not asked	Not asked	Not asked	63	63

* Because they uncover scandals without mercy (1995, 1999).
** Because they are against the immigration of foreigners (1995, 1999).
Source: Plasser and Ulram (2000, 229–30).

and reveals that FPÖ voters are mainly attracted by the party's attempts to uncover scandals and privileges and its stand on the immigration issue. However, over time there appears to have been a slight development away from protest and towards more positive (though vaguely formulated) motives ('best represents my interests', 'wind of change').

Populism, electoral success, and inter-party relations

The discussion so far reveals that the FPÖ has indeed followed a populist strategy, as defined by Mény and Surel in this volume. The FPÖ claims that the politicians of the other parties have betrayed the people. In particular, the FPÖ has protested against the alleged misbehaviour of the political class – first and foremost the waste of public money and the corruption – and its policies, in particular the government's immigration policy. These factors account for the greater part of the FPÖ's electoral gains and stressing them means focusing on vertical rather than horizontal cleavages. In selecting these issues the FPÖ has responded to new objective problems. It has exploited both the structure of competition in the party system and internal contradictions in the electoral alliances of the SPÖ and ÖVP. In promoting its issues the FPÖ has assumed a very bold position, as the directional theory of voting would suggest, and has used a forceful (or offensive) rhetoric to put its message across. All this worked well, as long as the FPÖ was an opposition party. As a government party, however, it is now part of the political establishment. Some elements of its success strategy no longer fit, whereas others – such as bold policy positions – will prove unworkable, even if the party tries to push them through. The FPÖ may therefore abandon its populist strategy and try to become a party of government which is supported, not because it is against the government, but because it provides good governance. 'Taming' the FPÖ was indeed one of the ÖVP's goals when it entered into the coalition with it. This, however, is only one of the possible scenarios. Alternatively, the FPÖ may want to continue its successful strategy, only slightly adapted to the changed circumstances.

The FPÖ has also proved populist with regard to the claim that the people should be more involved in making political decisions (cf. Canovan 1999). Whilst I am sceptical that this is anything more than a means to win power and to promote the FPÖ's policies, it has clearly been important for the FPÖ's electoral performance (Müller 1998 1999). The penultimate item in Table 9.2 demonstrates that it is indeed a popular strategy (see also Table 9.6, third item from the bottom). FPÖ supporters are indeed more in favour of direct democracy than either the supporters of other parties or the population at large, and distinguish themselves quite clearly when it comes to evaluating aspects of representative democracy. Declared FPÖ supporters are much more critical of representative democracy and much more willing to consider non-democratic alternatives than the supporters of other parties or those who do not declare any party preference (see Table 9.6).[4]

How have the other parties reacted to the 'new' FPÖ? Table 9.7 reports the parliamentary voting patterns since the early 1980s (when the FPÖ first participated in government). Clearly, the party system has become more polarised. The share of laws enacted with the support of all parties has dramatically declined; whereas the share enacted with only the votes of the government parties has increased considerably. What is most interesting, in the present context, is the proportion of legislation which has received the support of the FPÖ, which declined from almost three quarters in the 1986–90 term to 38 per cent in the

Table 9.6 Popular attitudes towards the political process (1997)

	Declared party supporters					*Population*
	FPÖ	*SPÖ*	*ÖVP*	*Greens*	*Liberals*	
Parliament is not (very) important	21	7	7	3	5	11
Parliament is fulfilling its functions less well than 15 years ago	45	28	30	21	19	34
Parliament tends to have more influence than is appropriate for a democracy	22	7	7	5	14	9
Agree with the statement: 'Essentially, we don't need a parliament at the top, but a strong man who can make decisions quickly'	42	19	17	6	7	21
Agree with the statement: 'It is more important for people to vote directly and frequently on issues rather than electing MPs every four years'	81	53	56	67	59	64
Agree with the statement: 'MPs are not sufficiently independent-minded or pro-initiative, and generally only follow party instructions'	88	81	83	80	88	84
N	(279)	(518)	(406)	(120)	(69)	(2000)

Source: Representative survey of the IFES (November–December 1997).

1996–99 term. This indicates that the policy distance between the FPÖ and the government parties has increased considerably. However, it also shows that the FPÖ and the government parties can agree on a considerable number of issues despite the fact that this is not necessary for passing legislation. According to a survey conducted among Members of the Austrian Parliament in the 1995–99 legislature, the policy distance between the ÖVP and FPÖ was smaller than between the coalition partners, the SPÖ and ÖVP, with respect to socioeconomic and sociocultural issues (Müller and Jenny 2000).

Table 9.7 Voting patterns in parliament, 1983–99 (% of enacted laws)

	Parliamentary term				
	XVI. *1983–86*	*XVII.* *1986–90*	*XVIII.* *1990–94*	*XIX.* *1994–96*	*XX.* *1996–99*
All party support	80	47	28	36	26
FPÖ included in voting majority	100	73	58	60	38
Government parties' support only	20	21	26	15	34

Source: The Austrian Parliament.

Conclusion: populism and liberal democracy

> In a democracy, the function of a politician is to find an issue on which he or she can win, for thereby a politician expresses some part of the values of the electorate. Political opportunism is not evil, therefore, but is instead the engine of democracy. (Riker 1982, 216)

Returning to the question of whether the populist strategy of the FPÖ is the evil that many of its critics suggest, or, alternatively, Riker's 'engine of democracy', given that the FPÖ 'expresses some part of the values of the electorate' both with respect to policy issues (particularly immigration) and aspects of the political decision-making process, Mény and Surel suggest that there is a tension between two sources of legitimacy in any democratic system: populist (or popular) input and constitutional democracy. This is a new way to frame a classical question of democratic theory, 'where are the limits of majority rule?', or, as Sartori put it, democracy 'is not pure and simple popular power', 'democracy is *not* unqualified (and thereby limitless) majority rule' (1987, 31). Respect for minority rights and the fulfilment of some minimum standards for public decision-making is part and parcel of democracy.

The FPÖ's political opponents have indeed claimed that its policy proposals conflict with those liberal values central to modern democracies. The Greens and the Liberals point to a clash between FPÖ demands and human rights. Other observers believe that the FPÖ's political style undermines respect for representative political institutions. Most interesting, however, is the position of the ÖVP parliamentary party leader, Andreas Khol, who in 1995 classified the FPÖ as having placed itself outside the constitutional spectrum (*'außerhalb des Verfassungsbogens'*) by demanding sweeping constitutional reform ('Third Republic'), by its rejection of EU membership, by the lack of a clear distance from Nazism, and by its 'violent language and revolutionary phraseology' (Khol 1995).

However, since this criticism comes from the FPÖ's political competitors or ideological opponents one may suspect some degree of self-interest. Khol, for instance, has managed to adapt his view of the FPÖ's position relative to the constitutional spectrum according to the political needs of his party. Whenever the ÖVP wanted to play the FPÖ card, the latter was defined as approaching the constitutional spectrum again. In 2000, when the ÖVP–FPÖ coalition was formed, Khol argued that the FPÖ had re-entered the constitutional spectrum by signing the preamble to the coalition agreement, which contained clear statements on Nazism and EU membership, and by pushing back demands for sweeping constitutional reform and using more civilised language. The fact that other parties have not changed their views as rapidly may owe more to tactics than to questions of principle.

The disinterested or non-ideological observer faces the problem that clear yardsticks are required in order to say whether there is a conflict between the policy proposals of a specific party and the values which make up constitutional democracy (see, for example, Beetham 1992). Martti Ahtisaari, Jochen Frowein and Marcelino Oreja used the international legal framework to establish such yardsticks. Applying them to the FPÖ, they expressed concerns about its use of the courts 'to suppress criticism wherever that criticism is expressed in strong terms' (what is both a criticism of the FPÖ's behaviour and the Austrian legal framework), and the 'very ambiguous language' of leading FPÖ politicians, including 'statements that can be interpreted to be xenophobic or even racist'. Although the three wise men did eventually classify the FPÖ as 'a right-wing populist party with extremist expressions', they did not rule out the possibility that the FPÖ could in the future develop into a 'responsible government party'. As I have argued above, such a transformation would require the FPÖ to abandon precisely the strategy responsible for its electoral breakthrough. Whether this will prove the case remains to be seen and will probably depend on the FPÖ's ability to find another winning strategy, and not least on the implications such a strategy would have for intra-party power relations, in particular the weight of the 'ordinary party member' as Jörg Haider now describes himself since stepping down as party chairman.

Notes

1. Support for the FPÖ rose from 5 per cent of the vote in 1983 to 26.9 per cent in 1999 (see Table 9.1).
2. In 1998, 59 per cent blamed foreigners for a rise in the crime rate, 47 per cent considered them a burden on the welfare state, 42 per cent thought that they compete with Austrians on the labour market, 46 per cent thought they caused problems on the housing market, and 40 per cent of respondents claimed that they increasingly felt like foreigners themselves due to the high number of foreign nationals living in Austria (Lebhart and Münz 1998, 22–3).
3. An IMAS survey of May 1992 showed that the term 'party' was among the words evoking the least degree of sympathy (12 per cent), and the highest degree of antipathy (32 per cent) (*IMAS Report,* No. 13, June 1992).
4. It should be noted FPÖ supporters tend to underdeclare their party preference.

Part III

Comparing National Cases

10
Popular Dissatisfaction with Democracy: Populism and Party Systems

Herbert Kitschelt

Introduction

Dissatisfaction with democratic institutions in well-developed post-industrial polities varies across countries and over time and is expressed in both conventional and unconventional forms of political participation. Some of this dissatisfaction is clearly related to the economic performance of contemporary democracies. Beyond the instrumental 'effectiveness' of democracies, however, their normative and procedural 'legitimacy' leaves an imprint on levels of democratic satisfaction. Where the quality of democratic procedures becomes a target, I will speak of 'populist' politics, and by 'populism' I understand an expression of dissatisfaction with existing modes of organised elite–mass political intermediation and the desire to abandon the intermediaries that stand between citizens and rulers. The ideal ruler should instead express some sort of 'volonté générale'. Citizens as 'principals' reject politicians and existing democratic institutions of representation empowered to serve as their 'agents' in the collective political decision-making process. Populism denotes a generalised distrust of principals toward their agents and populists call for the abolition of principal–agent relations in favour of a 'direct' and undistorted realisation of binding political decisions by the citizen-principals themselves. While this goal may be utopian (see, for example, Dahl 1956; Riker 1982), the populist aspiration manifests itself in many ways, one of which is the populist political party. This 'thin' procedural definition of populism, however, has nothing in common with substantive concepts of populism equating the phenomenon with anti-liberal market, protectionist economic and social policies (cf. Weyland 1999b).

Formally, populist politics in developed post-industrial capitalism have generally had a substantively anti-corporatist and anti-statist thrust. In the late 1990s, populist parties have generally added a xenophobic, particularist ethnocultural position on the immigration issue. There is an analytical difference, however, between parties designated New Radical Right (NRR), and populist anti-statist parties, both in terms of physiognomy and aetiology (see Kitschelt and McGann 1995, Chapters 1 and 2). The ideal-type of NRR party combines a commitment to greater market liberalism against redistributive policies and comprehensive welfare states, together with a socially and politically authoritarian and xenophobic agenda. Nonna Mayer's work on the French *Front national* (Mayer 1999) demonstrates how this combination of programmatic commitments relates to NRR parties throughout the 1990s, even though some observers have claimed that this issue combination no longer exists (see, for example, Schain 1997). NRR parties may place emphasis on job creation, but still rely on a neoliberal programme of deregulation and public spending cuts to achieve it. In terms of a socioeconomic coalition, NRR parties enjoy widespread support from the old petit bourgeoisie, which has been tranditionally hostile to the welfare state, and a young, predominantly male, blue-collar working class or lower white-collar employees unaffiliated to the traditional associations of socialist politics. The latter respond more to an authoritarian and xenophobic invitation than to neoliberal appeals. By contrast, highly educated professionals in the public or private service sector are under-represented in the NRR electorate. As the 'new entrepreneurialism' of the information age increasingly relies on self-employed professionals, the association of economic independence with preference for the NRR agenda disappears. Consequently, blue-collar and white-collar workers with a low level of education are over-represented in the NRR. The support for the extreme Right in these groups is a direct or indirect response to the failure of conventional Centre-Right or Centre-Left social democratic parties to adopt policies to reverse their declining economic fortunes, triggered by technological innovation and, to some extent, economic globalisation (Swank and Betz 2000). The NRR is equally a sociocultural phenomenon, expressing the fight against values and modes of social conduct usually associated with the highly educated: tolerance for different lifestyles and norms of personal conduct, active acceptance of different cultures, interest in deliberative, participatory modes of collective problem-solving, belief in gender equality in all social arenas, and a concern with ecology.

Anti-statist populists do not subscribe to the full agenda of the NRR and appeal to a broader social coalition. In programmatic terms, populist parties are mostly concerned with the public economy and the incestuous linkages between politicians, business, interest associations, and their societal constituencies. This predisposes populist parties towards market-liberal economic policies that undercut 'rent-seeking' political economic arrangements. The association of populist parties with a socioculturally authoritarian agenda is more coincidental. As a consequence of their broad anti-statism and less pronounced authoritarianism, populist parties bring together a broader socioeconomic support coalition than NRR parties. The most important difference between the two types of party is that the better-educated white-collar middle strata and professionals tend to be less under-represented in populist than in NRR parties. Educated professionals often embrace a market-liberal agenda directed against what may be perceived as a 'cartel' of established political parties (Katz and Mair 1995).

In terms of aetiology, both NRR and anti-statist populism require societal, economic and cultural conditions and a common strategic configuration of party systems. In both instances, the convergence between conventional moderate Left and Right parties opens up a space for unrepresented groups to opt for a new competitor. In this configuration, the costs of defection from established parties are slight, because the latter do not offer alternatives to voters. In an earlier publication, I argued that the emergence of an electorally successful NRR party, or an even more successful anti-statist populist party, depends primarily on the degree of convergence among conventional parties (Kitschelt and McGann 1995, 54–5). The greater the degree of convergence, the more voters are open to an anti-establishment appeal, and the greater the potential diversity of that electoral market, the more potentially diffuse the partisan appeal rallying such voters in programmatic terms. I also cited patronage politics in a rather loose conceptual sense, as a source of anti-statist, but not NRR populism (Kitschelt and McGann 1995, 25) and discussed clientelism and patronage as sources of the Austrian and Italian anti-statist populisms (Kitschelt and McGann 1995, 160–2). Nevertheless, clientelism is an ad hoc explanation. In the current analysis, I wish to focus on the contribution clientelist patterns of political exchange make to the uniqueness of anti-statist populist mobilisation.

Empirically, there is a continuum between NRR and populist parties. Observers often label both types of party 'extreme Right'. In Europe, however, traces of the populist momentum and logic inherent in a heterogeneous extreme Right sector are clearly detectable in Austria, Belgium, and Italy – precisely the three countries that have emerged from the strongest clientelist and patronage based political-economic systems.

Another country characterised by clientelism and a decline in conventional politics, but not by a rise of an anti-statist populist party, is Japan. Because Japan has a unique set of conditions that make it difficult to mobilise a new party, it is not dealt with in detail in the current analysis.

My analysis proceeds in four steps. First, I will demonstrate that sources of dissatisfaction with democracy in the early 1990s, when many of the new extreme Rightist parties emerged, were not purely economic and that political institutions must also be taken into account. Second, I will review the degree of anti-statist populism in political parties. Third, I will discuss the mechanisms that link clientelism to the rise of anti-statist populism. Finally, I will consider the possible limits to anti-statist populist mobilisation.

Sources of dissatisfaction with democratic institutions

In western democracies, there is an almost uniform support for basic democratic values, such as individual civil rights and liberties or political participation in the choice of representatives and rulers through universal suffrage (Dalton 1999; Klingemann 1999), but support for democratic institutions suffers when economic performance declines, particularly in established democracies. Over time, however, good performance may translate into a generalised belief in the 'legitimacy' of democracy and democratic institutions that is at least partially detached from day-to-day economic performance (Lipset 1963). What this model neglects, however, is the quality of democratic rules of interest intermediation as an independent element of legitimacy and support. Rules perceived as bad will exaggerate the influence of weak economic performance on democratic institutions, while rules perceived as good may have the reverse effect. When good rules are in place, weak economic performance indicates that politicians, as voter agents, are incapable of delivering on their promises. If the rules are considered bad, citizens may suspect that politicians lack the incentive to fulfil the promises that they have made. In the 1970s and 1980s, increasing numbers of citizens in Austria, Belgium, Italy and Japan have interpreted clientelist linkages between citizens and politicians as bad and these countries witnessed a rapid decline in support for democratic institutions until the early 1990s.

As an empirical illustration of that dynamic, let us compare citizens' trust in legislative institutions according to the second World Values Survey of 1990 (Table 10.1). The data was collected at a time when right-wing parties in the NRR and anti-statist populism were experienc-

Table 10.1 Popular satisfaction with legislative institutions in 14 advanced post-industrializing democracies in 1990 (%)

	Type of party system		
	Two-party or two-bloc competition	*Multi-party competition*	*Multi-party democratic competition with clientelistic linkages*
Severity of unemployment			
Light unemployment (national average below 8% of labour force)	Ireland: 50 United Kingdom: 46 United States: 47	Germany: 51 Netherlands: 52 Norway: 59 Sweden: 47	Austria: 41 Japan: 29
Severe unemployment (national average over 8% of labour force)	France: 48	Finland: 34	Belgium: 43 Italy: 32

ing a steep upward trajectory. As a result of economic performance, a low level of trust in legislatures should occur more in those countries with clientelist politics, prompting the rise of anti-statist populist party. Indeed, there is a rather large effect of unemployment on institutional trust, so that satisfaction with legislative institutions averages 46 per cent in low unemployment countries, as opposed to just over 39 per cent in high unemployment countries (see Table 10.1).

However, three of the four countries with clientelist party politics reveal below-average levels of satisfaction with comparable levels of unemployment. The effects of clientelist politics are most pronounced in Japan and Italy, with satisfaction rates of 17 per cent or 7 per cent below the group average, followed by Austria at 5 per cent below. Austria and Japan are outliers, even though their unemployment rates are low even by the standard of the light unemployment country cohort. Only Belgium reveals levels of popular satisfaction with legislatures slightly higher than the presence of clientelism would lead us to expect (+4 per cent). However, we must bear in mind that the challenges to established party politics started earliest in Belgium (in the early 1960s), and that patterns of clientelism in party politics are somewhat less clear-cut there than in the other three countries examined.

Other than clientelism, different configurations of party competition do not appear to effect levels of popular satisfaction with legislatures (see Table 10.1). One could argue, for example, that satisfaction should be higher in legislatures with two parties, or at least clear government and opposition blocs, because citizens can assign responsibility for economic performance more straightforwardly than in multi-party systems (Lewis-Beck 1988; Anderson 2000). I will go on to refine the analysis with regard to the dependent and independent variables starting with a examination of the nature of radical rightist parties in order to identify those with a populist appeal (the dependent variable), before characterising clientelism and discussing the political dynamics that makes clientelism controversial, as evidenced by the rise of anti-statist populism.

The New Radical Right and anti-statist populist parties

The parties that qualify most unequivocally as anti-statist populist are the Austrian Freedom Party (FPÖ) and the Italian *Lega Nord*, particularly during their period of spectacular take-off in the late 1980s and early 1990s (Kitschelt and McGann 1995, Chapter 5), since which time both have changed their character in ways which relate to the dynamics of party competition in each country. When Jörg Haider took over the FPÖ leadership the party took a radical turn against the grand coalition government and its clientelist practices in nationalised industries, housing, and public-sector employment. Given the depth of penetration of patronage in the Austrian political economy (Müller 1989), Haider's appeal proved hugely successful. Even though his anti-clientelist campaign had some distinctly anti-Semitic overtones, the broad political reform agenda attracted a heterogeneous constituency of citizens. Socioeconomic groups and strata were represented in a balanced fashion and party supporters did not nurture particularly authoritarian preferences on issues such as gender politics, law and order, or environmentalism. When Haider grafted xenophobic anti-immigrant slogans onto this anti-statist populist appeal, his cross-class support did not decline, but instead won him an additional increment of ex-social democrat working-class voters (Betz 1998b; Riedlsperger 1998).

The Italian *Lega Nord* and its precursors also gained momentum as an anti-clientelist party with strength in those regions of Northern Italy depicted by Bossi as the net fiscal financier of the clientelist networks which were particularly strong in Southern Italy. But whilst the anti-immigrant appeal has played a role in Bossi's rhetoric at different points in time, it has never clouded the party's principal message – that is, that the political establishment is corrupt and unaccountable. With the demise of the two main governing parties of the post-war Italian party system, the Christian Democrats and the Socialists, and the transformation of the major opposition party, the Communists, *Lega Nord*'s thunder has been partially stolen by the successor parties and Bossi has had to engage in some intricate manoeuvring to maintain the support of his own party between the emerging Centre-Right and Centre-Left blocs. There are few indications, however, that Bossi incorporated elements of the New Right discourse into that process.

A rejection of the clientelist network politics played out by the established Christian Democratic, Liberal, and Socialist parties was also the initial appeal of the *Vlaams Blok* in Flanders whose electoral fortunes began to improve dramatically in the late 1980s. Swyngedouw (1998a) shows how patronage-related municipal scandals in its stronghold Antwerp enabled party leaders to present the local party establishment as a self-serving elite that impoverished Flemish citizens and taxpayers through public waste and fraud. At the same time, from the outset the *Vlaams Blok* embraced a xenophobic anti-immigrant stance together with other sociocultural authoritarian themes of the NRR that show up in the profile of its voter support (Swyngedouw 1998a, 1998b; Billiet and De Witte 1995). The *Vlaams Blok* has always represented a hybrid of NRR and anti-statist populist appeal, complicated by a legacy of fascism and pro-Nazism rooted in the German occupation, and a militant rejection of Walloon domination of Belgium (Mudde 1995). In Wallonia, for reasons which will be discussed in the next section, both NRR and populist rightist parties had a much harder time taking off in the 1980s and 1990s and remained subdued until the turn of the millennium.

In other European countries, we encounter NRR parties more than anti-statist populism. In the Danish or Norwegian Progress Parties, the French *Front national*, or the Swiss right-wing parties of the 1980s and 1990s – particularly the Swiss *Autopartei*, later succeeded by the Swiss Freedom Party (Gentile and Kriesi 1998) – we find a right-wing market economics appeal, combined with socio-cultural authoritarianism, that generates an electoral coalition with an over-representation of the petit bourgeoisie, particularly blue-collar workers. In another set of countries, as in the young and economically less well-developed Southern European democracies (Greece, Portugal, Spain), and the older democracies such as Britain, the Netherlands, Sweden and Germany, neither anti-statist populists nor NNR parties have had any lasting success.

In a similar vein, in the democracies founded by European settlers, none of the new parties can be characterised as either NRR or anti-statist populist. In Canada, regionalism overpowers other divides. In Canada Preston Manning's Reform Party is populist in the sense that it calls for unmediated direct democracy, bypassing existing elites (Barney and Laycock 1999), and has some market-liberal, authoritarian sociocultural overtones (Nevitt et al. 1998), but in fact it is primarily a backlash against the mobilisation of Francophone Eastern Canada around the *Parti Québécois*, precipitating a net transfer of resources from Western Canada to Quebec. Even further removed from the NRR or anti-statist populist syndrome in Europe is the New Zealand First Party which spearheaded multiculturalism in championing the cause of the underprivileged Maori minority, and in defending the welfare state against the social retrenchment of Labour and National Party governments. In the United States, new rightist and anti-statist populist figures have appeared at the fringes of the two major parties, such as Pat Buchanan within and outside the Republicans (since 2000), and Lyndon LaRouche as a candidate in the Democratic primaries.

The aetiology of anti-statist populist success

I have already highlighted the importance of a programmatic convergence between the dominant moderate parties on the Left and Right parties around a comprehensive welfare state as a precipitating condition for the rise of NRR and anti-statist populist parties in my earlier work (Kitschelt and McGann 1995, see especially Chapter 2). Where this convergence makes the dominant parties almost indistinguishable from one another, political entrepreneurs can build anti-statist populist challenging parties that attract broader electoral coalitions than NRR parties. For this reason, the Italian *Lega Nord* and the Austrian Freedom Party were much more successful electorally than their NRR counterparts in Denmark, France, Norway or Switzerland before 1999. I will return later to the recent change of the Swiss party system in the 1999 elections. In the current analysis I will add another condition that explains the strong mobilisation of right-wing populism and accounts for the convergence between established parties in Austria, Italy, and partly in Belgium: clientelist voter–politician linkage strategies and their demise in the 1990s. After a general outline of the logic that links clientelism in post-industrial democracies to the rise of anti-statist populism, I will return to the comparison of individual cases.

In many democracies clientelist politics have constituted a well-worn technique of political exchange which has lasted for decades, if not centuries. This takes the form of politicians' accountability and responsiveness to their electorates, and is dismissed by normative democratic theory as a deficient, particularistic form of political conduct. Indeed, clientelism subordinates democratic politics to an economic power structure which involves the 'buying' and 'selling' votes for favours and reveals the fiction of citizenship equality, based on the fundamental rule of 'one person, one vote' that has long buttressed the legitimacy of democratic institutions. But the mere existence of clientelist network politics in well-developed post-industrialising democracies does not explain the demise of established parties and the rise of anti-statist populism. We must instead identify the specific mechanisms that precipitate the defection of large numbers of citizens from well-established political linkage practices at a particular moment in time (Kitschelt 2000).

Programmatic political parties promise voters indirect compensation for their electoral support. Contingent upon the party's strength in legislatures and executives, its politicians will enact policies that implement commitments made in the run-up to elections. These policies affect the costs and benefits of all citizens, irrespective of whether or not they voted for the governing party. This leaves room for 'free-riding' and means that programmatic parties only compensate voters indirectly due to the long-term causal chain between the act of voting and the ultimate policy results.

By contrast, clientelist parties compensate strategic voter constituencies directly for their support through pre-electoral incentives and post-electoral rewards. These take the form of gifts, monetary payments, public housing, public contracts or favourable regulatory decisions, and, most importantly, patronage politics in the form of civil service jobs. At least two types of clientelist exchanges typically work together. Resource-rich but vote-poor electoral constituencies provide financial support to electoral candidates in exchange for business favours once politicians have been elected (exchange circuit 1), and politicians employ the acquired funds in order to provide material advantages for resource-poor, but vote-rich mass electorates (exchange circuit 2). In the wake of elections, the politicians and parties which obtain leverage in the government executive employ public resources (such as jobs and housing) to reward supporters for their loyalty. Benefits accrue directly to specific individuals and small groups ('clients') known to support identifiable politicians and party machines ('patrons'). Techniques making voting ballots semi-public and party organisation, allow participants to monitor and enforce specific exchanges.

Most observers agree that clientelist practices are deeply entrenched in Austrian, Belgian, Japanese, and Italian politics and that techniques such as linkage-building were consolidated in the early post-war period. In all four countries clientelism is accompanied by deep penetration of the civil service by partisan appointments (patronage politics), and corresponding patterns of appointment in public or publicly regulated enterprises. The dominant parties are surrounded by an array of closely linked non-profit interest groups and quasi-public agencies such as chambers of commerce, health and unemployment insurance companies, and welfare associations to which public tasks are delegated, and tax resources allocated. Again, employment and promotion in the public sector depends on citizens' affiliation to a party 'pillar' and, in the cases of Austria and Belgium, access to subsidised public housing has been a major technique employed by parties to reinforce clientelist linkages.

The question then is why citizens and the mass media began to redefine the clientelist political-economic practices of citizen–elite linkage-building as a 'scandalous' and inherently problematic issue in the 1980s and 1990s. All four countries are evolved post-industrial democracies, and thus a developmentalist, modernisation theory cannot account for this sudden shift in recent decades (with the partial exception of Italy, where the North is more developed than the South; see Gobetti 1996). In addition, a historical legacy argument about the timing of bureaucratic professionalisation and universal suffrage does not apply (Shefter 1994). Both Austria and Japan had core bureaucratic institutions handed down from a quasi-absolutist state apparatus before democratisation and, according to Shefter, should never have become clientelist in the first place. Changes in electoral systems do not explain the challenge to clientelism in developed post-industrial democracies. First, the four countries have very different electoral systems, each of which has proved compatible with clientelist citizen–party linkages. Personality-based electoral systems coincided with the rise of clientelism in Italy (Katz 1980), and Japan (Ramseyer and Rosenbluth 1993), but not in Austria and Belgium. In Japan, clientelism was a problem before the reform of the electoral system and the new system does not appear to seriously inhibit clientelist practices (Rosenbluth 1996; see also McKean and Scheiner 1996). Furthermore, arguments about growing trade exposure making the maintenance of rent-seeking protectionist coalitions more costly (Rogowski 1987) cannot account for the demise of clientelism in our four countries, as well as a comparison of citizen–elite linkage practices across a broader set of developed post-industrial democracies. Austria and Belgium have always had a high degree of trade exposure, and so should theoretically never have developed clientelist politics (Katzenstein 1985).

Let me now propose an alternative political-economic theory of clientelist decline. In all four countries the post-industrial technological revolution has meant that those economic governance structures in public and private enterprise that generated the resources necessary to compensate economic losers and rent-seekers through clientelist arrangements have become less efficient. Leading national sectors that created domestic wealth and international competitiveness have declined. With the partial exception of Italy, these countries are characterised by institutions of co-operative market capitalism (Soskice 1999) that promote competitiveness among industries thriving on incremental innovation, long-term employment, and durable interlocking horizontal business and financial partnerships. By contrast, the current technological environment rewards firms in industrial and service sectors characterised by high employment flexibility, the mobilisation of venture capital, and continuous holistic innovations. The four countries thus face the imperative of restructuring their corporate and industrial relations institutions in order to take full advantage of these new opportunities and/or to find market niches in which they can profitably survive.

As a consequence, and given the pressure to adjust and restructure, a large part of the workforce in all four countries is finding the 'task' of sustaining those clientelistic practices which constitute the core of their country's democratic politics increasingly burdensome. Whether we examine large Japanese automobile and electronics companies, the 'Third Italy' (Gobetti 1996), or Austrian and Belgian engineering conglomerates, changes in production techniques and markets have eroded profitability and employment opportunities to the point that leading sectors generate ever less slack, thus increasing the burden of supporting rent-seeking clientelist political-economic linkage systems. The pressure to 'liberalise' governance structures, induced by domestic or international competition, raises the level of political controversy over rent-seeking clientelism that devours scarce resources in an environment characterised by rising unemployment and vanishing job opportunities.

The controversy over the societal costs of clientelism is amplified by a further factor: that of demography. All four countries face a fundamental demographic transition where a shrinking share of the population is gainfully employed and has to generate the resources to maintain 'pay-as-you-go' pension systems for a growing proportion of the population in retirement. Germany, Italy, and Japan have, or soon will have, the worst dependency ratio, that is, the highest ratio of retired people to gainfully employed, among all OECD countries. Their pension systems have incurred commitments that are extremely difficult to finance in an environment of low economic growth, leading to an increased fiscal pressure caused by the substantial overhead costs of a clientelist polity with powerful rent-seeking constituencies.

In this context, anti-statist populism strikes a chord with a large proportion of the gainfully employed population not employed in the public or quasi-public sector which has been propped up by clientelist practices. The combination of changing modes of production and demographic trends means that private-sector employers, employees and professionals demand political institutions of resource allocation that help a limited group of rent-seekers. Nowhere else in the western hemisphere have the economic privileges of rent-seekers and their associated politicians appeared so blatant and outrageous to average citizens as in the four countries considered here. The core of the problem that destabilises clientelism in developed post-industrialising democracies is thus a political-economic one rooted in technology and demography, but one which must be distinguished from a shallow notion of the impact of 'globalisation' on national economies, as indicated by the very different patterns of trade and international capital market exposure in Austria, Belgium, Italy and Japan.

Let us now re-examine the cases comparatively. In the post-war period strong clientelism has been a necessary, but not sufficient, condition for the decline of established democratic political parties (see Table 10.2). For our purposes it is irrelevant to know how the decline is distributed among established parties, but important to establish where the decline has created a vacuum subsequently filled by new competitors, and the character of those competitors.

The greatest decline in the electoral fortunes of establishment parties occurred in those countries where clientelism was most strongly entrenched (Table 10.2, Group A). Austria and Italy developed strong anti-statist populist parties filling some (Italy), or most (Austria), of the void left by the retraction of established parties. In Japan, the implosion of the Liberal Democrats and the Socialist Party left a vacuum which neither existing nor new parties have been able to fill permanently. Finally, Belgium is a borderline case with an NRR-anti-statist populist hybrid, alongside a range of other new parties, such as ethnoregional parties and Left-libertarians that preceded the *Vlaams Blok*. The penetration of anti-statist populism in Wallonia, in particular, has been contained by the fact that the province is the net beneficiary of cross-regional resource flows and not even populist politicians can risk going against regional economic self-interest. Moreover, the temporary polarisation of Belgian politics between Socialists and the Christian Democratic–Liberal coalition in the 1980s undercut populist mobilisation, especially in Wallonia, where there is a more militant socialist party.

There was a marked decline of the established parties – not commonly perceived as clientelist – in the countries in Group B (see Table 10.2). Consistent with my argument, in at least two cases (Canada, New Zealand), the successful new challengers cannot be characterised as anti-statist populist. Switzerland is a different matter. If we exclude the Swiss People's Party (*Schweizer Volkspartei*, SVP), the decline of conventional parties has been limited and mostly confined to Left-libertarian parties and Right-authoritarian NRR parties, precipitated by a convergence of the established parties. This situation changed in the run-up to the 1999 elections when one of the established parties, headed by a fiery local leader from Zurich, who embraced an anti-

Table 10.2 Performance of incumbent parties from the 1960s until latest election in the 1990s (% votes cast)

	1960–69 average performance	*Post-1995 performance*	*Change in performance*
Group A: Clientelistic polities			
Austria	96.4	60.1 (1999)	–36.3
Belgium	91.7	69.7 (1999)	–22.0
Italy	95.0	45.4 (1996)	–49.6
Japan	90.9	52.2 (1996)	–38.7
Group average	93.5	56.9	–36.6
Group B: Demise of established parties without clientelism			
Canada	90.1	68.3 (1997)	–21.8
New Zealand	99.1	62.0 (1997)	–37.1
Switzerland	90.6	80.8 [57.4] (1999)	–9.8 [-33.2]
Group average	93.3	70.4 [62.6]	–22.9 [-30.7]
Group C: Non-clientelistic democracies with strong NRR mobilisation			
Denmark	93.8	78.2 (1998)	–15.6
France	92.7	67.6 (1997)	–25.1
Norway	90.6	75.4 (1997)	–15.2
Group average	92.4	73.7	18.7
Group D: Non-clientelistic democracies without a strong New Right			
Australia	97.8	85.6 (1996)	–12.2
Finland	94.3	82.3 (1999)	–12.0
Germany	95.1	85.0 (1998)	–10.1
Netherlands	85.4	81.1 (1998)	–4.3
Sweden	93.2	81.1 (1998)	–12.1
UK	88.7	73.9 (1997)	–13.8
US	95.0	90.2 (1996)	–4.8
Group average	92.8	82.7	–10.1

Note:
See Table 10.3 for a list of the individual parties examined.

statist, populist appeal with a sufficient dosage of anti-immigrant rhetoric, pre-empted not only the NRR parties, but also attracted support from the Swiss mainstream. Swiss politics cannot be characterised as clientelist. Moreover, while Swiss politics represent an extreme convergence between the main parties, manifested by a permanent all-party government, the existence of direct democratic channels had so far pre-empted a populist challenge to Swiss democratic institutions (Gentile and Kriesi 1998, 129–31). For the time being, the SVP constitutes an amalgamation of its conventional centrist electorate, strands of the NRR constituency, and populists opposing the all-party government. It remains to be seen, however, exactly how the new party leadership will resolve the strategic dilemmas posed by the party's new electoral coalition. A further complication is the fact that the SVP is a government party and thus has limited opportunities to dissociate itself from the political establishment.

Countries in group C of Table 10.2 are those where convergence and power alternation between moderate leftist and rightist parties in the 1980s, sometimes coinciding with the existence of strong Left-libertarian parties, contributed to the rise of NRR parties. Finally, countries in group D have not experienced strong NRR nor anti-statist populist parties. In most of these countries, the convergence between conventional Left and Right was not sufficiently well-developed to trigger the defection of a large number of NRR or anti-statist populist voters. In some cases, such as Germany and Sweden, incipient NRR parties failed to adopt the 'winning' market-liberal and authoritarian formula of political appeals and therefore did not make big inroads in the electoral marketplace. Table 10.3 lists the parties counted as '1960s' incumbents' in this analysis.

The limits of anti-statist populist politics

Throughout the 1990s, anti-statist populist parties in Austria, Belgium and Italy attracted up to a quarter of the electorate and sustained political parties thriving on the critique of clientelism. However, there are reasons to believe that the potential mobilisation of anti-statist populists may be approaching its ceiling and it is far from certain that such parties will stay in power in the national systems of party competition. Most importantly, there is the risk that such parties only thrive when in opposition, and that once in government their attempts to dismantle clientelism or to introduce market-liberalising reforms will antagonise some of their followers – particularly those who may have voted for them on the basis of their anti-immigrant rhetoric.

Taking Austria as an example, the grand coalition of the People's Party and Social Democrats was a gift for Jörg Haider's Freedom Party, but one which disappeared once the FPÖ became a coalition partner with the Christian Democrats. The antagonistic position of the European Union *vis-à-vis* the new Austrian government did indeed have a rallying effect temporarily boosting Haider's support, but with market-liberal reforms and a toning down of the EU's stance, internal divisions may well open up within the anti-statist populist support coalition. In a way, this dynamic was foreshadowed by Umberto Bossi's brief interlude in government in the mid-1990s. Once in government, anti-statist populists, such as the *Lega Nord*, are immediately faced with difficult policy

Table 10.3 Parties counted as '1960s' incumbents'

Australia:	Labour, Liberals, Nationals, Democratic Labour;
Austria:	People's Party and Social Democrats, Freedom Party only in the 1960s;
Belgium:	Liberals, Christian Democrats, Socialists and Flemish People's Union;
Canada:	Progressive Conservatives, Liberals, New Democrats;
Denmark:	Conservatives, Liberals, Radicals, Social Democrats, Socialist People's Party;
Finland:	National Coalition, Swedish People's Party, Liberals, Agrarians, Social Democrats and Communists;
France:	Gaullists, Independent Republicans, Socialists and Allies, Communists;
Germany:	Christian Democrats, Social Democrats, and Free Democrats;
Italy:	Italian Social Movement, Christian Democrats, Liberals, Social Democrats, Socialists and Communists;
Japan:	Liberal Democrats, Socialists, Communists, Komeito;
Netherlands:	Religious Parties later combined in the Christian Democratic Appeal, United Freedom Party, Democrats '66 and Labour Party;
New Zealand:	Labour, National, Social Credit;
Norway:	Conservatives, Liberals, Center Christian People's, Labour, Left Socialists;
Sweden:	Conservatives, Liberals, Center, and Social Democrats;
Switzerland:	Catholics, Radicals/Liberals, Swiss People's Party, Independents, Social Democrats (bracket figures in Table 10.2 exlude the Swiss People's Party)
United Kingdom:	Conservatives and Labour Party;
United States:	Democrats, Republicans

choices which generate disillusion among supporters as to their ability to engineer a fundamental reform of the existing political system.

In political economy terms, the populist Right usually sides with supply-side market liberalism to fight unemployment, pursuing policies reminiscent of the infamous Laffer curve invoked in the United States in the early years of the Reagan administration – that is, the belief that a drastic tax cut will redirect funds to private investment and consequently cut unemployment and expand the volume of state revenue, at lower rates of taxation, sufficiently rapidly to pre-empt large public-sector deficits. The Laffer curve is the economic equivalent of the crock of gold at the rainbow's end: the chimera that social-democratic ends (full employment) can be obtained painlessly through market-liberal means (tax cuts for investors and high-income-earners). Because of the limited operational objectives of anti-statist populism in social and economic policies, it is unlikely to appeal to a majority of voters. Nevertheless, such parties may act as catalysts in helping neoliberal economic forces engineer a liberalisation of co-operative market economies. It is unlikely, however, that anti-statist populist parties will survive the resulting protracted transitional pains because many members of their core electoral constituencies, particularly those belonging to the marginal groups of young unskilled or semi-skilled blue-collar workers and white-collar employees, would be materially disadvantaged by such policies. The anti-statist populism, directed against clientelist linkage practices, allows parties to become 'catch-all' enterprises. But this construct breaks down as soon as economic policy-making forces party leaders to make hard choices that benefit some constituents and penalise many others.

In addition to the substantive political-economic limitations of anti-statist populism, its organisational structure and anti-institutional appeal impose a ceiling on its success. The critique of principal–agent relations in existing representative democracies corresponds to a populist party structure where a charismatic leader towers above party activists and reduces intermediary levels of party functionaries and regional leaders to insignificance. This 'charismatic populism' (Schedler 1996) increases the programmatic flexibility of parties, because leaders can 'reinvent' their substantive appeals contingent upon the exigencies of the situation. In this sense, it was easy for the likes of Haider or Bossi to inject elements of xenophobia and racism into the anti-statist message of their parties when such appeals became popular in the late 1980s. At the same time, the lack of institutionalisation of preference aggregation and organised interest intermediation within such parties creates all the problems of a 'routinisation' of leadership charisma indicated by Max Weber many decades ago. In the last instance leaders can only maintain the loyalty of their followers by substantive direct material (clientelist) exchange relations or the promise of an indirect (programmatic) exchange, where the party manages to participate in government, and not by the impact of their personality, however electrifying it may be. The construction of clientelist linkages is, by definition, inconsistent with the message of anti-statist populist parties, although it does not necessarily prevent their leaders from engaging in unrestrained patronage politics once in office. Furthermore, the programmatic formulation of the parties' commitments yields to political-economic dilemmas and trade-offs when some of the parties' constituencies prefer market liberalism while others oppose it. The chances are, therefore, that anti-statist populism is itself a transitional phenomenon that compels politicians in established parties to abandon traditional linkage strategies and to move on to what Dutch political scientists have described as a 'de-pillarisation' of politics. The disappearance of clientelist practices may well put anti-statist populists out of political business, or alternatively force them to transform themselves into parties of the New Radical Right with a more focused and narrower electoral constituency.

Conclusion

This, arguably rather speculative, analysis does not attempt to offer an explanation of populism in general insofar as I believe that no one theory can account for populist mobilisation in the formal sense of offering a critique of established political interest intermediation relying on principal–agent networks, with a single parsimonious set of arguments applicable to all concrete institutional and socioeconomic conditions. Neither does this analysis offer a general treatment of 'populism' in developed post-industrialising democracies. The anti-establishment parties in Austria, Belgium and Italy have a rather different character to those to be found in Canada or New Zealand, and both sets of cases cannot be accounted for in terms of the same theoretical argument.

Social theorists may be divided into 'lumpers' and 'splitters'. The first propose general parsimonious explanations for broad classes of phenomena, regardless of the reckless simplification required by such a strategy, whereas splitters prefer to treat each case as unique and are sceptical of parsimonious explanations, regardless of the loss of theoretical generality which this approach entails. Whilst I have great respect for lumpers and normally side with them because of their use of elegant and powerful general constructs that are insightful, even if individual cases do not always fit, in this chapter I tend to endorse the splitters. I do not believe there is much point in vague and generalised theorising about 'rightist' and 'populist' currents in developed post-industrialising democracies, or even about a general and popular decline of trust in or disenchantment with the institutions of representative democracy. I do believe, instead, that we need to examine the theoretically salient diversity among individual instances of 'populism' and, more generally, challenges to representative democracy. In the causal analysis of populism I propose treating the Austrian, Belgian and Italian anti-statist populists as a separate set of cases: Japan may be included in the set if and when its anti-statist populists overcome the unique obstacles currently blocking their electoral take-off.

11

Conditions Favouring the Success and Failure of Radical Right-Wing Populist Parties in Contemporary Democracies

Hans-Georg Betz

Introduction

One of the most important political developments in established capitalist democracies during the past two decades has been the mobilisation of popular support for parties on the far right of the political spectrum. The electoral gains of the Austrian Freedom Party (FPÖ) and Christoph Blocher's *Schweizer Volkspartei* in national elections, together with the showing of the *Vlaams Blok* in the 1999 European elections, suggests that rise of radical right-wing politics is more than a political flash in the pan. The fortunes of right-wing radical parties have, however, been mixed insofar as parties in Austria, Switzerland, Belgium, Norway, Denmark and Canada have done relatively well at the polls, whereas those in Italy, Germany, Sweden, Australia and New Zealand have fared rather badly. The electoral performance of New Zealand First is a case in point. Established in summer 1993, it won 8.4 per cent in the national election later that year, and its level of support rose to 13.4 per cent three years later.[1] However, this success was short-lived, and in the 1999 national elections, the party gained a mere 4.3 per cent of the vote and returned to parliament only because its leader, Winston Peters, narrowly managed to win his seat. In much the same way, the German *Republikaner*, Sweden's *Ny Demokrati*, and the Swiss Freedom Party (formerly the *Autopartei*) have seen a drop in their support, although, as the electoral history of the Scandinavian Progress parties demonstrates, a dramatic decline in electoral support does not necessarily mean political extinction.

Given the uneven electoral fortunes of radical right-wing parties in recent years, it is important to detect what factors determine their popular support not only initially but also over time insofar as a voter may initially vote for a new party out of curiosity or as an act of protest, but subsequently become disenchanted and no longer vote for it.

Despite the chequered electoral history of individual parties, radical right-wing parties, such as the French *Front national*, the *Vlaams Blok*, or the Scandinavian Progress parties, have generally been among the most successful new parties to emerge in established democracies in recent decades (Betz and Immerfall 1998). Undoubtedly, one of the main reasons for their initial success has been the strong populist stance adopted by almost all these parties in their attempt to attract popular interest and support. This fails to account, however, for changes in party fortunes over time and, more specifically, it does not help us to understand why some radical right-wing parties have gradually built up a loyal voter base, whilst others failed to retain their supporters and have faded away. In what follows, I will argue that a rational voter model may prove more suitable in explaining the divergent fortunes of right-wing radical populist parties after their initial breakthrough. In such an analysis, continuous voter support is seen to depends on whether or not a party manages to deliver politically, which in turn has important implications for the organisational structure of these parties and their programmatic development.

The populist appeal

The majority of radical right-wing parties that emerged during the past two decades in established capitalist democracies differ from other parties in their populist appeal. In its most essential form populism can be defined as 'a style of political rhetoric' (Kazin 1995, 3) designed to mobilise ordinary people as a political force against 'the established structure of power and the dominant ideas and values of the society', with the intention of devaluing the latter as the basis of political legitimacy, and replacing them with the 'common sense of the ordinary people' as a new basis for political legitimacy (Canovan 1999, 3). This suggests that populism is primarily a political strategy, whose political rhetoric is the evocation of latent grievances and the appeal to emotions provoked by them, rather than an ideology.

Populist rhetoric is designed to tap feelings of *ressentiment* and exploit them politically. And for good reason, insofar as *ressentiment* is an emotion characterised, above all, by its 'concern and involvement with power' (Solomon 1994, 103). Max Scheler has defined *ressentiment* as a 'psychic mechanism' based on the experience of individual inferiority and/or weakness (Scheler 1992; see also Bittner 1994). It is 'typically a reaction to an injury or slight' (intended or not) frequently reflecting an 'overwhelming sense of injustice' (Solomon 1994, 103), and 'an oppressive sense of inferiority' (Scheler 1992, 26). But *ressentiment* goes beyond the mere awareness or recognition of injury and actively seeks outlets for personal outrage and the attribution of blame and ways to gain redress, even if in reality this often ends up as little more than 'frustrated fantasies of revenge' (Solomon 1994, 102).

One reason for the success of contemporary radical right-wing parties is that they have promoted themselves as vehicles for the effective expression of popular frustration and have forced the political establishment to listen to their demands. It is no coincidence that these parties became popular at a time when there was a dramatic rise in public disenchantment with traditional parties, political leadership, the political process, and even the way democracy works in developed democracies. In this sense, the populist strategy has been to claim to be the spokesmen for the unarticulated opinions, demands, and sentiments of ordinary people, to give them voice and, as a well-known *Front national* slogan put it, to 'return the word to the people' (*rendre la parole au peuple*). Behind this claim is the implicit accusation that ordinary people, despite their moral superiority and innate common sense, are denied the opportunity to make themselves heard or worse, do not dare to speak their minds. This was the message behind Jörg Haider's 1994 election slogan that claimed 'He says what we [only dare] think'.

Following the populist logic, most contemporary radical right-wing parties reject intermediate institutions in favour of a, direct relationship between the people and its leaders, based on mutual trust and heavily reliant on plebiscitary mechanisms, such as referenda and popular initiatives, but also the direct election of executive organs, such as mayors and governors. Such measures are meant to provide citizens with more effective opportunities for input and control and a sense of being taken seriously. As the Austrian Freedom Party (FPÖ) put it, the goal is to transform the existing elite-dominated party state into a true 'citizens' democracy' and thus bring about a 'society of freedom' in which 'the rights of the people are respected' (Freiheitliche Akademie n.d., 7).

Mobilising *ressentiments*

In common with all political parties, radical right-wing populist parties try to gain political influence and power, but unlike most established parties, they do so by using a strategy designed to corrode the legitimacy of the established political and ruling elites to represent the people, to speak on their behalf, and to make decisions affecting their lives. As Margaret Canovan (1999) has noted, the core of the populist political strategy of the Radical Right strategy is to challenge 'not only established power-holders but also elite values' in order to devalue them as the basis of political legitimacy. To achieve their goals, populists rely heavily on rhetorical devices that establish them as being 'of the people but not of the system' (Taggart 1996, 32), and thus in a position to speak for the people. This strategy is designed to mobilise people to act politically by appealing to grievances and *ressentiments*, but in order for it to work the conditions must allow these rather diffuse and latent sentiments to take a more concrete form.

It is often argued that since radical right-wing parties are generally apposed to immigration, their success is largely a result of their ability to seize an issue that has become a key political question in most prosperous countries throughout the world. Whilst there is much to support this view, it fails to explain the initial success of many of these parties, which only discovered the 'foreigner issue' after having gained a discrete level of support at the polls. Indeed, a closer look at the initial phase of mobilisation reveals that radical right-wing populist parties tried to appeal to select, and often country-specific, instances of popular *ressentiments*.

A case in point is the German *Republikaner*, which initially marketed itself as the advocate of a new German identity and German unification. In the 1980s, the party's primary goal was the restoration of national self-esteem and German popular pride. In addition to the established German political parties, the *Republikaner* also attached the winners of the Second World War, whose interpretation of the Nazi period had shaped the way Germans think of themselves and their history. One of the party's major political demands at the time was to 'decriminalise' German history by rewriting it in such way that it could no longer be simply reduced to the image of Auschwitz. With these claims, the *Republikaner* tried to tap the widespread *ressentiments* associated with *Vergangenheitsbewältigung* 'confronting the past', suggesting that Germany should 'to put the past to rest', 'historicise' its Nazi legacy, and become a normal country again. This argument played a significant role in the public debate in the late 1980s (Betz 1988, 127–57). Although it is difficult to say whether the *Republikaner* would have become a significant factor in German politics had the Berlin Wall not come down in 1989, it is clear that unification certainly deprived the *Republikaner* of its central issue and partly explains the party's virtual collapse in the wake of this event.

Similar observations can be made with regard to other radical right-wing populist parties. The Canadian Reform Party, for example, was founded in the late 1980s with the explicit goal of giving voice to Western Canadian grievances against the central government in Ottawa. The precipitating event was the federal government's decision to grant a major military contract to a Quebec-based company, despite the fact that a Western company had made 'a cheaper and technically superior bid' (Nevitte et al. 1998, 175). This incident 'provided a rare symbol of alienation with which all Western Canadians could identify', a 'powerful symbol to Westerners of the perceived injustice of the current political system' (Harrison 1995, 105–6). This provided fertile ground for Preston Manning's right-wing populist campaign which, at least initially, appealed to long-standing Western *ressentiments* against the Francophone minority in Quebec and the special treatment received from an Eastern-dominated political elite.

A similar dynamic accounts for the rise and initial electoral success of the *Lega Nord* and its predecessor leagues in Northern Italy in the late 1980s. Here, the main factor was the growing sense of frustration over an inefficient, clientelistic, and corrupt state that transferred large sums of revenues from the North to fund projects in the South with little tangible benefit. In its initial phase of mass mobilisation, the *Lega* gave a rather crude and aggressive expression to Northern Italian *ressentiments* against Rome and Southerners in general.[2] At the same time, it promoted a 'cultural model of reference' reflecting the virtues and values espoused by the small industrial and artisan enterprises predominant in the *Lega*'s strongholds: 'hard work, thrift, honesty, and entrepreneurship' (Biorcio 1997, 60).

Finally, we will consider the example of the dramatic electoral gains of the *Schweizer Volkspartei* (SVP) after Christoph Blocher, the president of the Zurich wing, assumed leadership. It is, perhaps, no coincidence that the rise of Blocher occurred precisely when Switzerland was coming under international scrutiny with regard to its role and conduct during the Second World War. Mounting accusations that Swiss banks had reaped huge benefits from accounts held by Jews from Germany and the occupied countries, many of whom had perished in the Holocaust, came to a head when the Under-Secretary of the American Department of Commerce, Stuart Eizenstat, published a report containing accusations against the Swiss Confederation, including the charge it had acquired large amounts of gold from the German

Reichsbank during the war, part of which may have come from the victims of concentration camps. Perhaps more important was the tenor of charges which implied that Switzerland had hidden behind neutrality, whilst reaping enormous profits from the war.

Blocher, who also heads an organisation with the revealing title of 'Campaign for an Independent and Neutral Switzerland', had been instrumental in defeating the referendum on Switzerland's membership to the European Economic Area, and was quick to seize the opportunity to establish himself as the defender of Swiss national pride. In two speeches in the late 1990s, he strongly objected to the charges brought against Switzerland. At the same time, he voiced sympathy and understanding for the 'innumerable citizens' whose feelings 'for our native land are being repeatedly offended', and especially for the more elderly among them who 'are being hurt with respect to their lifelong efforts and achievements for this country' (Blocher 1997a). Declaring that '[W]e are not ashamed of our history' and vowing that '[T]he people of Switzerland cannot be blackmailed' he lashed out against Switzerland's critics at home ('young representatives of the Left, a few theologians, numerous sociologists, professors, artists and journalists') and abroad. He also singled out the Jewish World Congress as 'the leader of the campaign against Switzerland in the past and the present', and other Jewish organisations which 'are demanding money' whilst denying 'that they are interested in money' (Blocher 1997b), and he went so far as to compare the threats of these organisations to boycott Swiss goods with the Nazi-instigated boycott of Jewish business in Germany 'that initiated the atrocious extermination of the Jewish people' (Blocher 1997a).

The evidence suggests that the appeal to *ressentiments* plays a significant role in the initial phase of populist mobilisation. In some cases, what triggers popular *ressentiments* is a single event that serves as a focal point for expressions of anger and disenchantment, as was the case in Canada and Switzerland. In other cases, *ressentiments* are generated by negative experiences over an extended period of time. This was the case in Northern Italy, where long-standing frustration with the Italian state and the political establishment, together with mounting animosity toward the South, finally exploded in the late 1980s. A similar point can be made with regard to Belgium, where the *Vlaams Blok* sought to exploit deep-seated Flemish *ressentiments* against the Walloons.[3] Negative experiences also account for the rise of the FPÖ in Austria. Disenchantment with the country's entrenched *Proporzsystem* provided Haider with a political climate conducive to a populist anti-system campaign. One might also argue that this was, at least in part, the case in Germany, although it is difficult to say whether and to what degree the *Republikaner* managed to appeal to German *ressentiments* stemming from the efforts to come to terms with the past.

Among the sources of popular *ressentiments*, the perception that some social groups enjoy preferential treatment may well provide a particularly favourable ground for populist mobilisation.[4] It also appears to be the reason for the initial success of Pauline Hanson in the 1996 Australian parliamentary elections, described by Robert Manne as 'the strangest story in recent Australian political history' (Manne 1998, 3). Hanson, the owner of a fish-and-chip shop with no previous political experience, ran for the Liberal Party as the candidate for Oxley in Queensland, traditionally a safe seat for the Labour Party. Hanson gained notoriety when her Labour opponent got wind of a letter she had written to a local newspaper, in which she accused Australian politicians of causing a 'racist problem' by showering Aboriginals 'with money, facilities and opportunities that only these people can obtain' (Manne 1998, 3). After the Liberal Party withdrew her candidacy, fearing bad publicity, Hanson presented herself as an independent for Oxley and won the seat 'with the largest anti-Labour swing in the country' (Manne 1998, 3). Clearly, Hanson's outspokenness with respect to Aboriginal rights had hit a raw nerve among Queensland voters who rewarded her for having expressed what many of them were probably thinking.[5]

In April 1997 Pauline Hanson used the launching of her One Nation Party to explicitly appeal to these *ressentiments* when she declared that the new party would finally give the Australian people '[T]he chance to finally rid ourselves of the inequity that has grown from years of political correctness, where we have not been able to speak our mind, or express our views without being called names intended to make us look backward, intolerant or extremist' (Hanson 1997). These words echoed charges Hanson had made in her maiden speech to the Australian parliament where she accused 'those who control the various taxpayer funded "industries" that flourish in our society servicing Aboriginals, multiculturalists and a host of other minority groups' of bringing about 'a type of reverse racism' directed against 'mainstream Australians'. At the same time she accused government of 'encouraging separatism in Australia by providing opportunities, land, moneys, and facilities only available [...] to Aboriginals' (Hanson

1996). As a result, 'the majority of Australians' faced the threat of becoming 'second-class citizens in their own country, under a government who panders to minority interests and denies the majority the right of decision' (Hanson 1997).

The Hanson phenomenon is contemporary radical right-wing populism in its purest form. Claiming that her views on issues were 'based on common sense', she marketed herself as 'voicing the views of many Australians who have for so long gone unheard and unhelped' (Hanson 1996). With the emergence of One Nation, Australian voters finally had a real choice and could decide 'if it is the elite of the media, of academia and those others who see themselves above ordinary Australians who dictate our future, or whether it will be the people themselves who decide our fate' (Hanson 1997).

Another reason why the case of Pauline Hanson is particularly interesting is that, together with New Zealand First, One Nation was the first radical right-wing populist party to try to build a broad populist movement on an anti-globalisation platform – a strategy which has increasingly been adopted by other radical right-wing parties.[6] Hanson argued that the established parties, 'with their policies of globalisation and economic rationalism', had 'positioned Australia so our industries would close and our jobs would be exported to benefit the workers and families of foreign lands at the expense of our own people' (Hanson 1997). She then presented a number of broad measures designed to reverse previous government policies of open trade in order to restrict the foreign ownership of Australian companies, restore protective tariffs, 'revitalise Australian manufacturing, and help small business and the rural sector' by promoting 'Australian made products from Australian owned companies', and halting all immigration 'except that related to investment that will lead to employment until Australia's unemployment is solved' (Hanson 1997).

Hanson's economic programme, which essentially called for comprehensive protectionism, was very similar to that promoted by New Zealand First in the mid-1990s (see Miller 1998). In both cases, the appeal to economic nationalism was primarily directed against Asians, both as immigrants and as investors buying up companies and real estate. Indeed, one of New Zealand First's also main tenets was its staunch opposition to the sale of strategic assets to majority foreign ownership. At the same time, New Zealand First also appealed to more specific *ressentiments* such as hostility among the elderly to the fact that previous governments had continuously refused to abolish a surtax imposed on pensions in the 1980s, whilst simultaneously cutting benefits.[7]

Radical right-wing success at the polls, at least in the initial phase of mobilisation, depends largely on a party's ability to exploit existing popular *ressentiments*. In most cases, these are country-specific and not primarily related to immigration or other general macrostructural changes, such as post-industrialisation or globalisation. More often than not, the initial success of these parties reflected grievances and feelings of discontent generated both by official elite-sponsored policies, such as affirmative action programmes and the promotion of multiculturalism (Canada, India, Australia), and policies designed to regain economic competitiveness (Australia and New Zealand). In both cases, the populist appeal to *ressentiments* challenged the established elites and their values in order to devalue the latter as a basis of legitimacy. In other cases, the radical Right appealed to *ressentiments* stemming from domestic or external pressure to confront and deal with dark chapters in the national history.

This interpretation raises a question: what precisely accounts for the success of a political strategy to mobilise popular *ressentiments* against the established elite in the 1980s and 1990s? There are at least two possible explanations. In the first place, this strategy fits larger developments that are related to what has come to be known as the 'postmodern condition', that is, the fundamental questioning of the 'grand narratives' underlying modernity, the triumph of popular culture over elite culture, and the questioning of political elites by the electorate. But the strategy also fits a second development characteristic of the 1990s – that of questioning the established system of redistribution via a bureaucratised welfare state and, with it, questioning of the notion of social justice itself. This is closely tied up with the complexity of modern welfare states, where it is increasingly difficult to know exactly who gets what and from whom, as with recent attempts to contain or even cut welfare expenditure. In this sense, programmes clearly benefiting identifiable groups are an easy target for popular resentment.

Issue identification and political effectiveness

Whilst the ability of radical right-wing populist parties to exploit popular *ressentiments* may account for their initial success at the polls, it fails to explain why some parties have done well over time, whereas others have suffered a marked decline in popular support. Starting from the assumption that there is a significant difference between initial mobilisation, based on curiosity or protest, and sustained electoral support, it is reasonable to assume that the curiosity will tend to wear off and that protest may later be expressed through abstention rather than electoral support. In the long-term, voters will support a new party only if it demonstrates some degree of effectiveness, and, in order to be effective, it must first be associated with a specific issue where it is perceived as competent.

For radical right-wing populist parties, the main issue of policy competence has been immigration. Radical right-wing populist parties are, above all, anti-immigration parties, which express and appeal to popular 'resentment against migrants and the immigration policy of their government' (Fennema 1997, 474). This does not necessarily mean that their programmes are only concerned with immigration, but that, rather, voters identify these parties primarily with this specific issue. Surveys appear to support this contention and suggest that what distinguishes supporters of radical rightist parties from other party supporters is the high degree of importance they attribute to the immigration question. Thus, in 1995 less than a quarter (22 per cent) of the French electorate, but among supporters of Jean–Marie Le Pen, the figure was 53 per cent considered immigration to be a top political priority (Mayer 1999, 155). Similarly in Austria, in the 1995 and 1999 national elections, half the FPÖ voters considered the party's position against further immigration as one of the main reasons for their electoral choice, whereas for supporters of other parties, immigration played no role at all (Plasser et al. 1995, 13–21; Plasser et al. 1999). The same applies to the majority of Hanson's supporters who, when asked in 1998 what they liked best about One Nation, cited the party's views and policies on immigration (Goot 1998, 68). Growing anti-foreigner sentiment was an equally significant factor in the recent success of the *Schweizer Volkspartei*, which has increasingly been identified with a relatively narrow range of issues, including a restrictive asylum policy (Longchamp n.d. 1999).

Given these results, it is reasonable to assume that the success of radical right-wing parties the late 1980s and the 1990s has been primarily a reflection of mounting public dissatisfaction with official immigration policies. In Western Europe, this was largely a result of the dramatic increase in the number of asylum-seekers, and refugees, which was in turn a consequence of earlier policies that had virtually halted labour migration. Faced by the large influx of asylum-seekers, and taking into account the growing presence and visibility of foreign populations as a major public policy problem, large sections of the public in Western Europe and other prosperous capitalist democracies expected a quick and decisive solution from their governments. In order to push the established parties into finding a solution, a growing number of people deliberately voted for radical right-wing parties because of their severe anti-immigrant policies. From this perspective, support for the radical Right can be interpreted as a rational and strategic use of electoral power to influence official public policy with which the voter disagrees, but is unable to change by voting for the established parties.

There are a number of reasons that lend credibility to this argument. First, support for the radical Right at the polls had the desired effect. Starting in the early 1990s, most Western European governments introduced a number of measures to restrict immigration. The most striking and highly publicised case was the reform of Germany's Basic Law in 1993, which allowed German authorities to reject asylum-seekers at the borders if their claim was deemed fraudulent. In this way Germany regained control of a situation that the public had increasingly considered to be intolerable. Between 1993, the height of the influx, and 1998, the annual flow of refugees into Germany dropped from roughly 440 000 to less than 100 000. Germany's change of its generous asylum law provoked a 'copy-cat' effect in other Western European countries, which successively restricted access to migrants. In France, the Minister of the Interior, Charles Pasqua, went so far as to declare that France no longer wanted to be an immigration country and called for what he called 'zero immigration' (*Le Monde*, 2 June 1993).

Secondly, in both the French and the German cases, measures to restrict immigration were partly an attempt by the 'traditional' parties to stop, and eventually reverse, the advance of the Radical Right. In other countries, the established political parties, on both the Right and Left, tried to achieve similar results by adopting radical right-wing language and slogans on the issue of immigration.

Finally, radical right-wing parties have taken credit for having forced the established parties to impose immigration restrictions. Not surprisingly, Jörg Haider has publicly claimed the 'historical merit' on behalf of his party for having changed Austrian immigration policy by demanding 'Austria First' so that 'there is no Minister of the Interior' who could 'make an immigration policy' which would be in opposition to the measures proposed by the FPÖ (Haider quoted from the

1999 party conference). There can be no doubt that Haider considered this to be a major reason for his party's enduring success at the polls.

This may explain electoral support for a party after adopting immigration as its central issue, but it also raises the problem that once the electoral success of radical right-wing parties has pressured the established parties to toughen their stance on immigration, there is no reason why voters should not return to the established parties. This was the case, for example, in Germany and in Sweden where the collapse of *Ny Demokrati* was witnessed only a few years after its 'meteoric rise in popularity' in the 1991 Riksdag elections (Taggart 1996, 8). However, this explanation fails to explain the course of events in most of the other cases. The opposite occurred in Austria, France, and Norway: in these countries where radical right-wing parties have arguably been the most successful in the 1990s, electoral support for them has increased despite the tightening of immigration laws and a subsequent decline in the number of asylum-seekers.

The Norwegian case is a particularly intriguing one, given the dramatic gains of the Progress Party between 1993 and 1997. In the national election of 1993, the party polled 6.3 per cent of the vote, whereas in 1997 this figure leapt to over 15 per cent, making the Progress Party the second largest party in the Norwegian parliament. As in earlier election campaigns, the Progress Party voiced its strong opposition to immigration (Bjugan 1998, 178–80). Given the party's track record on immigration, its success may be interpreted as the reflection of a revival or intensification of anti-immigrant sentiments in Norway were it not for the fact that time-series data measuring public opinion on immigration tell an entirely different story and suggest that Norwegian society was significantly more, rather than less, tolerant toward immigrants in 1997 than in 1993. Thus, the number those of Norwegians supporting the statement that 'Norway should grant residence permits to at least as many refugees and asylum-seekers as today' increased from 49 per cent in 1993 to 67 per cent in 1997 (and 70 per cent in 1998), and the number of those supporting the statement that 'immigrants should have the same possibility to work as Norwegians' increased from 75 per cent to 86 per cent (and 91 per cent in 1998) (Blom 1998, 7).

The divergence between immigration reality and the electoral performance of prominent radical right-wing parties does not necessarily mean that there is no linkage between popular views on immigration and support for the Radical Right. It does suggest, however, that this relationship may be far less direct and significantly more complex than is generally assumed to be the case. Looking more closely at popular attitudes to immigration, surveys show that there is significant variation in the level of support or rejection of immigration depending on what the respondent is asked. Taking Norway as an example, one finds a noticeable difference between statements on granting residence permits or allowing foreigners to work in Norway, in which cases the great majority gave promigrant responses, and a statement about whether immigrants had 'too easy' access to social assistance compared to Norwegians where, although agreement with the statement has declined from 67 per cent in 1993, it was still supported by over half the population (53 per cent) in 1997 (Blom 1998, 7). Results from other countries reveal a similar pattern. For example, in Denmark, in 1993 and 1996, only a fifth of the population agreed that immigrants took jobs away from Danes and thus contributed to rising unemployment, but two-thirds agreed that many immigrants came to Denmark to exploit the welfare system (Togeby 1998, 1247). Similarly in France, considerably fewer respondents thought foreign workers took jobs away from the French (47 per cent in 1996), than those who thought that many immigrants came to France only to exploit the French welfare system (a figure of 73 per cent in 1997) (IFOP/L/Express survey, September 1996; CNCDH 1998).

These results suggest a somewhat differentiated reading of the continuous success of radical right-wing parties. This perspective suggests that, voters continue to support these parties precisely because previous support for them proved so effective. Thus, once most governments imposed severe restrictions on migrant flows that came close to the goal of zero immigration, popular anti-immigrant sentiments did not disappear but simply shifted to the question of social benefits. In the words of Anton Kuijsten, 'an unemployed guestworker is kind of a *contradictio in terminis*'; in this context immigrants are 'easily stigmatized as people who only cost the state money, which has to be provided by the native taxpayer' (Kuijsten 1997, 211). This is particularly striking in the case of asylum-seekers, who often receive significant levels of public financial support. One can suppose that this resentment has also been fuelled by government attempts to cut social benefits in the face of the increasing pressure of globalisation. At the same time, however, governments, at least in Western Europe, are not in a position to stop providing benefits to non-citizens given the universal nature of the European welfare state. In this situation, it is easy for radical right-wing parties to appeal to public anxiety in the context of growing insecurity associated with the effects of global competition, and popular resentment at the allegedly high financial burden of unemployed foreign workers and refugees on an already strained welfare state.

Whilst this would appear to be a feasible explanation for the continuous support of radical right-wing parties in Western Europe, despite the imposition of highly restrictive anti-immigration policies, it does not explain the dramatic differences in their electoral fortunes. This is particularly puzzling in the case of Germany which, even after the change of the Basic Law, continued to receive more refugees and asylum-seekers than all of Western Europe taken together and to spend a considerable amount of money on its refugee population. In such circumstances, one might expect a high level of support for radical right-wing parties, yet in Germany, the Radical Right has limped from one electoral disaster to another.

One possible solution to this puzzle is to consider the internal organisation of radical right-wing parties. The argument advanced so far maintains that voters support radical right-wing populist parties in order to force the established parties to modify or change their position on immigration. This, however, only makes sense if radical right-wing populist parties constitute a credible challenge to the established parties. I would argue that this presupposes, above all, internal coherence and effective leadership. This has been the case in Austria, France (at least until the break-up of the *Front national* in early 1999), Norway and Italy where the parties in question are not only highly centralised, but have also been led by a charismatic leader who has been the central point of reference for the supporters. In Germany, the opposite has been the case. Until today, the German Radical Right been unable to agree on one leading figure and has been internally fragmented and divided among competing organisations as a result. Whenever one of the parties managed to win seats at the regional or local level, its representatives invariably started to fight each other within a short period of time, leading to divisions within the group and consequent defections.

Internal cohesiveness is particularly important in populist parties because they tend to rely heavily on the charismatic qualities of single individuals to maintain control of the party and to 'maximise the impact of their relatively small electoral constituency' (Taggart 1996, 38). Internal conflicts, defections, and internal leadership challenges are particularly damaging for populist parties, since they hamper their effectiveness and, as result, their appeal. From the perspective of a rational voter it is simply irrational, given the costs and benefits of voting, to vote for a political party whose behaviour undermines its effectiveness. This may explain the differing fortunes of some radical right-wing parties in recent years. Thus it was not surprising that the Swedish *Ny Demokrati* collapsed in 1994, after the original party founders resigned their leadership position. In other cases, decline in popular support was followed by defection or party splits, as in the case in Germany, Denmark, Italy, New Zealand and, most recently, France. However, defections do not necessarily cause permanent damage. Both Jörg Haider and Pia Kjærsgaard not only survived significant challenges to their leadership and the defection of a wing of their parties, but also managed to emerge from these episodes in a stronger position which eventually translated into gains at the polls–clearly a warning to all those who have declared Jean-Marie Le Pen to be politically dead.

The ultimate test of a party's effectiveness is its performance in office. Among radical right-wing populist parties, only two have been in that position at the national level, both as partners in coalition governments: the *Lega Nord*, which agreed to joint Berlusconi's government after the 1994 elections; and New Zealand First, which formed a coalition government with the conservative National Party in December 1996. In both cases the experiment did not last the full legislative period. The *Lega Nord* withdrew from government after less than a year, bringing about the collapse of Berlusconi's government. New Zealand First withdrew from government in August 1998 after weeks of acrimonious in-fighting, half its deputies defected from the party to sit as independents, albeit supporting the government, thus guaranteeing the National Party a majority in parliament.

Given their overwhelmingly negative record in government, it is hardly surprising that both parties lost a large part of their former electorate and support at subsequent elections. This was particularly the case of New Zealand First whose charismatic leader, Winston Peters, was responsible for a series of blunders that compromised the party's credibility. Before the 1996 election, Peters had ruled out any post-election arrangement with the National Party, whose economic policies he had fiercely criticised whilst in opposition. After the election, he not only made a deal with the National Party, but also accepted its neoliberal programme. To make things worse, he opted to become treasurer, which made him responsible for the budget. In the process, he was increasingly seen as taking orders from the head of New Zealand's independent Central Bank, which had frequently been the target of his attacks during the election campaign. Nor did the party fare much better with respect to policy-making. Peters was elected in part due to his position on the pension issue, but once in government his proposed pension plan to replace state pensions with a compulsory private scheme proved highly unpopular and it was rejected in a popular referendum by 92 per cent of the voters. As a result, popular support for the coalition government fell to 32 per cent, and to 2 per cent for New Zealand First. Given these developments, it was hardly surprising when Peters finally withdrew his party from the coalition.

The disastrous record of New Zealand First in recent years is indicative of the vulnerability of all radical right-wing populist parties. It shows that even a charismatic and highly popular political figure can rapidly fall from popular grace. New Zealand First's performance as a government party generated growing voter resentment of those who had previously mobilised voter resentment themselves. Ironically, it took a popular referendum to show New Zealand First and its leader the extent to which the public had become disenchanted with their performance. The case of New Zealand First, and to a certain degree that of the *Lega Nord*, suggest that one way to deal with radical right-wing populist parties may be to put them in a position where they have to assume real political responsibility. From this perspective, the strategy of the two major Austrian parties to exclude the FPÖ as a potential coalition party may have been short-sighted and, in the last instance, counterproductive, because it allowed Haider to criticise and make political claims and demands, without having to put his policies to the test.

Conclusion

In this chapter, I have argued that several factors account for the recent successes and failures of radical right-wing populist parties in contemporary democracies. Perhaps the most important is the ability to appeal to, and mobilise, popular *ressentiments* generated by specific events or experiences. This accounts, to a large degree, for the initial success of such parties at the polls. Another key factor is a party's ability to identify itself with a specific issue. In most cases discussed here that issue has been immigration and secondary issues associated with immigration, such as multiculturalism. Finally, there is the factor of internal party cohesion and leadership stability without which (i) other parties would be unlikely to take the radical right-wing populist challenge seriously, and where (ii) voters would be unlikely to lend support to a party because its existence had no serious party-political consequences, since it could be ignored by other established parties.

In trying to explain the differences in electoral performance of radical right-wing populist parties over the past two decades, I have consciously ignored structural factors, which have figured prominently in recent accounts of the rise of the Radical Right. In my opinion, these factors are indeed important in explaining the characteristics of the social basis of radical right-wing populist parties, particularly changes in the composition of their constituency, such as the growing 'proletarisation' of the radical right-wing vote, or, more generally, the preponderance of males among their voters, but they are much less pertinent in explaining why some parties have done significantly better than others. To understand these differences, we need to gain a better understanding of the specifics of each individual case, with respect to both the conditions which gave rise to these parties and to their behaviour once they gained some visibility at the polls.

Notes

1. Pre-election opinion polls had reported support for the party of up to 30 per cent of eligible voters.
2. One of the *Lega's* most famous slogans was '*Roma ladrona*' (Rome, the big thief).
3. As in Germany, Austria, and Switzerland, these *ressentiments* are linked to the past – in this case Flemish collaboration with the Germans during the Second World War. In June 1997, the Flemish regional parliament passed a bill awarding compensation to Flemish citizens convicted of collaboration during the war. The bill provoked an uproar among the Walloons and was only passed with support of the *Vlaams Blok* which had always been the most vocal advocates of an amnesty for Flemish collaborators (see Rosenzweig 1998).
4. In the run-up to the 1997 elections in Norway, Carl Hagen tried to mobilise *ressentiments* against the Lapp (*Sami*) minority in Northern Norway by denouncing the special rights granted to them (see Madeley 1998, 190).
5. In her maiden speech in Parliament, Hanson made this point herself declaring that she 'won the seat of Oxley largely on an issue that has resulted in me being called a racist. That issue related to my comment that Aboriginals received more benefits than non-Aboriginals' (Hanson 1996).
6. In 1998, the Danish People's Party's programme consisted of three simple points: 'against immigration, against the EU, and in favour of protecting the weakest in society' (Aylott 1999, 70).
7. In 1997, Carl Hagen campaigned on a similar platform, demanding 'that more money be spent on welfare of Norwegians for example through health care, pensions and education, the extra expenditures to be funded out of oil revenues in preference to locking them up in the Oil Fund' (Madeley 1998, 190).

12
In the Name of the Peasantry, the Proletariat, and the People: Populisms in Eastern Europe

Cas Mudde

Introduction

In the last decade, many scholars have proclaimed the re-emergence of populism in European politics. In Western Europe the term is generally used to denote postmodern or 'more moderate' types of 'Extreme Right' or 'Radical Right' parties, but in Eastern Europe it is considered to be a more general phenomenon, spread across the ideological spectrum.[1] Like nationalism, populism has become a catchword for both the western media and the academic community that deal, often only in passing, with the post-communist East. For example, as early as 1990 *Time* ran a story under the title 'Populism on the March' (Walsh 1990), while seven years later the journal *Communist and Post-Communist Studies* published an article entitled 'Slovakia and the Triumph of Nationalist Populism' (Carpenter 1997).

In this chapter I will critically evaluate the general claim that populism has returned to the centre of Eastern European politics. However, rather than looking at one specific interpretation of populism, I will discuss three different types in order to discover whether populism is relevant at all in the post-communist context, if so, to assess which populisms are relevant, and finally to assess the role of the 'Leninist legacy' (Jowitt 1992) in contemporary Eastern Europe.

The concept of populism

I will not dwell on the well-worn observation that populism is a highly contentious concept with more enemies than friends in the social sciences (Piccone and Ulmen 1995; Taguieff 1995; Knight 1998). The fact is that populism is a term frequently used in both social science and public debate to denote a specific form of politics. Leaving the normative discussion aside, much can be said about what 'populism' means or should mean. The most important question in 'populism studies' is whether there is a single overarching form of populism or (only) different populisms (see Ionescu and Gellner 1969; van Niekerk 1972; Canovan 1981; Conniff 1982b; Ernst 1987; Weyland 1999b).

The claims of a resurgence of populism in Eastern Europe have often been made on the basis of a variety of implicit definitions, and it is arguable that a more flexible framework may clarify more than it obscures. I will examine three ideal-types of populism most often mentioned in the literature, the two broad categories of agrarian and political populism cited in Margaret Canovan's classic 1981 text, and a third category, that of economic populism, primarily based on populism in Latin America. These categories tend to overlap in both theory and practice and should be used as theoretical tools to help provide better insight into a complex situation rather than as a definitive conceptual response to the question of how to define populism.

Agrarian populism

The origins of agrarian populism are found in two rather different movements from the end of the nineteenth century: the People's Party, a political movement constituted mainly though not exclusively by farmers in the 'heartland' of the United States (Hofstadter 1969; Wilson 1995), and the *narodniki*, a cultural movement of mainly urban intelligentsia in Tsarist Russia (Walicki 1969). What these movements shared was an anti-elitist ideology in which the peasant was considered the source of morality and agricultural life, the basis of a well-functioning society (MacRae 1969; Breitling 1987; Held 1996b). Agrarian populists are vehemently opposed to the urban elites and the centralising tendencies and materialist basis of capitalism, and they strive for the preservation of small family farms by founding co-operatives, for strengthening (rural) communities, and for self-governance (Piccone and Ulmen 1995). Often misperceived as defensive or backward-looking (Wilson 1995; Lackó 1996; Brass 1997), agrarian populism also had a progressive side (Goodwyn 1991; Bozóki 1994). For example, populists demanded radical economic reforms to maintain the position of small farm agriculture as the backbone of the entire economy, and fought to 'raise' the peasantry, by increasing and improving educational and health facilities in rural areas.

Political populism

The more recent notion holds that populism is, first and foremost, a particular *style* of politics, referring to 'the people' ('*das Volk*') as a homogeneous entity, proclaiming a direct link between the people and the populist actor, and using a distinctly plebeian *Stammtisch* discourse (Pfahl-Traughber 1994; Ernst 1987; Canovan 1999).[2] For good reasons, this definition has been attacked because of its generality and vagueness, which suggest that political populism is virtually identical to basic political campaigning techniques. To make political populism more distinct, I define it here as a political style that builds on the rigid dichotomy between the 'pure people' and a 'corrupt elite'. It is important to note that these categories are not defined in strictly formal terms – rather they are moral constructs. The fact that both categories are 'imagined' is less relevant than the centrality, consistency, and rigidity of this dichotomy. Rather than being truly 'anti-political' (Schedler 1997), populists have an ambiguous relationship towards politics; on the one hand, they consider it a 'dirty job', characterised by the amoral elite, while on the other hand, they need it to return the power to 'the people'. In short, political populists are reluctantly political (Taggart 2000), considering politics to be a necessary evil. At the same time, and somewhat paradoxically, they are among the staunchest believers in the primacy of (national) politics, rejecting any alleged limitations set by international pressure or economics. In terms of policies, they support forms of direct democracy, such as referenda. However, rather than presenting alternative policies, political populism politicises already existing or newly created emotions and sentiments, most notably resentment and rancour (Ernst 1987; Betz 1994; Tismaneanu 1996).

This type of 'politicians' populism' (Canovan 1981) has been predominantly linked with the right wing, most notably in recent studies of the phenomenon in Western Europe (see, inter alia, Betz 1994; Pfahl-Traughber 1994; Taggart 1995). Indeed, political populism's reference to the undivided people sits well with nationalists' belief in 'the nation', and the two are often mixed in the dichotomy of the 'national people' versus the 'anti-national elite' (Germani 1978; Taguieff 1995). However, this is not necessarily so, because non-nationalist and left-wing political actors have at times also excelled in political populism.

Economic populism

The heyday of this phenomenon dates back to Latin America in the 1920s, with a second upsurge in that region in the 1970s (see discussions in, for example, Conniff 1982a; Drake 1982; Weyland 1999a). In the Latin American tradition, populism is described as being 'a multi-class political movement, characterised by personalist, charismatic leadership, *ad hoc* reformist policies, and a repudiation of revolution' (Knight 1998, 237). This definition is only partly useful outside that tradition, especially when applied to post-communist Europe. For example, the 'multi-class political movement' is the norm in an area which has been 'de-classed' after decades of Communism. Moreover, the feature of 'personalist, charismatic leadership' has little discriminatory value in post-communist politics, particularly in the first decade, given the embryonic stage of party development and the general choice of party organisation (Kopecky 1995). Therefore, I define economic populism in the chapter in a broader manner, focusing on the *economic* dimension. Trying to achieve a 'Third Way' between capitalism and socialism, the core values of the economic populist programme in Latin America between the 1920s and the 1960s have been described as 'growth' and 'moderate redistribution' (Cardoso and Faletto 1979), with its core programme being 'import-substitution industrialisation' (Writh 1982). Generally speaking, populist economic policy includes a proactive role for the state in setting up protective tariffs, transferring income from the export to the domestic sector, redistributing wealth among the population, creating a supportive infrastructure, expanding consumption and welfare facilities, and coercing the social partners into co-operation (Cardoso and Faletto 1979; Drake 1982; Greskovits 1998).

The broad definition of economic populism is that of a phenomenon not restricted to a recent past or a specific area. At the same time, it is more distinct than contemporary usage of the term suggests. As Torcuato Di Tella (1997, 188) notes, 'in recent years [it] has become almost a by-word to imply irresponsible economic policies'. For example, the UN Secretary-General, Kofi Annan has declared that populism is one of the three types of backlash against globalism, the other two being nationalism and illiberalism. According to Annan (1999), economic populism, in the form of a host of protectionist measures, is increasingly used by 'embattled leaders' in a rhetorical sham fight with globalisation.

The similarities between political, economic and agrarian populism are, however, paralleled by clear differences. First of all, 'the people' are defined (or rather, 'imagined') in different ways: agrarian populists define 'the people' *exclusively* in terms of one group, the peasantry; political populists include virtually the entire population, with the notable exception of 'the elite'; while economic populists use a broader definition, though their critique favours the experience of the urban proletariat. Consequently, in contrast to agrarian populism, economic and political populism do not *exclusively* refer to the agricultural economy. Indeed, their sympathy does not go much further than a call for state support for the agricultural sector (through subsidies and tariffs), which has at least as much a nationalist (national independence in food production) as a populist component. The same applies to the overlap between economic and political populism, which is substantial, but not absolute. Moreover, the protectionist policies of contemporary 'national populist' parties have their origin in nationalism, as the economy is in general considered to be of secondary importance, subordinate to the overriding goal of protecting the rights of 'the nation' (Mudde 2000a).

The relevance of these three different notions will be assessed on the basis of a critical but necessarily superficial analysis of the past and present political situation in Eastern Europe. The main focus is on whether populism is a relevant feature of post-communist politics, and, if so, whether a special approach is taken to additionally evaluate the importance of the 'Leninist legacy' on the specific phenomenon of post-communist populism.

Agrarian populism in Eastern Europe

The Eastern Europe of the pre-communist period was largely backward, rural, and only marginally democratic. This meant that for most of the time agrarian populist movements were severely restricted in their attempts to mobilise supporters or influence politics. Not surprisingly, the first movements were mainly regionally organised, mobilising farmers in parts of the country in opposition to the often deplorable situation of the rural population. Given the authoritarian structure of the Eastern European regimes at the time, these actions generally involved clashes with the government authority, such as in Bulgaria at the turn of the century (Bell 1996).

At the beginning of the twentieth century, however, the political situation in most Eastern European countries improved somewhat, as the feudal nobility increasingly allowed some forms of democratic participation while still retaining power for themselves. Not surprisingly, 'where the majority of the population were peasants, peasant parties came to power' (Worsley 1993, 731), and agrarian populism became the dominant ideology. While in some countries, such as Hungary, the populists' influence was mainly intellectual or cultural (Bozóki 1994; Lackó 1996), most Eastern European populists developed action-oriented political movements (Ionescu 1969; Held 1996a). These movements, however, were very broad and encompassed both intellectual and peasant leaders, right-wing and left-wing ideologies, pro- and anti-regime wings, and so on. What all agrarian populists had in common was:

> [t]he philosophic foundation ... that the peasants were biologically and morally the healthiest stratum of society and that they were destined to create a society more balanced and more just than the existing system ... dominated by the urban bourgeoisie and a corrupt bureaucracy dependent upon its favours. (Dziewanowski 1996, 171)

In practice this led to the demand for an 'agrarianist' programme, in which agriculture was seen as the foundation of the entire economic system, and small farms were to be rescued from fragmentation through the formation of rural co-operatives (Ionescu 1969; Dziewanowski 1996). Like their counterparts in the United States, Eastern European populists were strongly anti-capitalist and anti-liberal (Hanák 1996). However, in addition to the usual critique of the anti-social and materialist features of capitalism, Eastern European populists also criticised its 'alien' roots. Capitalism was seen as a foreign element forcefully implanted in Eastern European societies by anti-national elites. In virtually all countries, the usual suspects were the Jews (Csepeli 1996; Treptow 1996) who the Eastern Europeans considered as archetypal speculators, making money without actually producing anything.

Despite resistance from the bourgeois elite and the aristocracy, populist agrarian parties gained overwhelming electoral victories across Eastern Europe in the early twentieth century (Ionescu 1969; Held 1996a), but their governments were generally short-lived, falling prey to authoritarian *coups d'état* in the 1920s and 1930s (for example, in Bulgaria and Poland). The consequence was a split in, rather than the demise of, the agrarian populist movement, with one part opposing the new rulers and the other collaborating with them. This process repeated itself when the Communists seized power after the Second World War. Though various populist leaders had originally believed in a sincere co-operation with the Communists, they were soon disappointed and more often than not landed in prison for 'subversive activities'. Once the Communists had taken full power in a country, peasant organisations were either forcefully integrated into the ruling Communist Party (as happened in Bulgaria), or co-opted as so-called 'bloc' or 'satellite' parties (as was the case in, for example, Czechoslovakia and Poland). These parties were more communist-oriented than populist or even agrarian, functioning as the Communist Party's 'transmission belt to the masses' (Dziewanowski 1996, 182).

After the fall of Communism, peasant parties reappeared in all Eastern European countries. These included some 'historic' parties – that is, those dating back to the pre-communist period (such as the Bulgarian Agrarian National Union, BANU, or the Slovenian People's Party, SLS), some reformed bloc parties (for example, the Polish Peasant Party, PSL), and some completely new parties (such as the Latvians Farmers' Union, LZS). With a few notable exceptions, agrarian parties have not been particularly successful in post-communist elections and those that have been successful have not followed a populist agenda – for example, the PSL.[3] Among the few successful populist agrarians we find two very different parties, the Hungarian Independent Smallholders' Party (FKgP), and Self-Defense in Poland.

The FKgP, lead by József Torgyán, started as a 'quasi-historic party' (Tóka 1997), referring in its label, symbols and ideology to the pre-war rural party of the same name. Initially, the party championed the rights of all people that had been 'robbed' and 'looted' by the former Communist regime and subsequently by the post-communist elite (Kovács 1996). In the 1990 'founding elections' the FKgP gained 12 per cent of the vote and joined a coalition government with the national-conservative Hungarian Democratic Forum (MDF), and the Christian-Democratic People's Party (KDNP). However, Torgyán acted as the leader of a semi-oppositional party, which led to a split in the party in 1992. After the split the FKgP increasingly resorted to agrarian (and political) populism, although the party and its leader are too politically superficial and unreliable to be labelled as agrarian populist (Bozóki 1994). In 1998 the FKgP again joined the government, this time with the liberal-conservative Federation of Young Democrats-Hungarian Civic Party (FIDESZ) and the MDF. Although the FKgP has now regained the Ministry of Agriculture, it seems to have toned down its stance, implementing some agricultural reforms aimed at EU accession rather than at the exclusive defense of the small Hungarian peasantry.

The only post-communist country in which agrarian populism has truly survived – and indirectly even defeated – the Communist regime, is Poland. There, 'the populist movement still speaks for nearly four million individual peasants as well as a group of skilled professionals, and a large number of peasant-workers who maintain their link with the countryside' (Fischer-Galati 1996, 246). However, it is not so much the parliamentary agrarian party, the PSL, which is the mouthpiece of populism – this party had already lost its populism under Communism, when it operated as the bloc party United Peasant Party (USL) – but the radical extra-parliamentary organisation, Self-Defense, which has on various occasions rallied disenchanted farmers in violent protest against government policies (Ost 1999). Its charismatic leader, Andrszej Lepper, has become a hero among small farmers, and Public Enemy No. 1 for the Polish government. With its action-oriented political style, Self-Defense places itself in the rich tradition of agrarian populist revolt in Poland, which includes violent strikes in the 1930s as well as successful opposition to collectivisation during Communist rule (see Narkiewicz 1976; Dziewanowski 1996).

Finally, elements of agrarian populism, such as the myth of the honest peasant, can be found among some old-style fascist organisations in post-communist Eastern Europe.[4] For example, the Russian National Unity (RNE) of Alexandr Barkashov attaches great importance to the 'rebirth of the Russian peasantry', which it considers to be 'the healthiest and genetically purest part of the Nation' (Shenfield 2001). This link between 'fascism' and the 'peasant myth' dates back to Hitler's '*Blut und Boden*' (blood and soil) philosophy, which the Nazis had taken from the popular *völkische* ideologies of eighteenth- and nineteenth-century German thinkers. Having said this, fascism (including national socialism) is not truly populist – for example, its elitism and totalitarianism are in sharp contrast with the more egalitarian and regionalist populist ideal of self-governance (Wiles 1969).

The marginalisation of agrarian populism in Eastern Europe is, as in the West, closely related to the process of industrialisation and the consequent demise of the peasantry in the region (Fischer-Galati 1996; Held 1996b).[5] But unlike the West, where the capitalist 'survival of the fittest' merely decreased the number of individual farms, in the East the Communists' process of collectivisation was like a 'tornado [that] swept the traditional family farm off the face of the earth' (Havel 1988, 385). The collective farm (*kolkhoz*) had little in common with the old family farm, and peasants became rural workers with little personal relation to the land they farmed. This rural proletariat is now more susceptible to the socialist ideal of a 'workers' paradise' than to the populist ideal of the 'peasant society'. Consequently, rural areas in many post-communist countries form the backbone of (not so) reformed communist successor parties, or of non-populist peasant parties which function as special interest groups rather than a support base of agrarian populist parties (Bell 1996; Kligman and Verdery 1999). Not surprisingly, agrarian populism only survived in those post-communist societies where collectivisation was either successfully resisted by the rural population (as in Poland; see Dziewanowski 1996), or moderated by 'goulash socialism' (as in Hungary; see Agócs and Agócs 1994).

Economic populism in Eastern Europe

Economic populism is a relatively modern phenomenon, dating back to the Latin America of the 1920s, and it did not play a key role in pre-communist Eastern Europe. Moreover, with economic policy at the core of the Communist model, economic populism was one of the many unacceptable alternatives to the official 'socialist economic policy'. However, Communist policies entailed some important overlap with economic populist policies (Drake 1982; Greskovits 1998).

With the fall of Communism, many western observers warned of the emergence of economic populist politics in the East. Not surprisingly, neoliberal economists were at the fore, arguing for the rapid introduction of neoliberal policies so as block the potential advance of the populists followed by social scientists who warned of a 'populist threat', but did so in reaction to the increasingly unpopular neoliberal policies (Greskovits 1998). Only a few scholars actually focused on the populists themselves and those that did so noted the marginal nature of economic populism in post-communist politics. With the probable exception of Slovakia (Carpenter 1997), economic populism rarely gained a foothold in Central and Eastern Europe. It remained by and large a rhetorical phenomenon (even in Slovakia), in economic terms closer to other (non-populist) political strands of post-communist politics than to traditional Latin American populism (Greskovits 1998). In the post-Soviet context the situation has been much the same, albeit often for entirely different reasons. Possibly one of the closest fits is Belarus, though this may be due to the many similarities between Communism and populism. In addition, Central Asian countries appear to be more prone to populist leadership.

Béla Greskovits (1998) explains this absence of 'a populist episode' in post-communist Eastern Europe through a comparison with Latin America of the 1970s–1980s and the 1990s. It is particularly the latter period which helps us to discern what is occurring in Eastern Europe. While the economic crisis in Latin America led to violent protests and neopopulist leaders in the 1970s–1980s, a more or less similar economic situation in the 1990s did not lead to either in Latin America or Eastern Europe.[6] He sees the explanation in term of the worldwide domination of neoliberal theory and practice in the 1990s, not least through the powerful Bretton Woods organisations, on the one hand, and a far less favourable socioeconomic breeding ground in the East than in the South, on the other.

Greskovits concludes that '[w]hile there has as yet been no convergence of political and economic factors favourable to populism, this may occur in the future' (Greskovits 1998, 100).

This is even more probable if one takes into account the importance of socioeconomic *values* among the masses. Largely as a result of the 'Leninist legacy', a significant potential for economic populist measures exists at the mass level in contemporary Eastern Europe. Socialised under the Communist regime, which claimed to take care of the people from the cradle to the grave, Eastern Europeans have become accustomed to the idea of a protective welfare state. Surveys show that the support of extensive state involvement in providing welfare is far higher in Eastern Europe than in the West (for example, Rose and Haerpfer 1996; Plasser, Ulram and Waldrauch 1998).

In addition, the main defences against economic populism are crumbling. Though still strong, the international consensus on neoliberalism has come under increasing attack, both from the centre and the periphery. In Eastern Europe itself, various political actors have started to openly question the former dogma, calling for a 'middle way'. More radically, the introduction of market capitalism, and the specific way in which it has developed in the region, have given way to 'social polarisation' (Williams 1999). Most notably, in the lesser developed parts of Eastern Europe, such as the Balkans and the former Soviet Union, this could create a situation similar to those of the heyday of Latin American populism, when '[g]roups disadvantaged and alienated by modern urban, oligopolistic capitalism and foreign penetration looked to the state to restore the protection and cohesion of older communities' (Drake 1982, 236–67).

Political populism in Eastern Europe

Political populism has been considered to be a particularly powerful phenomenon in post-communist Europe. As noted by western media and academics, 'right-wing' or 'national' populist parties have gained some striking electoral successes in post-communist elections (Mudde 2000b). The 23 per cent won by Vladimir Zhirinovsky's Liberal Democratic Party of Russia (LDPR) in 1993, the 18 per cent of Volislav Seselj's Serbian Radical Party (SRS) in 1996, or the 15 per cent of Joachim Siegerist's Popular Movement for Latvia (TKL) in 1995 are evidence of this.

What is most stunning, given the particular concern about 'national populism' in Eastern Europe, is that, in electoral terms, the situation is similar to that to be found in the West. For example, these electoral results have been matched by similar parties in Western Europe, such as Jörg Haider's Austrian Freedom Party (FPÖ), or Gianfranco Fini's *Alleanza Nazionale* (AN) in Italy. Moreover, and contrary to many writings, as in the West, contemporary national populism is not a 'ghost from the past', but a modern phenomenon. The successful parties are all new parties with their ideological and organisational origin in the post-communist period. Indeed, very few national populist parties with a pre-communist or communist identity have gained any significant success at the polls (Mudde 2000b).

What does set the two parts of Europe apart is the way in which national populism is treated by the political environment. Contrary to the situation in most of Western Europe, where national – and to some extent all political – populists are considered to be political pariahs, like-minded parties in Eastern Europe are often looked upon as potential coalition partners (*koalitionsfähig*). For example, the Greater Romania Party (PRM), the Party of Romanian National Unity (PUNR), the Slovak National Party (SNS), and Serbia's SRS all profit from the fact that political populism, broadly defined, plays an important role in the Eastern European political mainstream (von Beyme 1996). The key is once more found in the historical legacy.

Although Eastern Europe had many right-wing nationalist regimes in the pre-communist period, their influence on post-communist politics in general, and post-communist populism in particular, has been marginal. This is not surprising, as most regimes, both fascist and authoritarian, were highly elitist in both social composition and ideology and sit uneasily with the strong egalitarian composition and values of post-communist societies. It is instead the Leninist legacy that has made post-communist societies particularly prone to political populism. On the one hand, it reinforced long-standing anti-political sentiments at the mass level (Jowitt 1992; Tamás 1994), and on the other it gave rise to an intellectual variant of populism. This also explains the most significant difference between the East and the West – that is, not so much the potentially or allegedly higher levels of electoral success of populist parties, but rather the success of political populism at the elite level in the sense that while 'politicians' populism' is mainly the weapon of the outsider in Western Europe, in the East it is pursued by intellectuals (such as György Konrád), and even presidents (such as Václav Havel and Lech Walesa).

Communist rule created a perfect social environment for the mass support of political populism. As many authors have noted, 'real socialism' created nihilistic and atomised societies in which egalitarianism mixed with deep-rooted social envy (Tismaneanu 1996; Ulc 1996; Braun 1997). This, in combination with the stained reputation of 'state and party institutions, which were, rightfully at the time, considered identical to the Communist regime', created a deeply felt dichotomy between 'the moral non-Communist people' and 'the corrupt Communist elite' – incidentally, very similar, if not identical, to the dichotomy between (moral) 'civil society' versus (corrupt) 'state' (Tamás 1994; Sztompka 1998).

What most authors do not note, however, is that, intellectually speaking, this dichotomy has been highlighted by the discourse of famous dissidents. Because the Communist systems left little space for political opposition, dissidents tried to voice their opposition while officially staying away from 'politics' (Tamás 1994). Against the all-encompassing politics of the Communist Party, dissidents developed the concepts of 'anti-politics' (Konrád 1984) and 'anti-political politics' (Havel 1988). Together with many other key concepts in the writings of Eastern European dissidents, such as 'Central Europe' or 'civil society', 'anti-politics' was a rather vaguely-defined term and while this was not particularly problematic in the 'virtual reality' in which dissidents lived under Communism, it did become an immediate and clear problem in the post-communist period. What could 'anti-politics' add to democracy, given that it was defined as 'the political activity of those who don't want to be politicians and who refuse to share in power' (Konrád 1984, 230), or as 'one of the ways of seeking and achieving meaningful lives, of protecting them and serving them' (Havel 1988, 397)?

However, the populist element of 'anti-politics' is not so much its voluntary separation from classic politics in terms of government, or its 'watchdog' attitude towards 'real politics', but its claim to political propriety in politics, on which 'the people' exert pressure 'on the basis of their cultural and moral stature alone, not through any electoral legitimacy' (Konrád 1984, 231). This position is understandable under

Communism, if only because electoral legitimacy was impossible to achieve for dissidents, but 'moral anti-politics' (Schedler 1997) was never meant to apply solely to the communist regime. In the words of Konrád (1984, 321):

> If the political opposition comes to power, anti-politics keeps at the same distance from, and shows the same independence of, the new government. It will do so even if the new government is made up of sympathetic individuals, friends perhaps; indeed, in such cases it will have the greatest need for independence and distance.

After the fall of Communism, many dissidents were initially very active in practical politics during the transition period (see Bozóki 1999), and often shared key convictions, such as a belief in 'moral politics', a strong anti-elite rhetoric, and a deep hostility to political parties, with populists. Virtually all anti-communist umbrella organisations that defeated the old Communist Party in the first post-1989 elections defined themselves explicitly as 'movements' rather than parties. The argumentation was captured in the slogan of the Czech Civic Forum (OF) when they declared that 'Parties are for party members, [the] Civic Forum is for everybody' (Kopecky 2000).

Though most dissidents were pressured out of leading positions shortly after the first free elections, either by more skilled 'old-style' politicians or by straightforward electoral defeat, their legacy of anti-politics increasingly gained ground. Ironically, while anti-politics had been the exclusive territory of a small group of isolated dissidents under Communism, in the transition to democracy it achieved large-scale popularity under democracy. Moreover, captured by opportunists and anti-democrats, anti-politics was stripped of its rather naïve positive underpinnings and reduced to its more negative features. The struggle of the post-communist anti-political actor is not so much *for* something – such as a private space free from political or state intervention – but primarily *against*.

Post-communist political populists contest 'the power monopoly of the political class', arguing that the revolution has been stolen by former Communists and opportunists. In opposition to 'the political class' stand 'the people', which, in the tradition of both political populism and anti-politics, have a higher moral stature than amoral politicians (Greskovits 1998; Weyland 1999a). This fits well with the mood of Eastern European society, which can be defined as that of a 'victimised majority' eager to 'absolve itself from the need for normal political intercourse and compromise' (Braun 1997, 150; Tismaneanu 1996). Consequently, in line with both communist and anti-communist practice and morality, post-communist politics is to a large extent a struggle of good against evil, of all or nothing, in which compromise is not accepted.

In this atmosphere of polarisation and conspiracy, the rhetoric of the 'stolen revolution' is a fertile breeding ground. Its populist variant is mostly represented by right-wing rather than left-wing populist parties. The reason is simple: in most cases the argument is that the revolution has been stolen by former Communists, which fits well with the traditional anti-communism of the right. A good example are the Czech 'Republicans' (SPR-RSC) of Miroslav Sládek. Originally, the party had campaigned on a platform that included a call for very severe legislation designed to 'purge' former Communists. Later, the party broadened its 'politics of anti-politics' by targeting 'imaginary communists' (Dvoraková 2000). This led to the absurd situation of Sládek, a former Communist censor, accusing Havel, the former leading dissident, of being a 'traitor to the velvet revolution'.

Some Communist (successor) parties have also taken up the 'stolen revolution argument' against the new elite. Having disposed of, or at least toned down, their traditional elitist theory of class struggle under a Communist vanguard, they now defend 'the people' against 'the elite'. Obviously, this strategy is most successful in countries where former Communists are not particularly visible as such in post-communist politics and economy. In the Czech Republic, for example, the Communist Party of Bohemia and Moravia (KSCM) has made a stunning comeback with such a populist campaign. In other countries, former Communists are highly influential in post-communist politics, but no longer affiliate themselves with the Communist Party. Good examples are Russia and the Ukraine, where they have formed corrupt oligarchies, masquerading as defenders of democracy and the free market. Marginalised by the (super)presidentialist system in these countries, parties such as the Communist Party of the Russian Federation (KPRF) have resorted to populism rather than class politics in an attempt to gain a larger slice of the electoral cake (Gregor 1998; Hashim 1999).

Another way in which Communism has facilitated populist success in Eastern Europe is by its breakdown. Both economic and political crises reveal strong linkages with populism (Ernst 1987; Knight 1998). Moreover, as the democratisation movement in many countries fought two struggles at the same time – for freedom and against Communism and for national independence and against Soviet domination – the powerful combination of 'national populism' (Germani 1978; Taguieff 1995) surfaced in many countries. Though its nationalism has often been overstated, there is no doubt that the largest party in Slovak politics, the Movement for a Democratic Slovakia (HZDS), is a populist party. Centred on its charismatic leader, Vladimír Meciar, the 'quintessential populist demagogue' (Ulc 1996), the HZDS has from the outset championed the interests of 'the Slovak people'; first against 'the Czech elite', and later against 'the anti-Slovak elite' (Carpenter 1997; Leff 1998). This example also shows that populist politics in Eastern Europe is not purely an oppositional phenomenon, since Meciar's HZDS has been the major governmental party in independent Slovakia.

Studies have pointed to the positive relationship between presidentialism or semi-presidentialism and political populism (for example, Philip 1998; Weyland 1999a), particularly evident when populism is defined first and foremost as 'personalised politics'. Some post-communist presidents have at least used political populism, claiming to defend the general interest of 'the people' versus the special interests of the parties. Frequently noted examples of such populist presidents are Lech Walesa in Poland, Leonid Kuchma in Ukraine, and Boris Yeltsin in Russia (von Beyme 1996; Weyland 1999a), all of whom are functioning in semi-presidential, presidential or even super-presidential systems. However, presidents in parliamentary systems have also used political populism, including Václav Havel in the Czech Republic or Árpád Göncz in Hungary. In most cases, it had less to do with the *type* of political system than with the *maturity* of the system. The first decade of post-communist politics was characterised in most countries by a struggle over and between political institutions (Kopecky 1999). In their struggle against parliaments and political parties, presidents often choose to present themselves as the 'defenders of the whole people' rather than the 'defenders of special interests'.

However, as party systems, particularly in Eastern and Central Europe, increasingly resemble their western counterparts the phenomenon of populist politics is also changing. More of the leading intellectuals and mainstream party leaders are moving away from overt populist rhetoric, leaving it, as in the West, increasingly to the parties on the political fringe. According to Daniel Chirot (1996), this is because 'the forces of reaction' cannot find viable intellectual models in the West. This is highly debatable, since many national populist parties in Eastern Europe, such as the Hungarian Justice and Life Party

(MIÉP) and the Slovak SNS, are influenced by the ideas of the French *Front national* (FN).

Rather than having a lack of ideological inspiration from the West, I believe a more 'down-to-earth' political reason lies behind this recent conversion. Because most Eastern European countries are highly dependent on financial support from western-dominated organisations, and consider membership in the EU and NATO to be their highest foreign policy goal, they have to abide not only by the West's economic rules but also by its political norms. This only works when the institutions do not lower their standards and when EU membership is considered feasible in the short or medium term by local elites. In countries that will not be among the first wave of EU candidates, most probably Bulgaria and Romania, a populist backlash at both the mass and elite level is very likely to arise (Tanase 1999).

Conclusion

> It is the immediate past – the period since 1945 – together with the way in which the Communist era has been subsequently handled, that holds the key to an understanding of current developments. (Sunley 1996)

As in many other studies, any attempt to explain contemporary populism in Eastern Europe with reference to an 'age-old legacy' in the region is not particularly useful. What some scholars seem to underestimate is the profound way in which Communism has changed Eastern European societies and, consequently, their politics. But this 'Leninist legacy' is not as straightforward as is often assumed. This can also be seen in this short survey of different forms of populism in the region.

Agrarian populism was the leading political ideology among the people in pre-communist Eastern Europe. While the collaboration of leading figures of agrarian populism with both the right-wing authoritarian and the Communist regimes damaged its image among the people, the Communist policy of collectivisation transformed 'the people' so profoundly that there is virtually no space left for agrarian populism in post-communist Eastern Europe. Today, farmers in the region are 'rural workers' rather than 'peasants', and they give their support to (former) Communist parties rather than populist peasant parties.

As far as economic populism is concerned, this was not particularly relevant in pre-communist Eastern Europe, given the rural and backward character of most of the region. Communism changed this, not just through its radical industrialisation policies, but also through its welfare provisions and egalitarian rhetoric. At the same time, the reasonably equal division of (a lack of) goods among the people (excluding the *nomenclature*), as well as some other socio-economic features (such as the rise of the so-called 'grey society'), erected barriers to economic populism. But some of these barriers are already crumbling, as the market is rapidly dividing people into 'winners' and 'losers', 'haves' and 'have-nots', while it puts increasing strains on the old welfare state system. This, in combination with the strong support for equality and a strong welfare state at the mass level, is a fertile breeding ground for economic populism in post-communist Europe.

Finally, political populism, albeit that is was not prominent in the pre-communist era, is not entirely new to the region. As in the West, Eastern European populists in the 1920s–1930s generally fell prey to more specific ideologies, fascism and Communism, which both used populism to establish elitist regimes. Nevertheless, the period of Communism did leave an important legacy with regard to political populism, in the form of the 'anti-political politics' of the dissident movement. This intellectualised form of popular resentment against the Communist regime and its totalitarian politics only gained real notoriety in the *post*-communist period when it blended in perfectly with another 'Leninist legacy' – the myth of the 'victimised majority', cumulating in the rhetoric of the 'stolen revolution'.

Despite the fertile breeding ground for both economic and political populism, both forms have been only moderately successful in post-communist politics and this is attributable not to the historical legacy or the character of post-communist politics, but, to a large extent, to external factors. The post-communist 'triple transition' (Offe 1991) is a formidable task, in constant need of the support of regional leaders, of the regional masses, and the international environment. Most notably, the economic transition can only succeed with extensive funds from western states and international financial organisations such as the IMF and the World Bank. In return for financial support, Eastern European governments have to follow a rather strict economic policy that leaves little room for a policy of economic populism. A similar dynamics is at work in the political arena. Most Eastern European governments see EU membership as the highest foreign policy goal, accepting severe limitations in their political actions and style in order to achieve their ultimate aim.

Populism nevertheless plays a much more prominent role in contemporary Eastern European politics than in the West. The main problem in assessing its current role in more detail is twofold: the lack of clear-cut definitions for use in empirical research; and the shortage of empirical studies of populist praxis. For example, although Meciar's regime in Slovakia has almost unanimously been described as 'populist', the few studies made of the phenomenon of 'Meciarism' hardly use any clear conceptual or theoretical framework (for example, Leskó 1996; Fish 1999). This is, unfortunately, typical of the approach to the study of populism in general in which populism is used as a static label to vaguely qualify – and more often, to disqualify – a political actor. Yet were populism approached as a dynamic political phenomenon, it could arguably tell us much about both the political and the cultural environment in which it operates and which, in turn, generates it.

Notes

1. See, for example, Tismaneanu's (1999) collection of classic texts on the revolutions of 1989. A dissenting voice is Charles H. Fairbanks (1997, 97), who writes that 'The absence of *open* populist appeals is a distinctive feature of post-communist anti-politics; at a time when open populism, after the Cold War, is rising in the West, it is declining in the post-communist world'.
2. Some authors add an organisational feature, i.e. the fact that populists work outside the framework of political parties or within weakly organised (that is, personalised) parties (see, for example, Taggart 1995; Weyland 1999a, 1999b). However, as certain organisational and socioeconomic features accompanied populist politics in earlier periods, weakly organised political parties are more a sign of the times than a defining feature of political populism. Moreover, this organisational feature better describes the core of (related) phenomena such as 'charismatic leadership' or 'personalised politics'.
3. In the case of the Christian-Democratic Union-Czech(oslovak) People's Party (KDU-CSL) one may even doubt its description as a peasant party (rather than as a Christian Democratic party).
4. Tom Brass (1997) argues that the roots of agrarian populism can also be found in virtually all forms of 'postmodern theory', including ecofeminism, new social movements, post-Marxism, post-capitalism and so forth. I have not examined this claim in the post-communist context, as the similarities between agrarian populism and these movements, as described by Brass, are at such a high level of abstraction that it hardly still justifies the term 'agrarian populism'.

5. This also explains why in pre-war Eastern Europe, the Czech lands (notably Bohemia), then one of the most industrialised areas in Europe, was the only area in the region where agrarian populism was a marginal phenomenon (Ionescu 1969; Ulc 1996).
6. Authors claiming a resurgence of 'neopopulism' in Latin America in the 1990s, generally admit that these new populists differ significantly from their 'predecessors', associating 'neopopulism' instead with 'free-market economics' (Philip 1998), a particular political style (for example, Knight 1998), or both (Weyland 1999a).

Bibliography

Abromeit, H. (1998) *Democracy in Europe*. New York and Oxford, Berghahn Books.

Agócs, P. and Agócs, S (1994) '"The Change Was but an Unfulfilled Promise": Agriculture and the Rural Population in Post-Communist Hungary', *East European Politics and Societies*, 8 (1) 32–57.

Ahtisaari, M., Frowein, J. and Oreja, M. (2000) *Report*. Paris, mimeo.

Almond, G. A. and Verba, S. (1963) *The Civic Culture*. Princeton, Princeton University Press.

Anderson, B. (1991) *Imagined Communities*. London and New York, Verso.

Anderson, C. J. (2000) 'Economic Voting and Political Context: a Comparative Perspective', *Electoral Studies*, 19 (2/3), 151–70.

Anderson, P. (2000) 'Editorial: Renewals', *New Left Review*, (II) 1, 5–24.

Andeweg, R. B. (1999) 'Towards Representation *Ex Alto* and *Ex Post*?', paper presented at the conference on Multi-Level Party Systems, European University Institute, Florence.

Annan, K. A. (1999) 'The Backlash Against Globalism', *The Futurist*, 33 (3), 27.

Ashby, W. R. (1956) *An Introduction to Cybernetics*. London, Chapman & Hall.

Aylott, N. (1999) 'Paradoxes and Opportunism: the Danish Election of March 1998', *Government & Opposition*, 34, 70.

Barber, B. (1990) *Strong Democracy*. Berkeley, University of California Press.

Barney, D. D. and Laycock, D. (1999) 'Right-Populists and Plebiscitary Politics in Canada', *Party Politics*, 5 (3), 317–39.

Barry, B. (1965) *Political Argument*. London, Routledge & Kegan Paul.

Bartolini, S. (1999) 'Collusion, Competition, and Democracy, Part I', *Journal of Theoretical Politics*, 11 (4), 435–70.

Bartolini S. and Mair, P. (1990) *Identity, Competition, and Electoral Availability: the Stabilisation of European Electorates, 1885–1985*. Cambridge, CUP.

Beetham, D. (1992) 'Liberal Democracy and the Limits of Democratization' in D. Held (ed.), *Prospects for Democracy, Political Studies*, 40 (Special Issue), 40–53.

Bell, J. D. (1996) 'Populism and Pragmatism: the BANU in Bulgarian Politics' in J. Held (ed.), *Populism in Eastern Europe*. Boulder, East European Monographs, 21–61.

Benz, A. (1998) 'Postparlamentarische Demokratie? Demokratische Legitimation im kooperativen Staat' in M. T. Greven (ed.), *Demokratie – eine Kultur des Westens?* Opladen, Leske + Budrich, 201–22.

Berlin, I. et al. (1968) 'To Define Populism', *Government & Opposition*, 3 (2), 137–79.

Betz, H.-G. (1988) '"Deutschlandpolitik" on the Margins', *New German Critique*, 44, 127–57.

Betz, H.-G. (1994) *Radical Right-Wing Populism in Western Europe*. New York, St Martin's Press – now Palgrave.

Betz, H.-G. (1998a) 'Introduction' in H.-G. Betz and S. Immerfall (eds), *The New Politics of the Right*. London, Macmillan – now Palgrave, 1–10.

Betz, H.-G. (1998b) 'Against Rome: the Lega Nord' in H.-G. Betz and S. Immerfall (eds), *The New Politics of the Right*. New York, St Martin's Press – now Palgrave, 45–68.

Betz, H.-G. and Immerfall, S. (eds) (1998) *The New Politics of the Right*. New York, St Martin's Press – now Palgrave.

Beyme, K. von (1996) 'Rechtsextremismus in Osteuropa' in J. W. Falter, H.-G. Jaschke and J. R. Winkler (eds), *Rechtsextremismus. Ergebnisse und Perspektiven der Forschung*. Opladen, Westdeutscher, 423–42.

Billiet, J. and De Witte, H. (1995) 'Attitudinal Dispositions to Vote for a "New" Extreme Right-wing Party: the Case of "Vlaams Blok"', *European Journal of Political Research* (hereafter *EJPR*), 27 (2), 181–202.

Biorcio, R. (1991) 'La Lega come attore politico: dal federalismo al populismo regionalista' in R. Mannheimer (ed.), *La Lega Lombarda*. Milan, Feltrinelli, 34–82.

Biorcio, R. (1991/92) 'The Rebirth of Populism in Italy and France', *Telos*, 90 (Winter), 43–56.

Biorcio, R. (1997) *La Padania promessa*. Milan, Il Saggiatore.

Birenbaum, G. (1992) *Le Front national en politique*. Paris, Balland.

Birnbaum, P. (1979) *Le peuple et les gros*. Paris, Grasset.

Bittner, R. (1994) 'Ressentiment' in R. Schacht (ed.), *Nietzsche, Genealogy, Morality*. Berkeley, University of California Press, 127–38.

Bjugan, K. (1998) 'The 1997 Norwegian Parliamentary Election: a Swing Towards Parliamentary Power', *Political Quarterly*, 69 (2), 177–80.

Blinder, A. S. (1997) 'Is Government Too Political?', *Foreign Affairs*, 76 (6), 115–26.

Blocher, C. (1997a) 'Switzerland and the Second World War: a Clarification', speech given in Zurich, www.cins.ch/second.htm.

Blocher, C. (1997b) 'Switzerland and the Eizenstat Report', speech given in Bern.

Blom, S. (1998) *Holdning til innvandrere og innvandringspolitikk*. Oslo, Statistics Norway.

Bobbio, N. (1987) *The Future of Democracy*. Cambridge, Polity Press.

Boy, D. and Mayer, N. (eds) (1997) *L'électeur a ses raisons*. Paris, Presses de Sciences Po.

Bozóki, A. (1994) 'An Outline of Three Populisms: the United States, Argentina and Hungary', CEU, Department of Political Science, Working Paper No. 5.

Bozóki, A. (ed.) (1999) *Intellectuals and Politics in Central Europe*. Budapest, CEU Press.

Brass, T. (1997) 'The Agrarian Myth, the "New" Populism and the "New" Right', *Journal of Peasant Studies*, 24 (4), 201–45.

Braun, A. (1997) 'The Incomplete Revolutions: the Rise of Extremism in East-Central Europe and the Former Soviet Union' in A. Braun and S. Sheinberg (eds), *The Extreme Right: Freedom and Security at Risk*. Boulder, Westview Press, 138–60.

Breitling, R. (1987) 'Populismus' in A. Pelinka (ed.), *Populismus in Österreich*. Vienna, Junius, 26–34.

Broder, D. (2000) *Democracy Derailed: Initiative Campaigns and the Power of Money*. New York, Harcourt.

Buchanan, J. G. and Tullock, G. (1962) *The Calculus of Consent*. Ann Arbor, University of Michigan Press.

Budge, I. (1996) *The New Challenge of Direct Democracy*. Cambridge, Polity Press.

Butler, D. and Ranney, A. (eds) (1994) *Referendums Around the World*. Basingstoke, Macmillan – now Palgrave.

Canovan, M. (1981) *Populism*. New York, Harcourt Brace Jovanovich.

Canovan, M. (1984) '"People", Politicians and Populism', *Government & Opposition*, 19 (3), 312–27.

Canovan, M. (1993) 'Il populismo come l'ombra della democrazia', *Europa Europe*, 2, 43–62.

Canovan, M. (1999) 'Trust the People! Populism and the Two Faces of Democracy', *Political Studies*, 47 (1), 2–16.

Cardoso, F. H. and Faletto, E. (1979) *Dependency and Development in Latin America*. Berkeley, University of California Press.

Carey, J. M., Niemi, R. G. and Powell, L. W. (2000) *Term Limits in State Legislatures*. Ann Arbor, University of Michigan Press.

Carmines, E. G. (1991) 'The Logic of Party Alignments', *Journal of Theoretical Politics*, 3 (1), 65–80.

Carmines, E. G. and Stimson, J. A. (1993) 'On the Evolution of Political Issues' in W. H. Riker (ed.), *Agenda Formation*. Ann Arbor, University of Michigan Press, 151–68.

Carpenter, J. (1997) 'Slovakia and the Triumph of Nationalist Populism', *Communist and Post-Communist Studies*, 30 (2) 205–20.

Cerny, P. G. (1999) 'Globalization and the Erosion of Democracy', *EJPR*, 36 (1) 1–26.

Chirac, J. (1994) *La France pour tous*. Paris, Nil éditions.

Chirot, D. (1996) 'Why East Central Europe is Not Quite Ready for Perón, but May Be One Day', *East European Politics and Societies*, 10 (3), 536–40.

Conniff, M. L. (ed.) (1982a) *Latin American Populism in Comparative Perspective*. Albuquerque, University of New Mexico Press.

Conniff, M. L. (1982b) 'Introduction: Toward A Comparative Definition of Populism' in M. L. Conniff (ed.), *Latin American Populism in Comparative Perspective*. Albuquerque, University of New Mexico Press, 3–30.

Conniff, M. L. (ed.) (1999) *Populism in Latin America*. Tuscaloosa, University of Alabama Press.

CNCDH (1998) *La lutte contre le racisme et la xénophobie, 9éme enquête pour la Commission nationale consultative des droits de l'homme (CNCDH)*. Paris, La documentation française.

Crozier, M., Huntingdon, S. and Watanuki, J. (1975) *The Crisis of Democracy. Report on the Governability of Democracies to the Trilateral Commission*. New York, New York University Press.

Csepeli, G. (1996) 'In the Captivity of Narratives: the Political Socialization of Populist Writers in Hungary, and the Origin of National Narratives in Eastern Europe' in J. Held (ed.), *Populism in Eastern Europe*. Boulder, East European Monographs, 129–44.

Dahl, R. A. (1956) *Preface to Democratic Theory*. New Haven, Yale University Press.

Dahl, R. A. (1998) *On Democracy*. New Haven, Yale University Press.
Dahl, R. A. (1999) 'The Past and Future of Democracy', Occasional Paper No. 5/1999, Centre for the Study of Political Change, Università degli Studi di Siena.
Dalton, R. J. (1996) *Citizen Politics: Public Opinion and Political Parties in Advanced Industrial Democracies*. Chatham NJ, Chatham House.
Dalton, R. J. (1999) 'Political Support in Advanced Industrial Democracies' in P. Norris (ed.), *Critical Citizens*. Oxford, Oxford University Press, 57–77.
Dalton, R. J. and Küchler, H. (eds) (1990) *Challenging the Political Order: New Social and Political Movements in Western Democracies*. Cambridge, Polity Press.
Diamanti, I. (1993) *La Lega. Geografia, storia e sociologia di un nuovo soggetto politico*. Rome, Donzelli.
Didion, J. (1999) 'Uncovered Washington', *New York Review of Books*, 24 June.
Di Tella, T. S. (1965) 'Populism and Reform in Latin America' in C. Veliz (ed.), *Obstacles to Change in Latin America*. Oxford, Oxford University Press, 47–74.
Di Tella, T. S. (1997) 'Populism in the Twenty-first Century', *Government & Opposition*, 32 (2), 187–200.
Dobry, M. (1992) *Sociologie des crises politiques*. Paris, Presses de la Fondation Nationale des Sciences Politiques.
Drake, P. W. (1982) 'Conclusion: Requiem for Populism?' in M. L. Conniff (ed.), *Latin American Populism in Comparative Perspective*. Albuquerque, University of New Mexico Press, 217–45.
Dryzek, J. S. (1990) *Discursive Democracy: Politics, Policy, and Political Science*. Cambridge, Cambridge University Press.
Duran, P. (1999) *Penser l'action publique*. Paris, LGDJ.
Dvoraková, V. (2000) 'The Politics of Antipolitics? the Radical Right in the Czech Republic' in L. Sorenson (ed.), *Liberalism, Fascism and Social Democracy in Central Europe*. Aarhus, Aarhus University Press.
Dziewanowski, M. K. (1996) 'Polish Populism' in J. Held (ed.), *Populism in Eastern Europe*. Boulder, East European Monographs, 163–96.
Ellis, R. J. (1993) *American Political Cultures*. New York and Oxford, Oxford University Press.
Elster, J. (1998) 'Introduction' in J. Elster (ed.), *Deliberative Democracy*. Cambridge, Cambridge University Press, 1–18.
Elster, J. (1999) 'Accountability in Athenian Politics' in A. Przeworski et al. (eds), *Democracy, Accountability, and Representation*. Cambridge, Cambridge University Press, 253–78.
Ernst, W. W. (1987) 'Zu einer Theorie des Populismus' in A. Pelinka (ed.), *Populismus in Österreich*. Vienna, Junius, 10–25.
Fairbanks Jr., C. H. (1997) 'The Public Void: Antipolitics in the Former Soviet Union' in A. Schedler (ed.) *The End of Politics?* Basingstoke, Macmillan – now Palgrave, 91–114.
Faßmann, H. (1995) 'Der Wandel der Bevölkerungsstruktur in der Zweiten Republik' in R. Sieder, H. Steinert and E. Tálos (eds), *Österreich 1945–1995*. Vienna, Verlag für Gesellschaftskritik, 395–408.
Fennema, N. (1997) 'Some Conceptual Issues and Problems in the Comparison of Anti-Immigrant Parties in Western Europe', *Party Politics*, 3 (4), 473–92.
Finley, M. (1983) *L'invention de la politique*. Paris, Flammarion.

Fischer-Galati, S. (1996) 'Conclusions' in J. Held (ed.), *Populism in Eastern Europe*. Boulder, East European Monographs, 245–7.

Fish, M. S. (1999) 'The End of Meciarism', *East European Constitutional Review*, 8 (1/2), 47–55.

Fishkin, J. S. (1991) *Democracy and Deliberation*. New Haven, Yale University Press.

Foley, M. (1991) *American Political Ideas*. Manchester, Manchester University Press.

Fontana, B. (1994) 'Démocratie et histoire des idées', *Revue européenne des sciences sociales*, 32 (98) 189–93.

Fonvieille Alquier, F. (1984) *Une France poujadiste? De Poujade à Le Pen et à quelques autres ...* Paris, Éditions universitaires.

François, B. (1996) *Naissance d'une Constitution. La Cinquième République, 1958–1962*. Paris, Presses de Sciences Po.

Freeden, M. (1996) *Ideologies and Political Theory: a Conceptual Approach*. Oxford, Clarendon Press.

Freeden, M. (1998) 'Is Nationalism a Distinct Ideology?', *Political Studies*, 46 (4), 748–65.

Freiheitliche Akademie (n.d.) *Vom Parteienstaat zur Bürgerdemokratie*. Vienna, Freiheitliche Akademie.

Gaïti, B. (1998) *De Gaulle, prophète de la Cinquième République*. Paris, Presses de Sciences Po.

Gallagher, M. and Uleri, P. V. (eds) (1996) *The Referendum Experience in Europe*. Basingstoke, Macmillan – now Palgrave.

Gentile, P. and Kriesi, H. (1998) 'Contemporary Radical-Right Parties in Switzerland' in H.-G. Betz and S. Immerfall (eds), *The New Politics of the Right*. New York, St Martin's Press – now Palgrave, 125–42.

Gerber, E. R. (1999) *The Populist Paradox*. Princeton, Princeton University Press.

Germani, G. (1978) *Authoritarianism, Fascism, and National Populism*. New Brunswick, NJ, Transaction Books.

Gerring, J. (1998) *Party Ideologies in America, 1828–1896*. Cambridge, Cambridge University Press.

Giannini, G. (1945) *La Folla: seimila anni di lotta contro la tirannide*. Rome, Faro.

Giddens, A. (1998) *The Third Way: the Renewal of Social Democracy*. Cambridge, Polity Press.

Gobetti, D. (1996) 'La Lega: Regularities and Innovation in Italian Politics', *Politics and Society*, 24 (1), 57–82.

Goodwyn, L. (1976) *Democratic Promise: the Populist Movement in America*. New York, Oxford University Press.

Goodwyn, L. (1991) 'Rethinking "Populism": Paradoxes of Historiography and Democracy', *Telos*, 24 (2), 37–56.

Goot, M. (1998) 'Hanson's Heartland: Who's For One Nation and Why' in T. Abbot (ed.), *Two Nations: the Causes and Effects of the Rise of the One Nation Party in Australia*. Melbourne, Bookman Press.

Gregor, A. J. (1998) 'Fascism and the New Russian Nationalism', *Communist and Post-Communist Studies*, 31 (1), 1–15.

Greskovits, B. (1998) *The Political Economy of Protest and Patience: East European and Latin American Transformations Compared*. Budapest, CEU Press.

Guidorossi, G. (1984) *Gli italiani e la politica*. Milan, Angeli.

Habermas, J. (1989) 'Ist der Herzschlag der Revolution zum Stillstand gekommen?' in Forum für Philosophie Bad Homburg (ed.), *Die Ideen von 1789 in der deutschen Rezeption*. Frankfurt, Suhrkamp, 7–36.

Habermas, J. (1992) *Faktizität und Geltung*. Frankfurt, Suhrkamp.

Habermas, J. (1994) 'Three Normative Models of Democracy', *Constellations*, I, 1–10.

Habermas, J. (1996) *Between Facts and Norms: Contributions to a Discourse Theory of Law and Democracy*. Cambridge, Ma., MIT Press.

Hadenius, A. (ed.) (1997) *Democracy's Victory and Crisis*. Cambridge, Cambridge University Press.

Haider, J. (1995) *The Freedom I Mean*. Pine Plains, Swan.

Hanák, P. (1996) 'The Anti-Capitalist Ideology of the Populists' in J. Held (ed.), *Populism in Eastern Europe*. Boulder, East European Monographs, 145–61.

Hanson, P. (1996) 'Australia Wake Up!', maiden speech to Parliament, http://www.onenation.com.au/speeches/phtalk.htm.

Hanson, P. (1997) 'Launch of One Nation', speech delivered on 11 April.

Harrison, T. (1995) *Of Passionate Intensity*. Toronto, University of Toronto Press.

Hashim, S. M. (1999) 'KPRF Ideology and its Implications for Democratization in Russia', *Communist and Post-Communist Studies*, 32 (1), 77–89.

Haskell, J. (2000) *Direct Democracy or Representative Government? Dispelling the Populist Myth*. Boulder, Westview Press.

Hassenteufel, P. (1991) 'Structures de représentation et "appel au peuple". Le populisme en Autriche', *Politix*, 14 (2), 95–101.

Havel, V. (1988) 'Anti-Political Politics' in J. Keane (ed.), *Civil Society and the State*. London, Verso, 381–98.

Hayes, B. C. and McAllister, I. (1999) 'Who Voted for Peace? Public Support for the 1998 Northern Ireland Peace Agreement', paper presented at the Atlanta meeting of the APSA.

Hayward, J. (1996a) 'The Populist Challenge to Elitist Democracy in Europe' in J. Hayward (ed.), *Elitism, Populism, and European Politics*. Oxford, Clarendon Press, 10–32.

Hayward, J. (ed.) (1996b) *Elitism, Populism, and European Politics*. Oxford, Clarendon Press.

Held, D. (ed.) (1993) *Prospects for Democracy: North, South, East, West*. Stanford, Ca., Stanford University Press.

Held, J. (ed.) (1996a) *Populism in Eastern Europe*. Boulder, East European Monographs.

Held, J. (1996b) 'Antecedents' in J. Held (ed.), *Populism in Eastern Europe*. Boulder, East European Monographs, 1–20.

Helms, L. (1997) 'Right-wing Populist Parties in Austria and Switzerland: a Comparative Analysis of Electoral Support and Conditions of Success', *Western European Politics* (hereafter *WEP*), 20 (2), 37–52.

Hermet, G. (1991) 'L'éducation des gouvernants par les gouvernés', *Cosmopolitiques*, 19, 47–53.

Hermet, G. (1992) 'Le populisme: concilier l'inconciliable', paper presented at the workshop 'Political Behaviour', Annual Congress of the Swiss Political Science Association, Balsthal, 13 November.

Hermet, G. (1997) 'Populisme et nationalisme', *Vingtième siècle*, 56, Oct.–Dec., 34–47.

Hermet, G. (2001) *Les populismes dans le monde: une histoire sociologique XIXe–XXe siècle*. Paris, Fayard.

Hertzke, A. (1993) *Echoes of Discontent: Jesse Jackson, Pat Robertson, and the Resurgence of Populism*, Washington, Congressional Quarterly Press.

Hine, D. (1996) 'Political Parties and the Public Accountability of Leaders' in J. Hayward (ed.), *Elitism, Populism, and European Politics*. Oxford, Clarendon Press, 121–42.

Hinich, M. J. and Munger, M. C. (1997) *Analytical Politics*. Cambridge, Cambridge University Press.

Hofstadter, R. (1969) 'North America' in G. Ionescu and E. Gellner (eds), *Populism*. London, Weidenfeld & Nicolson, 9–27.

IFOP/*L'Express* survey (1996) 'L'évolution du racisme en France'.

Ignazi, P. (1992) 'The Silent Counter-Revolution: Hypotheses on the Emergence of Extreme Right-Wing Parties in Europe', *EJPR*, 22 (1), 3–34.

Ignazi, P. (1996) 'The Intellectual Basis of Right-Wing Anti-Partyism', *EJPR*, 29, 279–96.

Ignazi, P. (1999) 'Les partis d'extrême-droite: les fruits inachevés de la société post-industrielle', paper presented at the 6th Congress of the French Political Science Association, Rennes, 28 Sept.–1 Oct.

IMAS (1992) *Report*, No. 13, June.

Immerfall, S. (1998) 'The Neo-Populist Agenda' in H.-G. Betz and S. Immerfall (eds), *The New Politics of the Right*. London, Macmillan – now Palgrave, 249–61.

Incisa di Camerana, L. (2000) *Fascismo Populismo Modernizzazione*. Rome, Pellicani.

Ionescu, G. (1969) 'Eastern Europe' in G. Ionescu and E. Gellner (eds), *Populism*. London, Weidenfeld & Nicolson, 97–121.

Ionescu, G. and Gellner, E. (eds) (1969) *Populism: its Meanings and National Characteristics*. London, Weidenfeld & Nicolson.

Jowitt, K. (1992) *The New World Disorder: the Leninist Extinction*. Berkeley, University of California Press.

Katz, R. S. (1980) *A Theory of Parties and Electoral Systems*. Baltimore, Johns Hopkins University Press.

Katz, R. S. (1986) 'Party Government: a Rationalistic Conception' in F. G. Castles and R. Wildenmann (eds), *Visions and Realities of Party Government*. Berlin, de Gruyter, 31–71.

Katz, R. S. (1997) *Democracy and Elections*. New York, Oxford University Press.

Katz, R. S. and Mair, P. (1995) 'Changing Models of Party Organization and Party Democracy: the Emergence of the Cartel Party', *Party Politics*, 1 (1) 5–28.

Katzenstein, P. (1985) *Small States in World Markets*. Ithaca, NY, Cornell University Press.

Kazin, M. (1995) *The Populist Persuasion: an American History*. New York, Basic Books.

Khol, A. (1995) 'Die FPÖ im Spannungsfeld von Ausgrenzung, Selbstausgrenzung, Verfassungsbogen und Regierungsfähigkeit', *Österreichisches Jahrbuch für Politik 1995*, 193–221.

King, D. (2000) *Making Americans: Immigration, Race and the Origins of Diverse Democracy*. Cambridge, Ma. and London, Harvard University Press.

Kitschelt, H. (1986) 'Political Opportunity Structure and Political Protest. Anti-Nuclear Movements in Four Democracies', *British Journal of Political Science*, 16 (1), 57–85.

Kitschelt, H. (2000) 'Linkages Between Citizens and Politicians in Democratic Polities', *Comparative Political Studies*, 33 (6–7), 845–79.

Kitschelt, H. and McGann, A. J. (1995) *The Radical Right in Western Europe: a Comparative Analysis*. Ann Arbor, University of Michigan Press.

Kligman, G. and Verdery, K. (1999) 'Reflections on the "Revolutions" of 1989 and After', *East European Politics and Societies*, 13 (2), 303–12.

Klingemann, H.-D. (1999) 'Mapping Political Support in the 1990s: a Global Analysis' in P. Norris (ed.), *Critical Citizens*. Oxford, Oxford University Press, 31–56.

Klingeman, H.-D. and Fuchs, D. (1995) *Citizens and the State*. Oxford, Oxford University Press.

Knight, A. (1998) 'Populism and Neo-Populism in Latin America, especially Mexico', *Journal of Latin American Studies*, 30 (2), 223–48.

Knopff, R. (1998) 'Populism and the Politics of Rights: the Dual Attack on Representative Democracy', *Canadian Journal of Political Science*, 31, 683–705.

Kobach, K. W. (1993) *The Referendum: Direct Democracy in Switzerland*. Aldershot, Dartmouth.

Konrád, G. (1984) *Antipolitics*. London, Quartet Books.

Kopecky, P. (1995) 'Developing Party Organizations in East-Central Europe: What Type of Party Is Likely to Emerge?', *Party Politics*, 1 (4), 515–34.

Kopecky, P. (1999) 'Political Competition and the Institutionalisation of Parliaments: the Czech and Slovak Republics', PhD thesis, University of Leiden.

Kopecky, P. (2000) 'The Limits of Whips and Watchdogs: Parliamentary Parties in the Czech Republic' in K. Heidar and R. Koole (eds), *Behind Closed Doors: Parliamentary Party Groups in European Democracies*. London, Routledge, 177–94.

Kornhauser, W. (1959) *The Politics of Mass Society*. Glencoe, Ill., Free Press.

Kovács, J. M. (1996) 'Haider in Ungarn. Notizen zum postmodernen Populismus', *Transit. Europäische Revue*, 11, 182–98.

Kräh, G. (1996) *Die Freiheitlichen unter Jörg Haider*. Frankfurt am Main, P. Lang.

Kriesi, H. (1994) 'La défi à la démocratie directe posé par les transformations de l'espace public' in Y. Papadopoulos (ed.), *Présent et avenir de la démocratie directe. Actes du colloque de l'Université de Lausanne*. Geneva, Georg, 31–72.

Kriesi, H. (1998) 'The Transformation of Cleavage Politics. The 1997 Stein Rokkan Lecture, *EJPR*, 33 (2), 165–85.

Kriesi, H. (1999) 'Movements of the Left. Movements of the Right: Putting the Mobilization of Two New Types of Social Movements into Political Context' in H. Kitschelt et al. (eds), *Continuity and Change in Contemporary Capitalism*. Cambridge, Cambridge University Press, 398–423.

Kuijsten, A. (1997) 'Immigration and Public Finance: the Case of the Netherlands' in E. M. Uçarer and D. C. Puchale (eds), *Immigration into Western Societies*. London, Pinter, 209–28.

Lackó, M. (1996) 'Populism in Hungary: Yesterday and Today' in J. Held (ed.), *Populism in Eastern Europe*. Boulder, East European Monographs, 107–28.

La Palombara, J. (1965) 'Italy: Fragmentation, Isolation and Alienation' in L. W. Pye and S. Verba (eds), *Political Culture and Political Development*. Princeton, Princeton University Press, 282–329.

Lasch, C. (1991) *The True and Only Heaven: Progress and its Critics*. New York, Norton.

Lavau, G. (1969) *À quoi sert le PCF?* Paris, Fayard.

Laycock, D. (1994) 'Reforming Canadian Democracy? Institutions and Ideology in the Reform Party Project', *Canadian Journal of Political Science*, 27 (2), 213–47.

Lebhart, G. and Münz, R. (1998) 'Die Österreicher und ihre "Fremden"' in H. Faßmann, H. Matuschek and E. Menasse (eds), *Abgrenzen, ausgrenzen, aufnehmen: Empirische Befunde zu Fremdenfeindlichkeit und Integration*. Klagenfurt, Drava, 9–32.

Leca, J. (1996) 'La démocratie à l'épreuve des pluralismes', *Revue française de science politique*, 46 (2), 225–79.

Leff, C. S. (1998) *The Czech and Slovak Republics: Nation Versus State*. Boulder, Westview Press.

Lefort, C. (1986) *The Political Forms of Modern Society: Bureaucracy, Democracy, Totalitarianism*. Cambridge, Polity Press.

Lefort, C. (1988) *Democracy and Political Theory*. Cambridge, Polity Press.

Leskó, M. (1996) *Meciar a meciarizmus*. Bratislava, VMV.

Lewis-Beck, M. (1988) *Economics and Elections: the Major Western Democracies*. Ann Arbor, University of Michigan Press.

Lijphart, A. (1984) *Democracies: Patterns of Majoritarian and Consensus Government in Twenty One Countries*. New Haven, Yale University Press.

Lijphart, A. (1999) *Patterns of Democracy – Government Forms and Performance in Thirty-Six Countries*. New Haven, Yale University Press.

Lipset, S. M. (1963) *Political Man: the Social Bases of Support*. New York, Anchor.

Lipset, S. M. and Raab, E. (1971) *The Politics of Unreason: Right-Wing Extremism in America, 1790–1970*. London, Heinemann.

Lipset, S., and Rokkan, S. (1967) 'Cleavage Structures, Party Systems, and Voter Alignments: an Introduction' in S. Lipset and S. Rokkan (eds), *Party Systems and Voter Alignments*. New York, The Free Press, 1–64.

Longchamp, C. Ulrich, G., Bieri, U. and Bösch, L. (n.d.) *Umgruppierung der WählerInnen-Landschaft*, http://www.polittrends.ch/nachanalyse/welcome.html.

Luther, K. R. (1997) 'Die Freiheitlichen' in H. Dachs (ed.), *Handbuch des politischen Systems Österreichs*. Vienna, Manz, 286–303.

Luzzatto Fegiz, P. (1956) *Il volto sconosciuto dell'Italia. Dieci anni di sondaggi Doxa*. Milan, Giuffrè.

Luzzatto Fegiz, P. (1966) *Il volto sconosciuto dell'Italia. Seconda serie*. Milan, Giuffrè.

Lynch, J. (1969) *Presidential Address to the Fianna Fáil Árd Fheis*. Dublin, Fianna Fáil.

McCormick, R. L. (1986) *The Party Period and Public Policy: American Politics from the Age of Jackson to the Progressive Era*. Oxford, Oxford University Press.

McKean, M. and Scheiner, E. (1996) 'Can Japanese voters ever throw the rascals out? Electoral reform enhances permanent employment for politicians', unpublished MS, Duke University, November.

McMath, R. C. Jr. (1993) *American Populism: a Social History, 1877–1898*. New York, Hill & Wang.
MacRae, D. (1969) 'Populism as an Ideology' in G. Ionescu and E. Gellner (eds), *Populism*. London. Weidenfeld & Nicolson, 153–65.
Madeley, J. (1998) 'The Politics of Embarrassment: Norway's 1997 Elections', *WEP*, 21 (2), 190.
Magleby, D. B. (1984) *Direct Legislation: Voting on Ballot Propositions in the US*. Baltimore, Johns Hopkins University Press.
Mair, P. (1993) 'Myths of Electoral Change and the Survival of Traditional Parties', *EJPR*, 24 (2), 121–33.
Mair, P. (1995) 'Political Parties, Popular Legitimacy and Public Privilege' in J. Hayward (ed.), *The Crisis of Representation in Europe*. London, Frank Cass, 40–57.
Mair, P. (1997) *Party System Change: Approaches and Interpretations*. Oxford, Clarendon Press.
Mair, P. (2000) 'Partyless Democracy and the "Paradox" of New Labour', *New Left Review*, (2) (March–April), 21–35.
Majone, G. (ed.) (1996) *Regulating Europe*. London, Routledge.
Malloy, J. M. (1977) 'Authoritarianism and Corporatism in Latin America: the Modal Pattern' in J. M. Malloy (ed.), *Authoritarianism and Corporatism in Latin America*. Pittsburgh, University of Pittsburgh Press, 3–19.
Manin, B. (1994) 'Checks, Balances and Boundaries: the Separation of Powers in the Constitutional Debate of 1787' in B. Fontana (ed.), *The Invention of the Modern Republic*. Cambridge, Cambridge University Press, 27–62.
Manin, B. (1995) *Principes du gouvernement représentatif*. Paris, Calmann-Lévy.
Manin, B. (1997) *The Principles of Representative Government*. Cambridge, Cambridge University Press.
Manne, R. (1998) 'Foreword' in T. Abbot (ed.), *Two Nations: the Causes and Effects of the Rise of the One Nation Party in Australia*. Melbourne, Bookman Press, 3–9.
Manning, P. (1992) *The New Canada*. Toronto, Macmillan.
Maravall, J. M. (1999) 'Accountability and Manipulation' in A. Przeworski, B. Manin and S. C. Stokes (eds), *Democracy, Accountability, and Representation*. Cambridge, Cambridge University Press, 154–96.
Maravall, J. M. (2000) 'Rule of Law', paper for a workshop on Democracy and the Rule of Law organized by the Juan March Foundation, Madrid, 22–4 June.
March, J. G. and Olsen, J. P. (1995) *Democratic Governance*. New York, Free Press.
Marquand, D. (1999) 'Progressive or Populist? The Blair Paradox' in D. Marquand, *The Progressive Dilemma*, 2nd edn. London, Phoenix House, 225–46.
Mayer, N. (1999) *Ces Français qui votent FN*. Paris, Flammarion.
Mayer, N. and Perrineau, P. (eds) (1996) *Le Front national à découvert*, 2nd edn. Paris, Presses de la Fondation nationale des sciences politiques.
Mazower, M. (1998) *Dark Continent: Europe's Twentieth Century*. London, Allen Lane.
Mégret, B. (1997) *L'alternative nationale*. Saint-Cloud, Éditions nationales, on Front national, www.front-nat.fr.
Mény, Y. (1992) *La corruption de la République*. Paris, Fayard.

Mény, Y. (1998) 'The People, the Elites and the Populist Challenge', Jean Monnet Chair Papers, Florence, European University Insitute.

Mény, Y. and Surel, Y. (2000) *Par le peuple, pour le peuple.* Paris, Fayard.

Merkel, W. (1999) 'Defekte Demokratien' in W. Merkel and A. Busch (eds), *Demokratie in Ost und West.* Frankfurt, Suhrkamp, 361–81.

Merrill, S. III and Grofman, B. (1997) 'Directional and Proximity Models of Voter Utility and Choice: a New Synthesis and an Illustrative Test of Competing Models', *Journal of Theoretical Politics*, 9 (1), 25–48.

Miller, R. (1998) 'New Zealand First' in H.-G. Betz and S. Immerfall (eds), *The New Politics of the Right.* New York, St Martin's Press – now Palgrave, 203–10.

Morand, C.-A. (1999) *Le droit néo-moderne des politiques publiques.* Paris, LGDJ.

Morlino, L. and Tarchi, M. (1996) 'The Dissatisfied Society: the Roots of Political Change in Italy', *EJPR*, 30 (1), 41–63.

Mudde, C. (1995) 'One against All, All against One!: a Portrait of the Vlaams Blok', *Patterns of Prejudice*, 29 (1), 5–28.

Mudde, C. (1996) 'The Paradox of the Anti-party Party: Insights from the Extreme Right', *Party Politics*, 2 (2), 265–76.

Mudde, C. (2000a) *The Ideology of the Extreme Right.* Manchester, Manchester University Press.

Mudde, C. (2000b) 'Extreme Right Parties in Eastern Europe', *Patterns of Prejudice*, 34 (1), 5–27.

Müller, W. C. (1989) 'Party Patronage in Austria' in A. Pelinka and F. Plasser (eds), *The Austrian Party System.* Boulder, Westview Press, 327–56.

Müller, W. C. (1998) 'Party Competition and Plebiscitary Politics in Austria', *Electoral Studies*, 17 (1), 21–43.

Müller, W. C. (1999) 'Plebiscitary Agenda-Setting and Party Strategies: Theoretical Considerations and Evidence from Austria', *Party Politics*, 5 (3), 305–17.

Müller, W. C. and Jenny, M. (2000) 'Abgeordnete, Parteien und Koalitionspolitik: Individuelle Präferenzen und politisches Handeln im Nationalrat', *Österreichische Zeitschrift für Politikwissenschaft*, 29 (2), 137–56.

Müller, W. C., Plasser, F. and Ulram, P. A. (1999) 'Schwäche als Vorteil, Stärke als Nachteil' in P. Mair, W. C. Müller, and F. Plasser (eds), *Parteien auf Komplexen Wählermärkten.* Vienna, Signum, 201–45.

Narkiewicz, O. A. (1976) *The Green Flag: Polish Populist Politics 1867–1970.* London, Croom Helm.

Neveu, E. (1997) *Une société de communication?* Paris, Montchrestien (Coll. Clefs).

Nevitt, N., Blais, A., Gidengil, E., Johnson, R. and Brady, H. (1998) 'The Populist Right in Canada: the Rise of the Reform Party in Canada' in H.-G. Betz and S. Immerfall (eds), *The New Politics of the Right.* New York, St Martin's Press – now Palgrave, 173–202.

Newton, K. (1997) 'Social and Political Trust', paper presented at the John F. Kennedy School of Government Workshop on Confidence in Democratic Institutions: America in Comparative Perspective, Washington, DC.

Nie, J. S., Zelikow, P. D. and King, D. C. (eds) (1997) *Why People Don't Trust Government.* Cambridge, Ma, Harvard University Press.

Norris, P. (ed.) (1999) *Critical Citizens.* Oxford, Oxford University Press.

Ober, J. (1989) *Mass and Elite in Democratic Athens.* Princeton, Princeton University Press.

Offe, C. (1987) 'Democracy Against the Welfare State? Structural Foundations of Neo-conservative Political Opportunities', *Political Theory*, 15 (4), 501–37.

Offe, C. (1991) 'Capitalism by Democratic Design: Democratic Theory Facing Triple Transition in East Central Europe', *Social Research*, 58 (4), 865–92.

Offe, C. (1992) *Thesen zur öffentlichen Anhörung des gemeinsamen Verfassungskommission zum Thema Bürgerbeteiligung/Plebiszite*, mimeo, Bonn.

Offe, C. and Preuss, U. (1991) 'Democratic Institutions and Moral Resources' in D. Held (ed.), *Political Theory Today*. Cambridge, Polity Press, 143–71.

Ossipow, W. (1994) 'Le système politique suisse ou l'art de la compensation' in Y. Papadopoulos (ed.), *Elites politiques et peuple en Suisse*. Lausanne, Réalités sociales, 9–55.

Ost, D. (1999) 'The Radical Right in Poland: Rationality of the Irrational' in S. Ramet (ed.), *The Radical Right in Central and Eastern Europe Since 1989*. University Park, Pennsylvania State University Press, 85–107.

Page, J. A. (1983) *Perón: a Biography*. New York, Random House.

Papadopoulos, Y. (1996) 'Les mécanismes du vote référendaire en Suisse: l'impact de l'offre politique', *Revue française de sociologie*, 37 (1), 5–35.

Papadopoulos, Y. (1998) *Démocratie directe*. Paris, Economica.

Papadopoulos, Y. (2000) '"Gouvernance" et transformations de l'action publique: quelques notes sur l'apport d'une perspective de sociologie historique', paper prepared for the conference 'L'historicité de l'action publique. Activités pratiques et histoire des dispositifs publics', University of Amiens, 12–13 October.

Papadopoulos, Y. (2001) 'Transformations du style de l'action publique et responsabilité politique', *Politiques et management public*, 19(1), 165–83.

Pegram, T. R. (1992) *Politicians and Progressives: Private Interest and Public Policy in Illinois*. Urbana and Chicago, University of Illinois Press.

Perrineau, P. (1997) *Le symptôme Le Pen. Radiographie des électeurs du FN*. Paris, Fayard.

Pettit, P. (1997) *Republicanism: a Theory of Freedom and Government*. Oxford, Clarendon Press.

Pfahl-Traughber, A. (1994) *Volkes Stimme? Rechtspopulismus in Europe*. Bonn, Dietz.

Pharr, S. and Putnam, R. (2000a) 'Preface' in S. J. Pharr and R. D. Putnam (eds), *Disaffected Democracies. What's Troubling the Trilateral Democracies*. Princeton, Princeton University Press, xv–xxv.

Pharr, S. and Putnam, R. (ed.) (2000b) *Why Western Citizens Don't Trust their Governments*. Princeton, Princeton University Press.

Philip, G. (1998) 'The New Populism, Presidentialism and Market-Oriented Reform in Spanish South America', *Government & Opposition*, 33 (1), 81–97.

Phillips, K. (1999) *The Cousins Wars: Religion, Politics and the Triumph of Anglo–America*. New York, Basic Books.

Piccone, P. (1994) 'From the New Left to the New Populism', *Telos*, 101 (Autumn), 173–208.

Piccone, P. and Ulmen, G. (1995) 'Populism and the New Politics', *Telos*, 103 (Spring), 3–8.

Pierre, J. and Peters, B. G. (2000) *Governance, Politics and the State*. London, Macmillan – now Palgrave.

Pitkin, H. (1967) *The Concept of Representation*. Berkeley, University of California Press.

Pizzorno, A. (1981) 'Interests and Parties in Pluralism' in S. Berger (ed.), *Organizing Interests in Western Europe*. Cambridge, CUP, 249–84.

Plasser, F. (1997) 'Massenmedien und Politikvermittlung' in H. Dachs (ed.), *Handbuch des politischen Systems Österreichs*. Vienna, Manz, 463–82.

Plasser, F., Sommer, F. and Ulram, P. A. (1990) 'Eine Kanzler- und Protestwahl', *Österreichisches Jahrbuch für Politik*, 95–149.

Plasser, F. and Ulram, P. A. (1994) 'Meinungstrends, Mobilisierung und Motivlagen bei der Volksabstimmung über den EU-Beitritt' in A. Pelinka (ed.), *EU-Referendum*. Vienna, Signum, 87–119.

Plasser, F., Ulram, P. A. and Seeber, G. (1996) '(Dis-)Kontinuitäten und neue Spannungslinien im Wählerverhalten: Trendanalysen 1986–1995' in F. Plasser, P. A. Ulram and G. Ogris (eds), *Wahlkampf und Wählerentscheidung*. Vienna, Signum, 155–209.

Plasser, F., Ulram, P. A. and Sommer, F. (1999) *Analyse der Nationalratswahl*. http://www.gfk.at.

Plasser, F., Ulram, P. A. and Sommer, F. (eds) (2000) *Das österreichische Wahlverhalten*. Vienna, Signum.

Plasser, F., Ulram, P. A., Neuwirth, E. and Sommer, F. (1995) *Analyse der Nationalratswahl 1995*. Vienna, Fessel+GfK, 13–21.

Plasser, F., Ulram, P. A. and Waldrauch, H. (1998) *Democratic Consolidation in East-Central Europe*. Basingstoke, Macmillan – now Palgrave.

Poggio, P. P. (1994) 'Il naturalismo sociale e l'ideologia della Lega' in G. De Luna (ed.), *Figli di un benessere minore. La Lega 1979–1993*. Scandicci, La Nuova Italia, 137–96.

Poguntke, T. (1996) 'Anti-Party Sentiment. Conceptual Thoughts and Empirical Evidence: Explorations into a Minefield', *EJPR*, 29 (3), 319–44.

Poguntke, T. and Scarrow, S E. (eds) (1996) *The Politics of Anti-Party Sentiment* (Special Issue), *EJPR*, 29 (3), 257–62.

Pombeni, P. (2000) 'L'appello al popolo', *Ideazione*, 7 (2), 34–49.

Pujas, V. and Rhodes, M. (1999) 'Party Finance and Political Scandal in Italy, Spain and France', *WEP*, 22 (3), 41–63.

Rabinowitz, G. and Macdonald, S. E. (1989) 'A Directional Theory of Issue Voting', *American Political Science Review*, 83 (1), 93–121.

Ramseyer, J. M. and Rosenbluth, F. M. (1993) *Japan's Political Marketplace*. Cambridge, Ma., Harvard University Press.

Reeve, A. and Ware, A. (1992) *Electoral Systems*. London, Routledge.

Revelli, M. (1996) *Le due destre*. Turin, Bollati Boringhieri.

Ricolfi, L. (1993) *L'ultimo Parlamento. Sulla fine della Prima Repubblica*. Rome, La Nuova Italia Scientifica.

Riedlsperger, M. (1998) 'The Freedom Party of Austria: From Protest to Radical Right Populism' in H.-G. Betz and S. Immerfall (eds), *The New Politics of the Right*. New York, St Martin's Press – now Palgrave, 27–44.

Riker, W. H. (1982) *Liberalism against Populism: a Confrontation between the Theory of Democracy and the Theory of Social Choice*. San Francisco, W.H. Freeman.

Riker, W. H. (1986) *The Art of Political Manipulation*. New Haven, Yale University Press.

Rogowski, R. (1987) 'Trade and the Variety of Democratic Institutions', *International Organization*, 41 (2), 203–23.

Rosanvallon, P. (1993) 'L'histoire du mot démocratie à l'époque moderne' in M. Gauchet et al. (eds), *La pensée politique. Situations de la démocratie.* Paris, Gallimard-Le Seuil, 11–29.

Rose, R. and Haerpfer, C. (1996) 'New Democracies Barometer IV: a 10-Nations Survey', Glasgow, Centre for the Study of Public Policy, SPP, no. 262.

Rosenbluth, F. M. (1996) 'Internationalization and Electoral Politics' in R. O. Keohane and H. V. Milner (eds), *Internationalization and Domestic Politics.* Cambridge, Cambridge University Press, 137–57.

Rosenzweig, L. (1998) 'Une loi indemnisant d'anciens collaborateurs des nazis provoque un tolle en Belgique', *Le Monde*, June 23.

Sartori, G. (1968) 'The Sociology of Parties: a Critical Review' in O. Stammer (ed.), *Party Systems, Party Organizations, and the Politics of the New Masses.* Berlin, Freie Universität Berlin, 1–25.

Sartori, G. (1987) *The Theory of Democracy Revisited.* Chatham, NJ, Chatham House.

Sartori, G. (1994) *Comparative Constitutional Engineering.* London, Macmillan – now Palgrave.

Saussez, T. (1992) *Tapie–Le Pen. Les jumeaux du populisme.* Paris, Édition no.1.

Schain, M. A. (1997) 'Review of Kitschelt's *The Radical Right in Western Europe*', *Comparative Political Studies*, 30 (3), 375–80.

Scharpf, F. (1970) *Demokratietheorie zwischen Utopie und Anpassung.* Constance, Universitätsverlag.

Scharpf, F. (1993) 'Versuch über Demokratie im verhandelnden Staat' in R. Czada and M. Schmidt (eds), *Verhandlungsdemokratie, Interessenvermittlung, Regierbarkeit.* Opladen, Westdeutscherverlag, 25–50.

Scharpf, F. (1999a) *Governing in Europe. Effective and Democratic?* Oxford, Oxford University Press.

Scharpf, F. (1999b) 'Legitimacy in the Multi-Actor European Polity' in M. Egerberg and P. Laegreid (eds), *Organizing Political Institutions.* Oslo, Scandinavian University Press, 261–88.

Schedler, A. (1996) 'Anti-Political-Establishment Parties', *Party Politics*, 2 (3), 291–312.

Schedler, A. (1997) 'Introduction: Antipolitics – Closing and Colonizing the Public Sphere' in A. Schedler (ed.), *The End of Politics?* Basingstoke, Macmillan – now Palgrave, 1–20.

Scheler, M. (1992) *On Feeling, Knowing and Valuing.* Chicago, University of Chicago Press.

Schimank, U. (1996) *Theorien gesellschaftlicher Differenzierung.* Opladen, Leske + Budrich.

Schmitter, P.C. (2000) *How to Democratize the European Union... And Why Bother?* Oxford, Rowman & Littlefield.

Setta, S. (1995a) *L'Uomo qualunque. 1944–1948.* Rome and Bari, Laterza.

Setta, S. (1995b) 'Il qualunquismo' in G. Pasquino (ed.), *La politica italiana. Dizionario critico 1945–95.* Rome and Bari, Laterza, 365–75.

Shapiro, I. and Hacker-Cordón, C. (1999) *Democracy's Edges.* Cambridge, Cambridge University Press.

Shefter, M. (1994) *Political Parties and the State: the American Historical Experience.* Princeton, NJ, Princeton University Press.

Shenfield, S. (2001) *Russian Fascism: Traditions, Tendencies, and Movements.* Armonk, NY, M. E. Sharpe.

Shils, E. (1956) *The Torment of Secrecy: the Background and Consequences of American Security Policies.* Glencoe, Ill., Free Press.

Silbey, J. H. (1991) *The American Political Nation, 1838–1893.* Stanford, Ca., Stanford University Press.

Smith, D. A. (1998) *Tax Crusaders and the Politics of Direct Democracy.* New York, Routledge.

Smith, G. (1976) 'The Functional Properties of the Referendum', *EJPR,* 4 (1), 1–23.

Smith, R. M. (1993) 'Beyond Tocqueville, Myrdal, and Hartz: the Multiple Traditions in America', *American Political Science Review,* 87 (3), 549–66.

Solomon, R. C. (1994) 'One Hundred Years of *Ressentiment*' in R. Schacht (ed.), *Nietzsche, Genealogy, Morality.* Berkeley, University of California Press, 95–126.

Soskice, D. (1999) 'Divergent Production Regimes: Coordinated and Uncoordinated Market Economies in the 1980s and 1990s' in H. Kitschelt, P. Lange, G. Marks, and J. Stephens (eds), *Continuity and Change in Contemporary Capitalism.* Cambridge, Cambridge University Press, 101–34.

Stimson, J. (1995) 'Opinion and representation', *American Political Science Review,* 89 (1), 179–83.

Strøm, K. (1997) 'Democracy, Accountability, and Coalition Bargaining', *EJPR,* 31 (1/2), 47–62.

Sunley, J. (1996) 'Post-Communism', *National Interest,* 44, 3–16.

Swank, D. and Betz, H.-G. (2000) 'Globalization, the Welfare State, and Right-Wing Populism in Western Europe', unpublished MS, Marquette University and Center for European Studies, New York University.

Swyngedouw, M. (1998a) 'Anvers: une ville a la portee du Vlaams Blok?' in P. Delwit, J.-M. De Waele and A. Rea (eds), *L'Extrême droite en France et en Belgique.* Brussels, Editions Complex, 291–314.

Swyngedouw, M. (1998b) 'The Extreme Right of Belgium: of a Non-existent Front National and an Omnipresent Vlaams Blok' in H.-G. Betz and S. Immerfall (eds), *The New Politics of the Right.* New York, St Martin's Press – now Palgrave, 59–76.

Szczerbiak, A. (2000) 'Public Opinion and Eastward Enlargement: Explaining Declining Support for EU Membership in Poland', *SEI Working Paper,* No. 34, Brighton, Sussex European Institute.

Sztompka, P. (1998) 'Mistrusting Civility: Predicament of a Post-Communist Society' in J. C. Alexander (ed.), *Real Civil Societies: Dilemmas of Institutionalization.* London, Sage, 191–210.

Taggart, P. (1995) 'New Populist Parties in Western Europe', *WEP,* 18 (1), 34–51.

Taggart, P. (1996) *The New Populism and the New Politics.* London, Macmillan – now Palgrave.

Taggart, P. (1998) 'A Touchstone of Dissent: Euroscepticism in Contemporary Western European Party Systems', *EJPR,* 33 (3), 363–88.

Taggart, P. (2000) *Populism.* Buckingham, Open University Press.

Taguieff, P.-A. (1995) 'Political Science Confronts Populism', *Telos,* 103 (Spring), 9–43.

Taguieff, P.-A. (1997) 'Le populisme et la science politique. Du mirage conceptuel aux vrais problèmes', *Vingtième siècle,* 56 (Oct./Dec.), 4–33.

Tamás, G. M. (1994) 'The Legacy of Dissent', *Uncaptive Minds,* 7 (2), 19–34.

Tanase, S. (1999) 'Changing Societies and Elite Transformation', *East European Politics and Societies,* 13 (2), 358–63.

Tarchi, M. (1998) 'The Lega Nord' in L. de Winter and H. Türsan (eds), *Regionalist Parties in Western Europe.* London and New York, Routledge, 143–57.

Tarchi, M. (1999) 'La Lega tra destra e sinistra', *Trasgressioni,* 28, 3–29.

Taylor, C. (1998) 'The Dynamics of Democratic Exclusion', *Journal of Democracy,* 9 (4), 143–56.

Tismaneanu, V. (1996) 'The Leninist Debris, or Waiting for Perón', *East European Politics and Societies,* 10 (3), 504–35.

Tismaneanu, V. (ed.) (1999) *The Revolutions of 1989.* London, Routledge.

Tóka, G. (1997) 'Political Parties and Democratic Consolidation in East Central Europe', Glasgow, Studies in Public Policy no. 279.

Togeby, L. (1998) 'Prejudice and Tolerance in a Period of Increasing Ethnic Diversity and Growing Unemployment: Denmark since 1970', *Ethnic and Racial Studies,* 21 (6), 1137.

Tönnies, F. (1991) *Gemeinschaft und Gesellschaft.* Darmstadt, Wissenschaftliche Buchggesellschaft.

Traïni, C. (2000) 'Les braconniers de la politiques', *Cahiers du CEVIPOF,* no. 28.

Trechsel, A. H. and Sciarini, P. (1998) 'Direct Democracy in Switzerland: Do Elites Matter?', *EJPR,* 33 (1), 99–124.

Treptow, K. W. (1996) 'Populism and Twentieth Century Romanian Politics' in J. Held (ed.), *Populism in Eastern Europe.* Boulder, East European Monographs, 197–218.

Ulc, O. (1996) 'Populism, Racism, and Society in Czechoslovakia' in J. Held (ed.), *Populism in Eastern Europe.* Boulder, East European Monographs, 63–106.

Urfalino, P. (2000) 'La délibération et la dimension normative de la décision collective' in J. Commaille et al. (eds), *La juridicisation du politique. Leçons scientifiques.* Paris, LGDJ, 165–93.

van Niekerk, A. E. (1972) *Populisme en politieke ontwikkeling in Latijns Amerika.* Rotterdam, Universitaire Pers Rotterdam.

Walicki, A. (1969) 'Russia' in G. Ionescu and E. Gellner (eds), *Populism.* London, Weidenfeld & Nicolson, 62–96.

Walsh, J. (1990) 'Populism on the March', *Time,* 136, 27, 44.

Weale, A. (1999) *Democracy.* Basingstone, Macmillan – now Palgrave.

Weber, M. (1978) *Economy and Society.* Berkeley, Ca., University of California Press.

Westlind, D. (1996) *The Politics of Popular Identity: Understanding Recent Populist Movements in Sweden and the United States.* Lund, Lund University Press.

Weyland, K. (1999a) 'Neoliberal Populism in Latin America and Eastern Europe', *Comparative Politics,* 31 (4), 379–403.

Weyland, K. (1999b) 'Clarifying a Contested Concept: "Populism" in Latin American Studies', paper presented at the 95th Annual Meeting of APSA, Atlanta, 2–5 September.

Wildenmann, R. (1986) 'The Problematic of Party Government' in F. G. Castles and R. Wildenmann (eds), *Visions and Realities of Party Government.* Berlin, de Gruyter, 1–30.

Wiles, P. (1969) 'A Syndrome, Not a Doctrine: Some Elementary Theses on Populism' in G. Ionescu and E. Gellner (eds), *Populism: Its Meaning and National Characteristics.* London, Weidenfeld & Nicolson, 166–79.

Williams, C. (1999) 'Problems of Transition and the Rise of the Radical Right' in S. Ramet (ed.), *The Radical Right in Central and Eastern Europe Since 1989.* University Park, Pennsylvania State University Press, 29–44.

Wills, G. (1996) 'What Happened to the Revolution?', *New York Review of Books*, 6 June.

Wilson, C. (1995) 'Up at the Fork of the Creek: In Search of American Populism', *Telos*, 104 (Summer), 77–88.

Wolfgruber, E. (1994) 'Parteipolitischer Diskurs und Strategien in der Ausländer/innen/politik in Österreich 1989 bis 1993', *Österreichische Zeitschrift für Politikwissenschaft*, 23, 299–313.

Worsley, P. (1969) 'The Concept of Populism' in G. Ionescu and E. Gellner (eds), *Populism.* London, Weidenfeld & Nicolson, 212–50.

Worsley, P. (1993) 'Populism' in J. Krieger (ed.), *The Oxford Companion to Politics of the World.* New York, Oxford University Press, 730–1.

Writh, J. D. (1982) 'Foreword' in M. L. Conniff (ed.), *Latin American Populism in Comparative Perspective.* Albuquerque, University of New Mexico Press, ix–xiii.

Zaller, J. R. (1992) *The Nature and Origins of Mass Opinion.* Cambridge, Cambridge University Press.

Zolo, D. (1992) *Democracy and Complexity.* Cambridge, Polity Press.

Zürn, M. (1996) 'Über den Staat und die Demokratie im europäischen Mehrebenen System', *Politische Vierteljahresschrift*, 37 (1), 27–55.

Index

20202142R00151

Printed in Great Britain
by Amazon